Terms and conditions

IMPORTANT – PERMITTED USE AND WARNINGS – READ CAREFULLY BEFORE USING

Recommended system requirements:

- Windows: XP (Service Pack 3), Vista (Service Pack 2), Windows 7 or Windows 8 with 2.33GHz processor
- Mac: OS 10.6 to 10.8 with Intel Core™ Duo processor
- 1GB RAM (recommended)
- 1024 x 768 Screen resolution
- CD-ROM drive (24x speed recommended)
- 16-bit sound card
- Adobe Reader (version 9 recommended for Mac users)
- Broadband internet connections (for installation and updates)

For all technical support queries, please phone Scholastic Customer Services on 0845 6039091.

Book End, Range Road, Witney, Oxfordshire, OX29 0YD
www.scholastic.co.uk

© 2014, Scholastic Ltd

2 3 4 5 6 7 8 9   4 5 6 7 8 9 0 1 2 3

British Library Cataloguing-in-Publication Data
A catalogue record for this book is available from the
British Library.

ISBN 978-1407-12763-7
Printed by Bell & Bain Ltd, Glasgow

Due to the nature of the web we cannot guarantee the
content or links of any site mentioned. We strongly
recommend that teachers check websites before using
them in the classroom.

Extracts from *The National Curriculum in English*, *English
Programme of Study* © Crown Copyright. Reproduced
under the terms of the Open Government Licence
(OGL). http://www.nationalarchives.gov.uk/doc/open-
government-licence/open-government-licence.htm

Author
Christine Moorcroft

Editorial team
Rachel Morgan, Melissa Somers, Tracy Kewley,
Gemma Cary

Cover Design
Andrea Lewis

Design Team
Sarah Garbett, Shelley Best and Andrea Lewis

CD-ROM development
Hannah Barnett, Phil Crothers, MWA Technologies
Private Ltd

Typesetting and illustrations
Ricky Capanni, International Book Management

Acknowledgements
The publishers gratefully acknowledge permission
to reproduce the following copyright material:

Curtis Brown Ltd for the use of the poem 'Night
Mail' by WH Auden. Poem © 1938 by WH Auden,
renewed.
David Cobb for the use of the haiku 'Icicle' by David
Cobb, first published in *Iron Book of British Haiku*.
Poem © 1998, David Cobb (1998, Iron Press).
Curtis Brown Group Ltd, London for the use of the
poem 'Sea Timeless Song' by Grace Nichols. Poem ©
1984, Grace Nichols.
David Higham Associates for the use of extracts
from *Kensuke's Kingdom* by Michael Morpurgo. Text
© 1999, Michael Morpurgo (1999, Egmont).
Egmont for the use of an extract from *Wreck of
the Zanzibar* by Michael Morpurgo. Text © 1995,
Michael Morpurgo (1995, William Heinemann Ltd
and Mammoth).
Guardian News and Media Limited for the use
of the article 'Assassination of Mr Gandhi' from
theguardian.com first published 31 January 1948.
Text © 1948, Guardian News & Media Ltd.
Hexham Courant for the use of the articles 'Science
Week' and 'Young MasterChefs cook to impress'
from the Hexaham Courant. Text © Hexham
Courant.
Marian Reiner Literary Agency for the use of the
poem 'Until I Saw the Sea' by Lilian Moore first
published in *I Feel the Same Way* by Lilian Moore.
Poem © 1967, 1995 Lilian Moore (1967, Atheneum
Publishers).
National Geographic Society for the use of an
adapted article 'On thin ice' by Susan McGrath
published by the National Geographic in 2011.
National Geographic Society for the use of an
adapted article 'Polar Bears Under Threat' by
John Roach published by the National Geographic.
Scholastic Inc for the use of an extract from *Lone
Wolf* by Kathryn Lasky. Text © 2010, Kathryn Lasky.
(2010, Scholastic Inc).
Aaron Shepard for the use of the playscript 'Savitri'
by Aaron Shepard www.aaronshep.com
The Society of Authors as the Literary
Representative of the Estate of John Masefield for
the use of the poem 'Sea Fever' by John Masefield
first published in *Salt-Water Ballads*. Poem © 1902,
John Masefield (1902, Grant Richards).
Philip Waddell for the use of the poem 'Important
Notice' by Philip Waddell, first published in *The
Works 2* edited by Brian Moses and Pie Corbett.
Poem © 2002, Philip Waddell (2002, Macmillian
Children's Books).
Whale and Dolphin Conservation for use of 'Stop
Whaling Campaign'.

Every effort has been made to trace copyright
holders for the works reproduced in this book,
and the publishers apologise for any inadvertent
omissions.

Contents

Introduction

About the series

The *100 English Lessons* series is designed to meet the requirements of the 2014 Curriculum, English Programmes of Study. There are six books in the series, Years 1–6, and each book contains lesson plans, resources and ideas matched to the new curriculum. It can be a complex task to ensure that a progressive and appropriate curriculum is followed in all year groups; this series has been carefully structured to ensure that a progressive and appropriate curriculum is followed throughout.

About the new curriculum

The curriculum documentation for English provides a single-year programme of study for Year 1 and Year 2, but joint programmes of study for Years 3–4 and Years 5–6.

There is a much greater focus on the technical aspects of language – including grammar, punctuation, spelling, handwriting and phonics. These are the building blocks to help children to read and write. It has been perceived that these aspects have to be taught discretely, however the approach encouraged in this series is to embed these elements into existing learning. For example, using a focus text to identify the use of punctuation and using that as a springboard to practise it.

There is a spoken language Programme of Study which outlines statutory requirements across Years 1–6. Within the English curriculum there are also attainment targets that involve 'discussion', 'talking', 'participating' and 'listening'. The aims of speaking and listening are below:

> *The National Curriculum for English reflects the importance of spoken language in children's development across the whole curriculum – cognitively, socially and linguistically. The quality and variety of language that children hear and speak are vital for developing their vocabulary, grammar and their understanding for reading and writing. Teachers should therefore ensure the continual development of children's confidence and competence in spoken language. Children should develop a capacity to explain their understanding of books and other reading, and to prepare their ideas before they write. They must be assisted in making their thinking clear to themselves as well as to others and teachers should ensure that children build secure foundations by using discussion to probe and remedy their misconceptions. Children should also be taught to understand and use the conventions for discussion and debate.*
>
> *Statutory requirements which underpin all aspects of speaking and listening across the six years of primary education form part of the National Curriculum. These are contextualised within the reading and writing domains which follow.*

Terminology

The curriculum terminology has changed; the main terms used are:

- **Domains:** The area of the subject, for English the domains are 'Reading' and 'Writing'.
- **Sub-domains:** The next level down to the domains. In English, Reading's sub-domains are 'Word reading' and 'Comprehension' and Writing's sub-domains are 'Transcription' and 'Composition'.
- **Curriculum objectives:** These are the statutory programme of study statements or objectives.
- **Appendix:** Any reference to an appendix refers to an appendix of the National Curriculum for English document. There are two appendices – one for spelling (Appendix 1) and one for vocabulary, grammar and punctuation (Appendix 2).

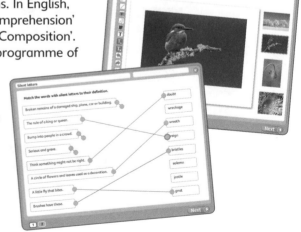

■■SCHOLASTIC

About the book

This book is divided into six chapters; each chapter contains a half-term's work and is based around a topic or theme. Each chapter follows the same structure:

Chapter introduction

At the start of each chapter there is a summary of what is covered. This includes:

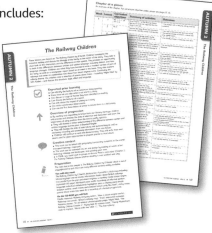

- **Introduction:** A description of what is covered in the chapter.
- **Expected prior learning:** What the children are expected to know before starting the work in the chapter.
- **Overview of progression:** A brief explanation of how the children progress through the chapter.
- **Creative context:** How the chapter could link to other curriculum areas.
- **Preparation:** Any resources required for the teaching of the chapter, including things that need to be sourced or prepared and the content that can be located on the CD-ROM.
- **Chapter at a glance:** This is a table that summarises the content of each lesson, including: the curriculum objectives (using a code system, please see pages 8–10), a summary of the activities and the outcome.
- **Background knowledge:** A section explaining grammatical terms and suchlike to enhance your subject knowledge, where required.

Lessons

Each chapter contains six weeks' of lessons, each week contains five lessons. At the start of each week there is an introduction about what is covered and the expected outcomes. The lesson plans then include the relevant combination of headings from below.

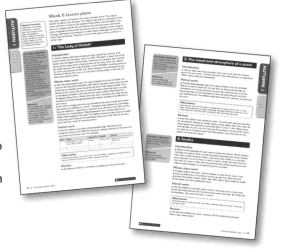

- **Curriculum objectives:** A list of the relevant objectives from the Programme of Study.
- **Resources:** What you require to teach the lesson.
- **Introduction:** A short and engaging activity to begin the lesson.
- **Whole-class work:** Working together as a class.
- **Group/Paired/Independent work:** Children working independently of the teacher in pairs, groups or alone.
- **Differentiation:** Ideas for how to support children who are struggling with a concept or how to extend those children who understand a concept without taking them onto new work.
- **Review:** A chance to review the children's learning and ensure the outcomes of the lesson have been achieved.

Assess and review

At the end of each chapter are activities for assessing and reviewing the children's understanding. These can be conducted during the course of the chapter's work or saved until the end of the chapter or done at a later date. There are four focuses for assess and review activities in each chapter:

- Grammar and punctuation
- Spelling
- Reading
- Writing

Elements of speaking and listening will be included where relevant within these four areas.

All four focuses follow the same format:

- **Curriculum objectives:** These are the areas of focus for the assess and review activity. There may be one focus or more than one depending on the activity.
- **Resources:** What you require to conduct the activities.
- **Revise:** A series of short activities or one longer activity to revise and consolidate the children's learning and ensure they understand the concept(s).
- **Assess:** An assessment activity to provide a chance for the children to demonstrate their understanding and for you to check this.
- **Further practice:** Ideas for further practice on the focus, whether children are insecure in their learning or you want to provide extra practice or challenge.

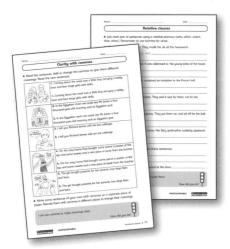

Photocopiable pages

At the end of each chapter are some photocopiable pages that will have been referred to in the lesson plans. These sheets are for the children to use; there is generally a title, an instruction, an activity and an 'I can' statement at the bottom. These sheets are also provided on the CD-ROM alongside additional pages as referenced in the lessons (see page 7 About the CD-ROM). The children should be encouraged to complete the 'I can' statements by colouring in the traffic lights to say how they think they have done (red – not very well, amber – ok, green – very well).

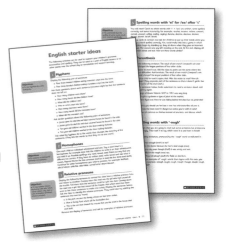

English starter activities

At the beginning of the book there is a bank of English starter activities (pages 11–14). These are games and activities that will help children familiarise and consolidate their knowledge of grammar, punctuation and spelling. The use of these will be suggested throughout the chapters, but they are also flexible and therefore could be used at any time.

■ **SCHOLASTIC**

About the CD-ROM

The CD-ROM contains:

- Printable versions of the photocopiable sheets from the book and additional photocopiable sheets as referenced in the lesson plans.
- Interactive activities for children to complete or to use on the whiteboard.
- Media resources to display.
- Printable versions of the lesson plans.
- Digital versions of the lesson plans with the relevant resources linked to them.

Getting started

- Put the CD-ROM into your CD-ROM drive.
  - For Windows users, the install wizard should autorun, if it fails to do so then navigate to your CD-ROM drive. Then follow the installation process.
  - For Mac users, copy the disk image file to your hard drive. After it has finished copying double-click it to mount the disk image. Navigate to the mounted disk image and run the installer. After installation the disk image can be unmounted and the DMG can be deleted from the hard drive.
- To complete the installation of the program you need to open the program and click 'Update' in the pop-up. Please note – this CD-ROM is web-enabled and the content will be downloaded from the internet to your hard-drive to populate the CD-ROM with the relevant resources. This only needs to be done on first use, after this you will be able to use the CD-ROM without an internet connection. If at any point any content is updated you will receive another pop-up upon start up with an internet connection.

Navigating the CD-ROM

There are two options to navigate the CD-ROM either as a Child or as a Teacher.

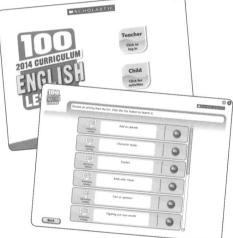

Child

- Click on the 'Child' button on the first menu screen.
- In the second menu click on the relevant class (please note only the books installed on the machine or network will be accessible. You can also rename year groups to match your school's naming conventions via the Teacher > Settings > Rename books area).
- A list of interactive activities will be displayed, children need to locate the correct one and click 'Go' to launch it.
- There is the opportunity to print or save a PDF of the activity at the end.

Teacher

- Click on the Teacher button on the first menu screen and you will be taken to a screen showing which of the *100 English* books you have purchased. From here, you can also access information about getting started and the credits.
- To enter the product click 'Next' in the bottom right.
- You then need to enter a password (the password is: login).
- On first use:
  - Enter as a Guest by clicking on the 'Guest' button.
  - If desired, create a profile for yourself by adding your name to the list of users. Profiles allow you to save favourites and to specify which year group(s) you wish to be able to view.
  - Go to 'Settings' to create a profile for yourself – click 'Add user' and enter your name. Then choose the year groups you wish to have access to (you can return to this screen to change this at any time). Click on 'Login' at the top of the screen to re-enter the disk under your new profile.
- On subsequent uses you can choose your name from the drop-down list. The 'Guest' option will always be available if you, or a colleague, wish to use this.
- You can search the CD-ROM using the tools or save favourites.

For more information about how to use the CD-ROM, please refer to the help file which can be found in the teacher area of the CD-ROM. It is a red button with a question mark on it on the right-hand side of the screen just underneath the 'Settings' tab.

Curriculum grid

This grid shows the full curriculum objectives for Year 5. The codes are referenced in the chapter introductions. Additional information is provided in italics, this includes the statutory information from the appendices and information about when certain objectives are introduced.

Domain	Code	Curriculum objective
Reading: Word reading	RWR1	To apply their growing knowledge of root words, prefixes and suffixes (morphology and etymology), as listed in Appendix 1, both to read aloud and to understand the meaning of new words that they meet.
Reading: Comprehension	RC1	To maintain positive attitudes to reading and understanding of what they read by continuing to read and discuss an increasingly wide range of fiction, poetry, plays, non-fiction and reference books or textbooks.
	RC2	To maintain positive attitudes to reading and understanding of what they read by reading books that are structured in different ways and reading for a range of purposes.
	RC3	To maintain positive attitudes to reading and understanding of what they read by increasing their familiarity with a wide range of books, including myths, legends and traditional stories, modern fiction, fiction from our literary heritage, and books from other cultures and traditions.
	RC4	To maintain positive attitudes to reading and understanding of what they read by recommending books that they have read to their peers, giving reasons for their choices.
	RC5	To maintain positive attitudes to reading and understanding of what they read by identifying and discussing themes and conventions in and across a wide range of writing.
	RC6	To maintain positive attitudes to reading and understanding of what they read by making comparisons within and across books.
	RC7	To maintain positive attitudes to reading and understanding of what they read by learning a wider range of poetry by heart.
	RC8	To maintain positive attitudes to reading and understanding of what they read by preparing poems and plays to read aloud and to perform, showing understanding through intonation, tone and volume so that the meaning is clear to an audience.
	RC9	To understand what they read by checking that the book makes sense to them, discussing their understanding and exploring the meaning of words in context.
	RC10	To understand what they read by asking questions to improve their understanding.
	RC11	To understand what they read by drawing inferences such as inferring characters' feelings, thoughts and motives from their actions and justifying inferences with evidence.
	RC12	To understand what they read by predicting what might happen from details stated and implied.
	RC13	To understand what they read by summarising the main ideas drawn from more than one paragraph, identifying key details that support the main ideas.
	RC14	To understand what they read by identifying how language, structure and presentation contribute to meaning.
	RC15	To discuss and evaluate how authors use language, including figurative language, considering the impact on the reader.
	RC16	To distinguish between statements of fact and opinion.
	RC17	To retrieve, record and present information from non-fiction.
	RC18	To participate in discussions about books that are read to them and those they can read for themselves, building on their own and others' ideas and challenging views courteously.
	RC19	To explain and discuss their understanding of what they have read, including through formal presentations and debates, maintaining a focus on the topic and using notes where necessary.
	RC20	To ask questions to improve their understanding of what they have read.
	RC21	To provide reasoned justifications for their views.

Domain	Code	Curriculum objective
Writing: Transcription	WT1	To use further prefixes and suffixes and understand the guidelines for adding them. *Including:* *'-cious' and 'tious'; '-cial' and '-tial'; '-ant', '-ent', '-ancy/'-ance', '-ency/'-ence'; '-able' and '-ible'; '-ably' and '-ibly'; adding suffixes beginning with vowel letters to words ending in '-fer'.*
	WT2	To spell some words with 'silent' letters.
	WT3	To continue to distinguish between homophones and other words which are often confused.
	WT4	To use knowledge of morphology and etymology in spelling and understand that the spelling of some words needs to be learnt specifically, as listed in Appendix 1. *Including:* *Words with the /ee/ sound spelled 'ei' after 'c'; words with the letter string '-ough; word list for Years 5 and 6 (see Appendix 1 of the curriculum).*
	WT5	To use dictionaries to check the spelling and meaning of words.
	WT6	To use the first three or four letters of a word to check spelling, meaning or both of these in a dictionary.
	WT7	To use a thesaurus. *This is introduced in Year 6, not in Year 5.*
	WT8	To write legibly, fluently, with increasing speed by choosing which shape of a letter to use when given choices and deciding, as part of their personal style, whether or not to join specific letters.
	WT9	To write legibly, fluently, with increasing speed by choosing the writing implement that is best suited for a task.
Writing: Composition	WC1	To plan their writing by identifying the audience for and purpose of the writing, selecting the appropriate form and using other similar writing as models for their own.
	WC2	To plan their writing by noting and developing initial ideas, drawing on reading and research where necessary.
	WC3	To plan their writing by in writing narratives, considering how authors have developed characters and settings in what they have read, listened to or seen performed.
	WC4	To draft and write by selecting appropriate grammar and vocabulary, understanding how such choices can change and enhance meaning.
	WC5	To draft and write by in narratives, describing settings, characters and atmosphere and integrating dialogue to convey character and advance the action.
	WC6	To draft and write by précising longer passages.
	WC7	To draft and write by using a wide range of devices to build cohesion within and across paragraphs.
	WC8	To draft and write by using further organisational and presentational devices to structure text and to guide the reader.
	WC9	To evaluate and edit by assessing the effectiveness of their own and others' writing.
	WC10	To evaluate and edit by proposing changes to grammar, vocabulary and punctuation to enhance effects and clarify meaning.
	WC11	To evaluate and edit by ensuring the consistent and correct use of tense throughout a piece of writing.
	WC12	To evaluate and edit by ensuring correct subject and verb agreement when using singular and plural, distinguishing between the language of speech and writing and choosing the appropriate register.
	WC13	To proofread for spelling and punctuation errors.
	WC14	To perform their own compositions, using appropriate intonation, volume, and movement so that meaning is clear.

Domain	Code	Curriculum objective
	WC15	To develop their understanding of the concepts set out in Appendix 2 by recognising vocabulary and structures that are appropriate for formal speech and writing, including subjunctive forms. *This is introduced in Year 6, not in Year 5.*
	WC16	To develop their understanding of the concepts set out in Appendix 2 by using passive verbs to affect the presentation of information in a sentence. *This is introduced in Year 6, not in Year 5.*
	WC17	To develop their understanding of the concepts set out in Appendix 2 by using expanded noun phrases to convey complicated information concisely.
	WC18	To develop their understanding of the concepts set out in Appendix 2 by using modal verbs or adverbs to indicate degrees of possibility.
	WC19	To develop their understanding of the concepts set out in Appendix 2 by using relative clauses beginning with *who, which, where, why, whose, that* or with an implied (omitted) relative pronoun.
	WC20	To develop their understanding of the concepts set out in Appendix 2 by learning the grammar in column 1 of Years 5 and 6 in Appendix 2. *Concepts for Year 5 include:* ● *Converting nouns or adjectives into words using suffixes.* ● *Verb prefixes.*
	WC21	To indicate grammatical and other features by using commas to clarify meaning or avoid ambiguity in writing.
	WC22	To indicate grammatical and other features by using hyphens to avoid ambiguity.
	WC23	To indicate grammatical and other features by using brackets, dashes or commas to indicate parenthesis.
	WC24	To indicate grammatical and other features by using semicolons, colons or dashes to mark boundaries between main clauses. *This is introduced in Year 6, not in Year 5.*
	WC25	To indicate grammatical and other features by using a colon to introduce a list.
	WC26	To indicate grammatical and other features by punctuating bullet points consistently.
	WC27	To use and understand the grammatical terminology in Appendix 2 accurately and appropriately in discussing their writing and reading. *Terminology for Year 5: modal verb, relative pronoun, relative clause, parenthesis, bracket, dash, cohesion, ambiguity.*

English starter ideas

The following activities can be used to support your children's grammar, punctuation and spelling. They can be used as a part of English lessons or at other points over the school day to consolidate and support learning.

1 Hyphens

Objectives
● To use hyphens to avoid ambiguity.

Display the following pair of sentences.

- *Four three-headed children eating monsters crept into the town.*
- *Four three-headed children-eating monsters crept into the town.*

Ask these questions about each sentence (answers might be that the sentence does not tell us).

- *How many children were there?*
- *How many heads did the children have?*
- *What did the children eat?*
- *Who or what crept into town?*
- *How many monsters were there?*
- *How many heads did the monsters have?*
- *What did the monsters eat?*

Ask similar questions about the following pairs of sentences.

- *James gave his dad the red dust-covered boxes he found in the attic.*
- *James gave his dad the red-dust covered boxes he found in the attic.*
- *Ten-year-old children worked in the shoe-making factories.*
- *Ten year-old children worked in the shoe making factories.*

Ask what the hyphens do to the words that changes the meaning of the sentences. (They link the words so that they act as one word.)

2 Homophones

Objectives
● To continue to distinguish between homophones.

Give each child an individual whiteboard and pen. Say a word that is a homophone, for example *toad*. Ask the children to write it on their whiteboards and hold it up. Possible spellings are: *toad, towed, toed*. Point out any that are different but correct. If they have all written *toad*, write *towed* and ask what it means. Repeat this for the less common *toed* (as in *toed the line, three-toed sloth*). Continue for other homophones you wish to practise, for example: *led/lead, who's/whose, aisle/isle, alter/altar, cereal/serial, desert/dessert*.

3 Relative pronouns

Objectives
● To use relative clauses beginning with *who, which, whose, where, why, that* or with an implied (omitted) relative pronoun.

Display the following sentence to remind the class how a relative pronoun links one clause to another: *Coming down the road was the girl who had caused all the trouble.* Tell them that the sentence could be split into two: *Coming down the road was a girl. She had caused all the trouble.* Ask which word has been used to link these sentences to make one (*who*). Display the sentences below. Ask the class to identify the relative pronouns. They could also try splitting the sentences into two (or more).

- *In the park we saw the family whose car had been stolen.*
- *Here is Sandy Park where all the footballers live.*
- *This is the cat that chased the mouse that ate the malt in the house that Jack built.*

Remove the display of sentences and ask for examples of relative pronouns.

4 Spelling words with 'ei' for /ee/ after 'c'

Objectives
● To understand that the spelling of some words needs to be learned specifically.

You will need: Cards on which words with 'c' + /ee/ are written, some spelled correctly and some incorrectly, for example: *receive, receeve, recieve; conceat, conceit, conceet; ceiling, ceeling, ceyling; deceive, deceive, deceave, deceive; deceet, deceat, deceit, deceit.*

Hold up cards at random and ask the children to put up their hands when you hold up a word spelled correctly. You could make this into a game in which the children begin by standing up; they sit down when they give an incorrect response. The winners are any left standing at the end. At the end, display all the correct words and ask: *How are these words similar?*

5 Parenthesis

Objectives
● To use brackets, dashes or commas to indicate parenthesis.

Display the following sentence: *The result of one match Liverpool's win over Arsenal changed the league positions of four other clubs.*

Ask someone to read it out. Ask the class to point out the parts where the reader had difficulties. Add brackets: *The result of one match (Liverpool's win over Arsenal) changed the league positions of four other clubs.*

Ask the same child to read it again. Ask: *Was this easier to read? How do brackets help?* (They separate part of the sentence so that it doesn't get in the way of the sense of the main part.)

Display the sentences below. Invite volunteers to read a sentence aloud, add brackets and try again.

- *The reign of Queen Victoria 1837 to 1901 was very long.*
- *We bought a cyclamen a type of plant at the market.*
- *We knew Ryan was there he was hiding behind the shed but we pretended not to.*
- *Mrs Sharp you should see her! has a new hat with butterflies all over it.*
- *Don't cross the main road it's dangerous unless you're with an adult.*

Try using pairs of commas or dashes instead of brackets, and discuss which work best.

6 Spelling words with '-ough'

Objectives
● To understand that the spelling of some words needs to be learned specifically.

Tell the children that you are going to read out some sentences but pronounce one word wrongly. Their task is to say which word it is and how it should sound.

Read the following sentences, pronouncing the '-ough' word as indicated in brackets.

- *Have you had enough (enoh) to eat?*
- *She went to the doctor because she had a bad cough (cow).*
- *It was a warm day even though (thoff) it was windy and wet.*
- *The ship rolled in the rough (row) sea.*
- *Tomorrow they will plough (pluff) the fields on the farm.*

At the end, ask for examples of '-ough' words that rhyme with the ones you read wrongly, for example: *enough, rough; cough, trough; though, dough; rough, tough; plough, bough.*

7 All in a noun phrase

Display the following sentences.

● *We saw _____ swimming in the sea.*
● *_____ sailed into the bay.*
● *Her birthday present was _____.*
● *The mountaineer said he had climbed to the top of _____.*
● *The footballer kicked the ball past _____.*
● *We could see _____ in the valley.*
● *Nobody had seen _____.*
● *In the pet shop were _____.*
● *_____ showed us how to change the speed of a pendulum.*
● *On Saturdays my parents go to _____.*

Read out the first one and point out that it is not a complete sentence. Ask: *What could you put in the gap for it to make sense? What kind of word is this?*

Display the following noun phrases alongside the sentences.

● *The old clock-maker*
● *the local farmers' market*
● *A tall ship*
● *the low-lying mist*
● *the highest mountain in England*
● *two young dolphins*
● *the other team's goalkeeper*
● *a pair of angora rabbits*
● *a pair of gold earrings*
● *the ghost with the green head*

Ask the children to choose a phrase to fill the gap. Point out that a noun phrase acts like a noun. Invite volunteers to choose noun phrases to fill the gaps in the other sentences and to read the sentences.

8 Make the opposite verb

Objectives
● To learn the grammar of word structure.

Write a verb whose opposite can be formed by adding a prefix. (See verb list, below.) Invite a volunteer to give its opposite by adding a prefix, verbally ('dis-', 'de-', 'un-'). Verb list: *agree, allow, appear, believe, clutter, connect, contaminate, dress, fasten, fold, freeze, hydrate, like, please, prove, qualify, select.*

Variations and adaptations
Try a similar activity with other verb prefixes such as 'mis-', 'over-' and 're-'.

9 Bullet points

Objectives
● To punctuate bullet points consistently.

Write the heading 'How to keep a secret' on the whiteboard.

Give the following instructions verbally: *Keep quiet about it; Don't even tell anyone you know a secret; Don't write it down; Don't tweet it.*

Invite volunteers to come out and write these instructions using bullet points.

Ask the others to check the spelling and punctuation.

Circle the (corrected, if necessary) punctuation marks in a different colour: a colon to introduce the list, no punctuation after each item and a full stop at the end.

Other topics you could use: *How to make friends; How to keep out of trouble.*

10 Spelling words with Greek suffixes and prefixes

Tell the children that you are going to read out some sentences and that each one contains a word with a suffix or prefix from Greek. Their task is to write that word on an individual whiteboard.

Read the following sentences.

1. Please photocopy this page.

2. My friend never goes in lifts because she has claustrophobia.

3. They treated his cut knee with an antiseptic.

4. We learned about Greece in a geography lesson.

5. An isotherm is a line on a map that joins places with the same temperature.

At the end, ask for examples of other words that include the same Greek prefix or suffix, for example:

1. photograph, photosynthesis; 2. *arachnophobia, agoraphobia;* 3. *antibiotic, antistatic, antihistamine;* 4. *geology, geothermal, geometry; autograph, photography; biography;* 5. *isobar, isosceles; thermal, geothermal, thermometer.*

Ask what the prefix or suffix means. Look it up.

11 Verb agreement

In advance of the lesson, prepare some large speech bubbles cut out of card, with short sentences that would be used in spoken language, some of which have verbs/subjects that do not agree and some with mismatched singular and plural verbs and subjects, for example:

● *I'm going to a party.*
● *I were going to do my homework.*
● *I bet you don't know who I saw.*
● *They was all playing football.*
● *He were just there where you are.*
● *Was Harry at the match?*
● *There were six massive dogs chasing us.*

Hold up a speech bubble and ask the children to stand up if they think the grammar is wrong. Ask a child who is standing to explain what is wrong and to put it right. Repeat this for as many speech bubbles as appropriate.

12 Spelling nouns with '-ssion' endings

Tell the children that you are going to read out some sentences and that each one contains a word with the suffix '-ssion'. Their task is to write that word on an individual whiteboard.

Read the following sentences.

1. The spaceship was on a mission to Mars.

2. I went to the first session of the dance class.

3. A drum is a percussion instrument.

4. The profession he has chosen is medicine.

5. A break or interval during a play is also called an intermission.

6. There was a sign on the door saying 'No admission'.

Ask what types of words these are (nouns). Point out that nouns with this suffix are usually words for ideas – things you cannot see. Remind the children that nouns for people's jobs whose ending sounds the same are usually spelled '-cian': *beautician, electrician, mathematician, optician, physician, technician.*

13 Grammatical terminology

Objectives
● To use and understand the grammatical terminology in Appendix 2 accurately.

Give the children clues for a grammatical term for example *bracket* could be *a symbol that encloses extra information*. Ask the children to think of the term described and to write it down on their individual whiteboards along with examples of it in use. Share the answers. Repeat with other grammatical terms such as: *modal verb, relative pronoun, relative clause, parenthesis, bracket, dash, cohesion, ambiguity*.

14 Spelling-bee

Objectives
● To learn to spell some words specifically.

Split the class into two to three teams. Invite one child from each team to stand up, give them a specific word to spell orally. If they get it correct then their team scores one point, if they get it wrong then discuss with the class where they went wrong and why – touching on any tricky spellings. Repeat with the other team and alternate so each child gets a turn. The word could be those that they have been struggling with or from the Years 5 and 6 word list in Appendix 2.

Variations and adaptations
Instead of saying the words, ask the children to write the words – different children from each team could race to spell them correctly on the board.

15 Commas for clarity

Objectives
● To use commas to clarify meaning or avoid ambiguity.

Display a piece of text without a comma such as:
Paul fed the hens and the rabbits hopped around the lawn.

Ask a child to read it out loud – did it make sense? Establish that on first reading it sounds like Paul fed the hens *and* the rabbits, but that the rest of the sentence shows that is not the case. Ask the children to come up to the board and place a comma in the correct position to clarify the sentence:
Paul fed the hens, and the rabbits hopped around the lawn.

Variations and adaptations
Collect examples from books, display these without the commas and repeat the exercise.

16 Indicating degrees of possibility

Objectives
● To use modal verbs or adverbs to indicate degrees of possibility.

Display a picture to the class that is very zoomed in, or blurry or obscured in some way. Ask the children to discuss the picture and say what they think it is and to share these thoughts. Highlight the language that they are using *perhaps, might, must be, surely* and so on. Gradually zoom out, sharpen or reveal the picture and repeat the exercise at each stage – does the children's language get more definite? Explore the language change and discuss the use of modal verbs and adverbs to indicate degrees of possibility.

17 The perfect form

Objectives
● To exemplify how the perfect form is used to mark relationships of time and cause.

Prior to the lesson write two or three sentences on the board, such as: **I have ordered lots of paint** *because the living room needs decorating.* **He has eaten a good lunch** *so he won't be hungry.* **They have played this team** *before and they lost ten–nil!* **You have been unhappy** *since that new teacher arrived.* Rub out either the first phrase (bold) or the second. Gather the children in front of the remaining parts of the sentences, and ask them to consider what the missing phrase could be for each. Elicit suggestions and discuss them, drawing attention to correct sentences and use of the perfect form where appropriate.

Myths and legends – King Arthur

This chapter begins with an exploration of legends and reading *Arthur High King of Britain* by Michael Morpurgo. The children explore how the author creates the main character and moves him from one 'world' to another. They then compare the novel to *King Arthur and the Knights of the Round Table* by Marcia Williams. Non-fiction reading involves examining the sources of the Arthur legend and discussing fact, myth, legend and opinion. The children also read a classic poem on the same theme – 'The Lady of Shalott' by Alfred, Lord Tennyson.

Expected prior learning
- Can outline the characteristics, themes and events of legends.
- Can use the organisational features of books and websites to locate information.
- Can arrange words in alphabetical order by the first and second letters.
- Can organise information into paragraphs and under headings.
- Can give examples of useful words for indicating time and linking paragraphs.
- Know some words with 'silent' letters.
- Know that words can be built from root words.

Overview of progression
- Children will discuss and evaluate how authors use language. They will look at how authors develop characters and setting, and make comparisons.
- They will practise retrieving, recording and presenting information from non-fiction and explore how to distinguish between statements of fact and opinion.
- They will practise how to plan and make notes in preparation for writing and be given opportunities to assess the effectiveness of their own and others' writing.
- They will apply their growing knowledge of morphology and etymology to read aloud and understand new words. They will explore the spelling of words ending in /shus/, homophones, and modal verbs and adverbs.

Creative context
- The lessons could be linked to work in geography on a contrasting UK locality (Cornwall/the Scilly Isles).
- Examining different types of evidence and understanding the difference between fact and opinion are key skills required in history.
- The Arthurian themes such as loyalty, honour and chivalry – and what these might mean today – could be discussed in PSHE.

Preparation
This chapter focuses on King Arthur two texts are suggested, you could use, if appropriate, *The Story of King Arthur and his Knights* by Howard Pyle, or other versions. Children's versions of 'Sir Gawain and the Green Knight', ideally including *Sir Gawain and the Green Knight* by Michael Morpurgo are also required.

You will also need:
Arthur High King of Britain by Michael Morpurgo; *King Arthur and the Knights of the Round Table* by Marcia Williams; *Sir Gawain and the Green Knight* by Michael Morpurgo; a map of Cornwall, showing Tintagel and the Scilly Isles; standard and etymological dictionaries; internet access; highlighter pens; stopwatches or timers; a selection of factual books and legends.

On the CD-ROM you will find:
Media resources 'King Arthur', Painting of the Lady of Shalott'; interactive activities 'Character scales', 'Ends with /shus/', 'Words ending '-able' and '-ible'; photocopiable pages 'Alphabetical words', 'Ambiguous sentences', 'King Arthur: an interview with a historian', 'Gelert', 'Homophone bank', 'Hyphen game', 'Narrative poem storyboard', 'The Lady of Shalott', 'William Tell', 'Words with silent letters', 'Holiday homophone letter'

Chapter at a glance

An overview of the chapter. For curriculum objective codes, please see pages 8–10.

Week	Lesson	Curriculum objectives	Summary of activities	Outcome
1	1	RC: 3, 5	Explore how the author creates a character and moves him into another 'world'. Plan own 'other-world' story opening.	• Can differentiate between myths/legends and other stories. • Can plan a myth/legend opening in which a character moves into another world.
	2	RC: 3, 15 WC: 5, 17	Write story openings, using language for impact.	• Can use language to create impact and engage the reader.
	3	RC: 11, 13, 21	Use adjectives and their opposites to describe characters in a story, supported by evidence from the text.	• Can describe a story character, justifying this with evidence from the text. • Can use adjectives and opposites effectively.
	4	RWR: 1	Read words ending /shus/ and identify different spellings of this suffix. Explore words from the same root.	• Can read common words ending /shus/. • Can spell some of these words using their knowledge of roots.
	5	RWR: 1 WT: 2	Read words with silent letters and explore their etymology to try to explain spellings. Invent mnemonics to help spell these words.	• Can read words with silent letters and spell them using mnemonics. • Can use an etymological dictionary to explore derivations and spellings.
2	1	RC: 16, 17, 20	Read an interview with a historian. Scan text to find information. Identify opinions, exploring how they are expressed.	• Can use features such as icons and headings to find information. • Can recognise facts and opinions. • Can ask questions that can be researched.
	2	WC: 19, 28	Identify modal verbs in a text and explore how they are used. Use modal verbs to change meanings.	• Can change the meaning of a verb using a modal verb to express an opinion about probability.
	3	RC: 16 WC: 19, 28	Identify adverbs in a text and explore how they are used. Use adverbs to modify meanings of verbs.	• Can change the meaning of a verb using an adverb in order to express an opinion about probability.
	4	RC: 17 WC: 2	Use websites to find answers to questions about King Arthur and associated characters, places and events. Make notes, including references.	• Can make notes including references. • Can ask questions to answer through reading. • Can contribute to group research to answers questions. • Can recognise facts and opinions.
	5	RC: 17 WC: 8, 19	Write a paragraph to say whether they think King Arthur was a real person, justifying their opinions with evidence from non-fiction.	• Can make notes that are meaningful to others. • Can use notes to write a paragraph expressing opinions using appropriate vocabulary.
3	1	RC: 15	Read about the battle of Mount Bladon, identifying figurative language in the text and explaining its meaning.	• Can identify figurative language.
	2	RC: 14, 15	Alter words in a passage to change its atmosphere.	• Can use powerful verbs and adjectives to create an effect.
	3	WT: 1	Read words that end with '-ible' and '-able'.	• Can spell adjectives that have the suffixes '-ible' and '-able'. • Can apply simple rules for choosing between '-able' and '-ible' when spelling these words.
	4	RC: 14 WC: 4, 9	Identify words and phrases the author uses to link different time settings in the story.	• Can identify words and phrases that an author uses to move between different time settings.
	5	WC: 4, 5, 7, 9	Write their own version of a scene from the legend of King Arthur, selecting words to create atmosphere.	• Can select words to create atmosphere.
4	1	RC: 2, 3, 6, 18	Compare a cartoon-strip version of the legend of King Arthur with Michael Morpurgo's novel.	• Can formulate opinions about stories they have read.
	2	RC: 18 WC: 1	Choose a scene from the cartoon-strip version of the story and plan a presentation of it for a younger audience.	• Can formulate opinions about stories they have read. • Can write own adaptation of a legend.
	3	WC: 1, 2, 14	Write a script for their presentation, including dialogue and stage directions. Comment on each other's writing.	• Can write own adaptation of a legend.
	4	WC: 3	Write their own cartoon-strip version of a scene from the story, based on the notes and plans they made for their presentations.	• Can write own adaptation of a legend.
	5	WT: 1	Read examples of adjectives ending '-ant' or '-ent' and nouns ending '-ance', '-ancy', '-ence' or '-ency' and look for spelling rules.	• Can use knowledge of suffixes to create nouns from adjectives.

Chapter at a glance

Week	Lesson	Curriculum objectives	Summary of activities	Outcome
5	1	RC: 1, 18	Groups read different versions of 'Sir Gawain and the Green Knight'. Answer questions; compare with other groups' answers.	• Can compare different versions of the same story.
	2	WT: 3, 4, 5	Look up homophones and find their derivations. Match homophones to definitions.	• Can use an etymological dictionary to find word derivations. • Can spell homophones correctly for meaning.
	3	WT: 5, 6	Look up difficult words in 'Sir Gawain and the Green Knight'. Write a glossary.	• Can use the first three letters of a word for alphabetical order.
	4	WC: 23	Play a game: explaining the meanings of pairs of words with/without hyphens.	• Can explain how hyphens change the meanings of words.
	5	WC: 2, 4, 7, 14, 28	Create a knight and make up a magical adventure.	• Can plan and write a story modelled on another read. • Can read the story aloud with expression.
6	1	RWR: 1 RC: 1, 9 WT: 5	Listen to the poem 'The Lady of Shalott'. Discuss the meaning of *narrative poem*. Complete a storyboard about the poem as if for a film.	• Can describe the features of a narrative poem.
	2	RC: 1, 7	Discuss and make notes about the atmosphere of a verse, how the poet uses language to create it. Learn a verse by heart and prepare a performance.	• Can describe the atmosphere of a poem. • Can learn a verse from a classic poem by heart.
	3	RC: 1	Identify similes in the poem and discuss/ write about their effects.	• Can identify a simile and make up some of their own.
	4	RC: 1, 8	Identify and describe contrast in the poem and how the poet uses it.	• Can identify contrasting images in a poem.
	5	WC: 14	Writing a prequel verse to the poem: how the Lady of Shalott came to be in the castle and cursed.	• Can write a verse for a narrative poem in a similar style to a poem read.

Background knowledge

Adjective: Sometimes called *describing words* because they pick out single characteristics. Because verbs, nouns and adverbs can do the same, you can identify adjectives by their uses: either before a noun (*a foggy morning*) to modify the noun or after the verb *be* (*is foggy*) as its complement.

Adverb: A word that modifies the meaning of a verb or other word (but not a noun), for example: *ran quickly; very hot*.

Adverbial: Part of a clause that behaves like an adverb in modifying a verb: it could be an adverb, preposition or subordinate clause, for example: *waking up that morning, he goes to the gym to get fit.*

Cohesion: A text has cohesion if it is clear how the meanings of its parts fit together.

Homophone: A word that sounds the same as another word but might have a different spelling.

Modal verb: A verb used for expressing tense, degrees of certainty or ability and obligation: for example, *will, shall, could, might, ought to, must.* (*It **might** rain. You **should** go.*)

Modify: If one word modifies another it is placed as near as possible to it and makes the other word's meaning more specific.

Mood: The mood of a poem refers to the feelings evoked: *sadness, humour, belligerence, cheerfulness, joy* and so on.

Root word: A word that does not contain any smaller words or affixes.

Simile: A figure of speech that compares objects, people, places, ideas and so on, for example, *flapping like a flag in the wind; as still as a painting.*

Suffix: An affix placed at the end of a word to change its meaning and make a new word.

Week 1 lesson plans

This week's lessons are based on *Arthur High King of Britain* by Michael Morpurgo. The story will be read to the class during the course of the week (and continued during later weeks). The children will discuss what is meant by a legend. They will explore different ways of introducing a story and the main character. They will look at the ways in which an author moves between different 'worlds' in a story. The children will also explore vocabulary that might be new and examine the spelling of words with silent letters and words ending with /shus/.

1: Magical worlds

Expected outcomes
● All children can write a story opening using another as model; with help, they can read words with silent letters and /shus/ endings.
● Most children can create a new way of entering a magical world, using vocabulary for impact; they can spell words with silent letters and /shus/ endings.
● Some children can also create a character for a magical world; they can spell new words with silent letters /shus/ endings.

Curriculum objectives
● To increase familiarity with a wide range of books, including myths, legends and traditional stories and modern fiction from our literary heritage.
● To identify and discuss themes and conventions in and across a wide range of writing.

Resources
Media resource 'King Arthur' on the CD-ROM; map of Cornwall; *Arthur High King of Britain* by Michael Morpurgo

Introduction
● Show the image of King Arthur from the CD-ROM and ask the children what they know about him. Ask: *Was he a real person? How could you find out?* Tell them that you will explore this in a later lesson. Remind them of the meanings of *legend* and *myth*: they are often used for the same stories, depending on what people believe.
● Introduce *Arthur High King of Britain* by Michael Morpurgo and read the first page. Ask: *Is this how you expected the legend to begin? Why/why not?* The book has a modern setting, which is unexpected. Ask which word in the first sentence suggests a modern setting (*rucksack*). Show a map of Cornwall and invite a volunteer to point out the Scilly Isles. Leave the map on display so that they can later find other places in the story and trace the boy's journey.

Whole-class work
● Read the rest of Chapter 1. Highlight other words that confirm the modern setting: *sausage rolls*; *jam sandwich*, '*See you, Morris*' and '*Flaming marathon, is it?*'
● Ask how the author introduces Arthur's magical world. (The boy seems to drown but is rescued.) Discuss other stories with characters that move from the normal world into magical worlds, for example: *Alice's Adventures in Wonderland* (Lewis Carroll), *The Lion, the Witch and the Wardrobe* (CS Lewis); *Northern Lights*, *The Subtle Knife* and *The Amber Spyglass* (Philip Pullman); the *Harry Potter* books (JK Rowling).

Independent work
● Ask the children to imagine a character and think about how he or she could move from a normal to a magical world, and to make notes about it. Write prompts on the board to help: main character, setting, what the character does, how he or she moves into a magical world, characters in the magical world, what they tell or show the main character.

> **Differentiation**
> ● Children who need more support could begin with a 'magical world doorway' from a familiar story (for example, a mirror or picture to step into) and adapt it to create their own.

Review
● Invite volunteers to read out their ideas. Ask the others: *What setting is the character in at the start? How does he/she move into a magical world? How is the magical world different?*
● After listening to a few ideas, ask the children to suggest words that will capture the readers' interest in the setting. List some of the suggestions. Explain that these will be useful in the next lesson.
● Re-read some descriptive passages from *Arthur High King of Britain*. Ask: *Which words make this interesting?* List examples: *the cold mud oozing between his toes*; *the fear that was taking root in the boy's heart*; *the ocean was closing in around him*.
● Continue with the story, as time allows, between lessons. If you have enough copies the children could read it independently.

Curriculum objectives
● To increase familiarity with a wide range of books, including myths, legends and traditional stories and modern fiction from our literary heritage.
● To discuss and evaluate how authors use language, including figurative language, considering impact on the reader.
● In narratives, to describe settings, characters and atmosphere and integrating dialogue to convey character and advance the action.
● To use the perfect form of verbs to mark relationships of time and cause.

Resources
Arthur High King of Britain by Michael Morpurgo; the list of words generated at the end of lesson 1; the children's notes from lesson 1 about how a character might move into a magical setting

2: Creating an impact

Introduction
● Recap the story so far and read Chapter 2. Ask: *What magical events take place? Does the author make these believable?* Discuss how the author sets events in a magical world where anything is possible. Revisit the word list from lesson 1 (creating the setting) and add others the children suggest.

Whole-class work
● Read out an idea for a 'normal world' to 'magical world' story opening: for example, where a character goes through a hole in a tree. Ask for some short sentences to say what happened. Write these up as very simple statements such as: *The girl went into the forest. She began to climb the giant oak. She wanted to get to the top. She found a big hole. She crawled into it.*
● Ask: *How can we make this more interesting?* Suggest adding adjectives, changing the verbs (recap the perfect tense, use starter activity 17 'The perfect form' if required), saying how the girl felt when she found the hole, and so on. Insert the most effective words and ask what difference they make. Introduce the term *impact*: the story opening now has impact.

Independent work
● Ask the children to write their story openings, using their plans from lesson 1 and choosing words for impact. Discuss the effect of their words as a class.

Review
● Read out some of the story openings. Ask what effect they create, how this was achieved, what was effective, which words created this effect.

Curriculum objectives
● To draw inferences and justify these with evidence from the text.
● To provide reasoned justifications for their views.
● To summarise the main ideas drawn from more than one paragraph, identifying key details that support the main ideas.

Resources
Arthur High King of Britain by Michael Morpurgo; interactive activity 'Character scales' on the CD-ROM; photocopiable page 40 'Character scales'

3: Characters

Introduction
● Read the next chapter of *Arthur High King of Britain*. Ask for an adjective to describe Arthur, using evidence from the story. If the children find this difficult, suggest an adjective. Ask if this describes him, and why.

Whole-class work
● Show the interactive activity 'Character scales' on the CD-ROM. Invite a volunteer to drag the marker along a scale from bad to good for Kay. Ask the others if they agree, and why. Remind them to use evidence from the story. Point out that not all characters fit at the ends of the bad/good line.

Paired work
● Give each pair photocopiable page 40 'Character scales'. Ask them to choose one of the following characters and decide where on the first scale the character fits: Arthur, Egbert, Kay, Merlin, King Pelinore, Morgana le Fay, Guinevere, Margawse or Lady Nemue.
● Encourage them to make a note of evidence from the story on a separate sheet of paper. Ask them to write their own words/labels for the blank scales to suit the character and to complete these too.

> **Differentiation**
> ● Provide words for character scales and explain their meanings: *brave/cowardly, ordinary/mysterious, gentle/harsh, honest/dishonest, open/sly, generous/mean, loyal/disloyal.*

Review
● Invite volunteers to use a character scale to help them to describe their character. Ask how the author creates this effect.

Curriculum objectives
● To apply their growing knowledge of root words, prefixes and suffixes (morphology and etymology), as listed in Appendix 1, both to read aloud and to understand the meaning of new words that they meet.

Resources
Arthur High King of Britain by Michael Morpurgo; dictionaries; interactive activity 'Ends with /shus/' on the CD-ROM; photocopiable page 41 'Ends with /shus/'

4: Adjectives ending with /shus/

Introduction
● Display the following adjectives ending in the sound /shus/ and invite volunteers to read them aloud: *ambitious, anxious, cautious, ferocious, gracious, malicious, obnoxious, vicious.*
● Model how to find each word in a dictionary, for example: *Ambitious will be near the beginning of the dictionary because it starts with 'a': The word at the top of this page is ample. Both begin 'am'. Look at the third letter. Ambitious comes before ample.* Ask them to look up some of the words – in a dictionary race.

Whole-class work
● Ask the children to match each adjective to a character in *Arthur High King of Britain* and explain their choices.

Independent work
● Hand out photocopiable page 41 'Ends with /shus/' (or allow children to use the interactive version on the CD-ROM). Ask the children to read the words in the list and to look up their meanings before sorting them into sets. They can then add their own words to each set.

Differentiation
● Children who need support could work with a more confident partner.

Review
● Write up some words from the lesson and ask which root words they come from, for example: *spacious/space; gracious/grace, cautious/caution, anxious/anxiety.* Circle the letter before '-ious' and its counterpart in the other word: *spa**c**e/spa**c**ious.* Discuss how this helps with spelling the suffix. (Note that very few words end in '-scious', the most common being *luscious* and *conscious*.)

Curriculum objectives
● To apply their growing knowledge of root words, prefixes and suffixes (morphology and etymology), as listed in Appendix 1, both to read aloud and to understand the meaning of new words that they meet.
● To spell some words with 'silent' letters.

Resources
Arthur High King of Britain by Michael Morpurgo; photocopiable page 'Words with silent letters' from the CD-ROM; etymological dictionaries or dictionaries that include etymological notes; for extra practice, see the photocopiable page 'Alphabetical words' from the CD-ROM

5: Silent letters

Introduction
● Display the following sentence from Chapter 1 of the story: *He knew the waters around the Scilly Isles like the back of his hand.* Ask: *Which three words have unusual spellings? Scilly, Isles* and *knew* have silent letters. Explain that no one is sure where the 'c' in *Scilly* came from. Use 'spell-speak' to help – sounding the 'c' as /k/.

Whole-class work
● Ask the class to open an etymological dictionary in approximately the right place for *isle*: *'I' is the ninth letter, so open it in the second quartile, almost at halfway.* Ask if it comes before or after *island*, and how they know. They could put the words *isle, islet* and *island* in alphabetical order.
● Read the information about *isle* (or *island*). The 's' might come from Latin *insula*. Similarly, look up *know*, which has several derivations, including Old Norse *kná*. Discuss mnemonics for spelling *isle* and *island*, for example: *An isle/island IS LAND.*

Paired work
● Display photocopiable page 'Words with silent letters' from the CD-ROM. Ask the children to look up the words to find out why they might be spelled like this and then think up mnemonics to help them and others to spell them.

Review
● Ask for other words from the story that have silent letters: *castle, damn, doubt, gnawed, knee, kneel, knight, knocked, listen, scent, sword, wrestled.*

Week 2 lesson plans

This week's lessons will focus on non-fiction texts about King Arthur, including the non-fiction text 'King Arthur: an interview with a historian', and websites that provide further information. The children will make notes and share the information they find with their groups before writing a paragraph stating their opinions about whether or not King Arthur was a real person.

1: King Arthur in history

Introduction

● Tell the children that for centuries people have written about King Arthur – and, more recently, made films about him. Ask: *Does this make you think he was really a king, or even a real person? Can we check?* We can read accounts by historians from the time, lists of kings and so on. We can look for evidence that someone existed but there is no real way of proving they didn't.

Whole-class work

● Remind the class that *Arthur High King of Britain*, like many stories, is about an old legend that may have some truth in it. Explain that some historians do not think Arthur was a real person, let alone a king, but others think he might have been. Tell the children that they are going to read an interview with a historian who has researched King Arthur, and make notes on any facts he has found and his opinions.

Paired work

● Give each pair photocopiable page 'King Arthur: an interview with a historian' from the CD-ROM. Read the first page with the children. Ask: *How can you tell which are the historian's words and which are the interviewer's words?* (They may notice that the interviewer's words end in a question mark, but so do some of the historian's words. It is the bold type that helps the reader to find each question.)
● Ask them for an example of a fact given by the historian. For example, *Tintagel was an important community in the fifth century.* Ask: *How do we know this is a fact?* (From excavations.) Point out that sometimes opinions are expressed as if they are facts, for example: *Arthur belongs in the late fifth or the early sixth century.* Ask: *Why might this not be a fact?* (Because some historians do not believe Arthur existed at all.) Point out that facts can be checked against other sources.
● Ask for an example of an opinion from the text, for example: *I think Arthur probably played a part in some battles against the Saxons.* Ask: *How do we know that this is an opinion?* (The historian says *I think* and *probably.* Then he says that there is not enough evidence.)
● The children can then read the text and list the facts it tells them and any opinions expressed by the historian. They could list these in two columns.

Facts		Opinions	
Fact	How I know it is a fact	Opinion	How I know it is an opinion

Review

● Ask each pair to compare their answers with those of another pair. Allow a minute or two and then ask if any have found anything they disagree on. Discuss these with the class to decide whether they are facts or opinions (or neither).

Curriculum objectives

- To use modal verbs or adverbs to indicate degrees of possibility.
- To use and understand the grammatical terminology in Appendix 2 accurately and appropriately in discussing their writing and reading.

Resources

Photocopiable page 'King Arthur: an interview with a historian' from the CD-ROM; the children's notes from lesson 1

2: Expressing opinions: using verbs

Introduction

- Remind the children of the text they read during the previous lesson. Tell them that they are going to re-read it to find out more about the kind of language used for expressing facts and opinions, or for trying to convince the listener or reader that something is a fact.

Whole-class work

- Display a paragraph from photocopiable page 'King Arthur: An interview with a historian' from the CD-ROM as a model and point out some of the modal verbs: *Archaeology **may** never prove anything about him; Something **might** turn up: his name on a memorial stone, or even a coin....*
- Note that these verbs include words like *may* and *might*. Ask why. (They give more information about the main verb in the sentence; they show that something is likely or possible, but not certain.) Ask the children how the meanings of these sentences would change if these verbs were changed, for example: *Archaeology will never prove anything about him; Something will turn up: his name on a memorial stone, or even a coin....*

Paired work

- Give the children a section of the interview and ask them to underline any verbs that change the meanings of other verbs. Ask them to rewrite the section of text, changing these verbs so that the meaning of the sentence changes.

Review

- Invite volunteers to read a changed paragraph of text. Ask: *Did anyone change that paragraph in a different way?* Ask them to read it out. Ask the class how the meaning has changed.

Curriculum objectives

- To distinguish between statements of fact and opinion.
- To use modal verbs or adverbs to indicate degrees of possibility.
- To use and understand the grammatical terminology in Appendix 2 accurately and appropriately in discussing their writing and reading.

Resources

Photocopiable page 'King Arthur: an interview with a historian' from the CD-ROM

3: Expressing opinions: using adverbs

Introduction

- Tell the class they are going to look at another type of word that can alter the meaning of other words. Remind them of adverbs, using examples in sentences, such as: *He wrote carefully; I worked hard; We knew him well.* Ask which word they could take out of each sentence to change its meaning but still leave a sentence. Explain that adverbs are also useful in expressing opinions.

Whole-class work

- Ask: *Which adverb in the following sentence changes the meaning of a verb? Excavations showed that Tintagel in Cornwall was an important community in the fifth century – probably a centre of local government.* Ask: *Which verb does **probably** change?* (Was.)

Independent work

- Give each child photocopiable page 'King Arthur: an interview with a historian' from the CD-ROM and ask them to underline all the adverbs they can find that help to express an opinion. They could choose some sentences to rewrite, changing these adverbs.

Differentiation

- If necessary, select and highlight some phrases or sentences for them to work on, point out the verb and ask them to find a word that changes its meaning, for example: *Something might turn up.* Ask: *What other words could we swap it for?* (Will, should.)

Review

- Invite feedback and ask how the adverbs changed the meanings of the verbs.

Curriculum objectives
● To retrieve, record and present information from non-fiction.
● To note and develop initial ideas, drawing on reading and research where necessary.

Resources
Computers and internet access – in preparation for the lesson, bookmark websites that give information about King Arthur for children

4: Was King Arthur a real person? (1)

Introduction

● Tell the children that they are going to collect some more information about King Arthur. Help them to come up with some questions that will help, for example: *If King Arthur was real, who were his parents? Where was he born? When did he live? How did he die? Where?*

Whole-class work

● Ask: *What answers would you get to these questions from* Arthur High King of Britain? Model how to use a website to find information that might help: use the headings and icons, site map and links. Model how to scan pages for headings, pictures and captions; then skim for key words.
● Ask: *How will I remember what I found out?* Recap how to make notes: writing short forms of words, omitting unimportant words but writing important words or names in full. Emphasise that they need to be able to read and make sense of them later!
● Ask: *How will I remember where I found this information?* Make a note of the website and page.

Group work

● Let the children search for information to answer their questions using the selected websites. They could share the task of writing notes, with different children writing different parts.

Review

● Invite each group to report a piece of information they found. Ask: *Is this a fact or an opinion? How can you tell?* Encourage other children to comment.

Curriculum objectives
● To retrieve, record and present information from non-fiction.
● To use further organisational and presentational devices to structure text and to guide the reader.
● To use modal verbs or adverbs to indicate degrees of possibility.

Resources
Children's notes from lesson 4; children's work on modal verbs (lesson 2) and adverbs (lesson 3)

5: Was King Arthur a real person? (2)

Introduction

● Tell the class that they are going to use the notes they made in the previous lesson to help them to write a paragraph to say whether they think King Arthur was a real person, and what evidence supports their opinion.
● Remind them of the verbs they learned about that change the meaning of other verbs and ask for examples that help to express opinions, for example: *might, should, could, seem, must.* Also ask what adverbs they learned about that change the meanings of verbs, for example: *probably, certainly, definitely, surely.*

Group and independent work

● Recap the meaning of *paragraph* and useful vocabulary for expressing opinions: *because, so, thus, the reason is.*
● Ask the children to begin by sharing the notes they made with their groups. Ask them to use the shared notes to help them to write their own paragraph about whether King Arthur was a real person.

Review

● Display the paragraphs so that the children can read one another's work and comment on it. If the children have different opinions about King Arthur, this could be discussed in a class debate in another lesson. Continue reading the story between lessons or, if you have enough copies, the children can read on independently.

Week 3 lesson plans

This week's lessons will continue to be based on *Arthur High King of Britain* by Michael Morpurgo and focus on key parts of the story: Arthur's first battle (Mount Bladon), his wedding, the sword in the lake, the Holy Grail coming to Camelot. The children will explore how the author creates settings and atmosphere. They will develop skills in the use of language for expressing facts or creating an atmosphere, in writing coherent paragraphs and spelling words with similar-sounding endings '-able' and '-ible'.

Expected outcomes
● All children can make some comment about writing style and begin to create atmosphere in writing. With help, they can write a version of part of King Arthur with supported choices.
● Most children can do this with little support.
● Some children will use a greater range of vocabulary in their discussion and writing.

Curriculum objectives
● To discuss and evaluate how authors use language, including figurative language, considering the impact on the reader.

Resources
Arthur High King of Britain by Michael Morpurgo

1: The battle of Mount Bladon

Introduction
● Re-read the story of the battle of Mount Bladon (Chapter 3 'Excalibur'). Ask: *As Arthur and his men set off for the battle, what did you feel about their chances of winning? What made you feel this?* (They seemed unbeatable and fearless, so readers are given the feeling that they will win.) *Which words create this effect?* (Arthur said that they felt as if anything was possible; more and more people joined them as they passed through each village.) Point out examples to explain figurative language and to show how authors use it to create effects, for example: *the new steel in our hearts.* Ask: *Did they really have steel in their hearts? What effect does this give?* (They were determined to win – steel gives the feeling of strength.)
● After reading the passage about the battle, ask: *How did you feel about the Saxons?* Were they just enemies to defeat or did the author make you have any feelings about them? (They were brave: *Say all you like about a Saxon, but he is no coward; They bled their blood into the soil of Britain and stained it for ever.*) The author makes us feel some sympathy for them.

Paired work
● Ask the children to read the paragraph of Chapter 3 that begins, *I take no pride in the blood we spilt, nor any pleasure in it either.* Ask them to write answers to these questions, with evidence from the text.
  ● *How did Arthur feel about killing people in battle?*
  ● *Arthur said that others said his actions 'showed courage but I knew it for what it was'. What did he mean?*
  ● *What do these words make you think about Arthur: 'As I hacked and thrust and slashed, I became as someone else'?*
  ● *What made Arthur stop and think about how the fighting was changing him?*
  ● *What do these pieces of figurative language mean: 'a red mist', 'kept my face heavenward'?*

> **Differentiation**
> ● Ask children who need more support to look for words that make us think Arthur was savage in battle: *hacked* and *thrust* and *slashed.* Ask: *Do you think he was starting to enjoy killing people? Which words tell us that he realised this and stopped himself?*

Review
● Listen to different children reading their answers and ask how Arthur began to change. Draw out that he seemed to be getting carried away by the fighting (*a red mist would come before my eyes*) but that he remembered Merlin's words: *keep your face heavenward.* Discuss what this means. (Thinking of what is right/good – not literally looking towards heaven.)

Curriculum objectives
● To discuss and evaluate how authors use language, including figurative language, considering the impact on the reader.
● To identify how language, structure and presentation contribute to meaning.

Resources
Arthur High King of Britain by Michael Morpurgo; photocopiable page 42 'Arthur's wedding'

2: Arthur's wedding

Introduction
● Invite volunteers to recap the story up to Arthur's wedding. Ask: *Will Arthur and Guinevere be happy? Why/why not?* What did Merlin mean when he said: *There are other fish in the sea.* Note the figurative language.

Whole-class work
● Re-read the first scene of Chapter 4. Ask: *What is the atmosphere here?*

Paired work
● Give each pair photocopiable page 42 'Arthur's wedding'. Allow five to ten minutes for them to underline words and phrases that create the happy atmosphere of joy and celebration.
● Repeat this for the next section beginning *I met Merlin on the ramparts*. Ask: *How does the atmosphere change? What words does the author use to create the feeling of foreboding?* For example, *mist-covered marshes*.

Independent work
● Ask the children to make changes to each passage to alter its atmosphere. Point out it's not just adjectives that can be changed. Changing other words, such as verbs, can also have an effect, for example: *ran – crept, said – muttered*.

Review
● Read out some of the altered passages and ask: *What is the atmosphere like now? Which words help to create this atmosphere?*

Curriculum objectives
● To use further prefixes and suffixes and understand the guidelines for adding them.

Resources
Photocopiable page 43 'Words ending '-able' and '-ible''; interactive activity 'Words ending '-able' and '-ible'' on the CD-ROM; dictionaries

3: Adjectives ending with '-able' and '-ible'

Introduction
● Remind the class how Arthur felt when he saw his half-sisters arriving: *a terrible sense of foreboding*. Invite a volunteer to write *terrible* on a whiteboard. Ask the class to check this in a dictionary. Recap root words and ask for other words with the same root: *terrify, terror*.

Whole-class work
● Ask: *What kind of word is* terrible*?* (Adjective.) Ask for other adjectives ending with the suffix '-ible', and their root words (*horrible/horror/horrid, visible/vision, sensible/sense/sensitive*). Repeat this for words with endings that sound the same but are spelled '-able' (*comfortable/comfort, movable/move*). Point out that for *most* adjectives ending '-able' the suffix is added to another English word (*eatable, drinkable*) but for most for adjectives ending '-ible' the suffix is added to a root word from another language, such as Latin or Greek (*edible, legible, visible*). Note that the endings of some words change before the suffix is added, for example: *move/movable, love/loveable*.

Independent work
● Ask the children to complete photocopiable page 43 'Words ending '-able' and '-ible'' (or the interactive version on the CD-ROM) and then to check their answers in a dictionary.

> **Differentiation**
> ● Support children by writing the words in the appropriate columns and ask them to add the suffixes '-ible' or '-able'. Remind them that the spelling of the root may change.

Review
● Discuss any tricky words on the photocopiable sheet with the class. Point out some correct alternatives: *collectible/collectable; dividable/divisible*.

4: The Round Table

Introduction
● Re-read the scene where Arthur talks about the Round Table, beginning where Guinevere's father, Leodegraunce, presents it to Arthur (Chapter 4). Ask: *How does the author remind us that Arthur is talking to the boy?*

Whole-class work
● Ask: *What is special and mysterious about the table?* Explain the Holy Grail. Ask: *How does this part of the story prepare readers for what will happen later?*

Group work
● Ask the children to discuss this part of the story and make notes about the different times in the past, present and future mentioned and how the author moves between these times.

> **Differentiation**
> ● For children who need more support, provide a chart for notes and help them to begin:
>
> | Before King Arthur's time | King Arthur's time | King Arthur's future | The boy's time |
> |---|---|---|---|
> | Merlin made table for Arthur's father | King Leodegraunce tells story of table | Merlin names future knights, says Holy Grail will come to Camelot | Old man shows table |

Review
● Recap how the author moves from the present (the boy with the old Arthur) to Arthur in the past, to his father and to his future. Re-read sentences with key words that link these times: *I remember*; *after his death*; *now the Round Table is back*; *here will sit.*

5: Setting the scene

Introduction
● Write up headings for scenes from the story: *The sword in the lake* (Chapter 3), *The Holy Grail comes to Camelot* (Chapter 9), *The final battle* (Chapter 10). Taking each scene in turn, read a few sentences aloud. Ask: *What was the atmosphere like? How did the author create it?*

Whole-class work
● Choose a scene from above. Ask: *What happened in this scene?* List the actions, for example: *Arthur went to a lake with Merlin. He saw a hand holding a sword*, and so on. Ask: *What could you add to create atmosphere?*

Independent work
● Hand out photocopiable page 44 'Describing a scene'. Ask the children to write a word for the atmosphere of each scene, for example: *mysterious, powerful, frightening, brutal*. They should then list some words that help to create this effect before writing their own version of the scene. Ask the children to swap scenes with a partner, then read and discuss what works well in one another's writing.

> **Differentiation**
> ● Help by comparing different verbs for the same actions, for example: *rode/charged.*

Review
● Ask the class if they think their partner wrote anything very effective, and to read it aloud.

Curriculum objectives
● To identify how language, structure and presentation contribute to meaning.
● To select appropriate grammar and vocabulary, understanding how such choices can change and enhance meaning.
● To assess the effectiveness of their own and others' writing.

Resources
Arthur High King of Britain by Michael Morpurgo

Curriculum objectives
● To select grammar and vocabulary and understand how such choices can change and enhance meaning.
● In narratives, to describe settings, characters and atmosphere and integrate dialogue to convey character and advance the action.
● To use a wide range of devices to build cohesion within and across paragraphs.
● To assess the effectiveness of their own and others' writing.

Resources
Arthur High King of Britain by Michael Morpurgo; photocopiable page 44 'Describing a scene'

Expected outcomes
● All children can contribute to discussions comparing books and planning a presentation, and write a simple cartoon strip.
● Most children can identify similarities and differences and model a comic strip on reading.
● Some children can take a leading part in discussions.

Curriculum objectives
● To increase familiarity with a wide range of books, including myths, legends and traditional stories and modern fiction from our literary heritage.
● To read books that are structured in different ways and reading for a range of purposes.
● To participate in discussions about books that are read to them and those they can read themselves, building on their own and others' ideas and challenging views courteously.
● To make comparisons within and across books.

Resources
Arthur High King of Britain by Michael Morpurgo, *King Arthur and the Knights of the Round Table* by Marcia Williams – if possible, several copies of each book so that the children can read independently or with a partner; children should be given opportunities to read both books before the lesson

Week 4 lesson plans

Another humorous comic strip version of the legend will be introduced this week – *King Arthur and the Knights of the Round Table* by Marcia Williams. The children will compare the two versions of the legend and then select a scene for which they will plan a script to present to a younger audience. Words from the story will be used to introduce the adjective suffixes '-ant' and '-ent' and the noun suffixes '-ance' or '-ancy' and '-ence' or '-ency'.

1: An alternative version of the legend

Introduction
● Ask the class if they enjoyed reading *King Arthur and the Knights of the Round Table* by Marcia Williams, and explain why/why not. Encourage them to listen to one another and then to say whether or not they agree, and why. Ask: *How does each author introduce the story?* Compare the different structures of the two Arthur stories: Michael Morpurgo's telling by Arthur to the boy, whose name we are not told, and Marcia Williams' straightforward 'traditional tale' approach, beginning *Once...*. Ask: *How are the endings different?* Discuss the effect of each ending: happy, mysterious, sad, hopeful.

Whole-class work
● Ask the children to think about the similarities and differences between the two versions of the legend. Ask: *What were the key events? Were these the same in both stories? What was different?* Help them to list their ideas on a chart.

Key events	Arthur High King of Britain	King Arthur & Knights of Round Table
Arthur pulled sword out of stone (as true king of Britain)	✓	✓
Arthur challenged Sir Pellinore	✓	✓
Arthur fought a battle at Mount Bladon	✓	✗

Paired work
● Tell the class that they are going to work in pairs to discuss the similarities and differences between the two different versions of the legend and to record these on charts like the one shown. Different groups could work on different aspects of the story: key events; characters; places.

Differentiation
● Children who need support could be paired with others with higher attainment in reading.

Review
● Ask each group to report their results to the class, who should listen for anything they disagree with or that the group has missed out. Ask: *Are the two books similar? In what ways?* The children should notice that both books tell the same story, with the same key events, although Michael Morpurgo's book includes more events than that of Marcia Williams, which omits the battles of Mount Bladon and Camlan. Also the endings differ: in Michael Morpurgo's tale, Arthur is mortally wounded in the battle of Camlan but in Marcia Williams' book he lives happily ever after. Both books feature the same main characters, apart from Mordred, who is absent from *King Arthur and the Knights of the Round Table*. Others, for example Bercelet, are not named or have slightly different names or different spellings (Sir Egbert/Sir Ector, Morgana le Fay/Morgan le Fay, Arthur Pendragon/Uther Pendragon). Some characters are different: Merlin is more of a comic figure in Marcia Williams' book but more mysterious in Michael Morpurgo's.

Curriculum objectives

● To identify the audience for, and the purpose of, the writing, selecting the appropriate form and using other similar writing as models for their own.
● To participate in discussions about books that are read to them and those they can read themselves, building on their own and others' ideas and challenging views courteously.

Resources

King Arthur and the Knights of the Round Table by Marcia Williams – if possible, one copy per group; stopwatches or timers

2: A scene from the story

Introduction

● Ask the class to think about *King Arthur and the Knights of the Round Table* by Marcia Williams. Did they find it funny? Invite them to read out funny parts. Ask: *Was it all funny?* Point out that authors use humour in serious stories and sadness in funny ones as a contrast. Look for examples of serious, sad, mysterious or frightening parts in the story.

Group work

● Ask each group to work together to choose a scene from the story. Remind them of the rules for group discussion.
● Allow five to ten minutes, then ask them to plan how to present their scene to a younger class. Talk about different ways of helping the audience to understand the scene – a narrator, dialogue, signs, props and so on. They will also need to think how to tell what has already happened in the story.
● Ask them to time their presentation – it should be no longer than five minutes – and make notes about what they will do.

Review

● Ask the children to leave their notes, along with a blank sheet of paper for comments, on their table. The groups can then move round the tables (perhaps clockwise or in some other orderly way) to read, discuss and leave comments on other groups' plans. Keep the plans and comments for the next lesson.

Curriculum objectives

● To identify the audience for, and the purpose of, the writing, selecting the appropriate form and using other, similar, writing as models for their own.
● To note and develop initial ideas, drawing on reading and research where necessary.
● To perform their own compositions, using appropriate intonation, volume and movement so that meaning if clear.

Resources

Children's planning notes and feedback from the previous lesson; *King Arthur and the Knights of the Round Table* by Marcia Williams – if possible, one copy per group; photocopiable page 45 'Playscript planner'

3: Presenting a scene for a younger audience

Introduction

● Remind the class of their work from the previous lesson. Ask them to read the comments made by others about their plans. Ask them to comment on the way in which these were expressed, and read out examples. Were these polite? Were they helpful? How did they help?

Group work

● Ask the class to work in groups to prepare their presentation for a younger class. Help them to identify the jobs to do: allocating roles, writing the script and preparing props (with appropriate limits, according to feasibility and time). Give them photocopiable page 45 'Playscript planner' to help with this.

Review

● As in the previous lesson, ask the children to leave their completed work on their table, along with a blank sheet of paper, and circulate around the tables to leave comments on other groups' work. They should comment on anything they think is good for the intended audience and anything they think should be changed, and why. If possible, find a time between lessons when the children can present their scenes to the younger class in chronological order, with appropriate narration to link them.

Curriculum objectives

● In writing narratives, to consider how authors have developed characters and settings in what they have read, listened to or seen performed.

Resources

Arthur High King of Britain by Michael Morpurgo

4: Cartoon strip

Introduction

● Recap the final chapter of *Arthur High King of Britain* with the class. Ask: *How has Arthur's character changed through the story?*

Independent work

● Show the children how to use a storyboard to plan a cartoon strip to retell this chapter. Limit the story to eight frames. They should decide what they need to show in each frame, any narrative, the characters' words and thoughts (including Bercelet's). Ask them to think about how they might use Bercelet's thoughts to give the reader information. They can then draw and write their stories.

Differentiation

● Help the children to split the story into eight scenes, for example: Arthur telling the boy what he would like him to do and the boy's answer; the question and answer about Lancelot and Guinevere; the next question and answer; walking down the tunnel; Lady Nemue and the boat; the acorn; sailing away; arriving home.

Review

● Ask the children to swap stories with a partner (chosen for them) and to make notes to write a review of it. They could write their reviews as a homework activity.

Curriculum objectives

● To use further prefixes and suffixes and understand the guidelines for adding them.

Resources

King Arthur and the Knights of the Round Table by Marcia Williams – if possible, one copy per group; photocopiable page 46 'Suffixes'; dictionaries

5: Suffixes '-ant', '-ance', '-ancy' and '-ent', '-ence', '-ency'

Introduction

● Tell the class that they are going to look at some words from the stories. Read examples of adjectives ending '-ent' and '-ant', along with the nouns: *arrogant Sir Pellinore; magnificent Round Table; gallant hero; reticent man.* Ask: *What kind of word are they?*

Whole-class work

● Write the adjectives on the board and ask the children to look them up. Invite volunteers to give the meanings and to use them in sentences. Demonstrate how to change the suffix to make a noun, for example: *arrogance.* Ask for a sentence using it, for example: *Sir Pellinore showed his arrogance by laughing at Arthur's challenge.* Ask: *Can you change **magnificent** into a noun and use it in a sentence?* (*Magnificence. They were amazed at the magnificence of the Round Table.*) Repeat this for the other words. *What do you notice about the spellings of the suffixes of the nouns?* ('-ent' and '-ence', '-ant' and '-ance'.)

Independent work

● Provide photocopiable page 46 'Suffixes' and ask the children to complete the nouns using a suffix. They should check them in a dictionary.

Differentiation

● Where necessary, read and complete the nouns with the children. Point out 'a' or 'e' in '-ant' and '-ent', and ask them to complete the noun suffix.

Review

● Ask: *Can you see a pattern in the spellings of the suffixes – 'a' or 'e'?* Point out the letters before '-ent'/'-ence'/'-ency'. How would '-ant'/'-ance'/'-ancy' suffixes change their sounds?

Week 5 lesson plans

During this week's lessons the children will read and enjoy different versions of a story linked with the legend of King Arthur – 'Sir Gawain and the Green Knight'. They will invent their own knight and write a magical adventure about him in the style of the story read, after looking up and learning new vocabulary, spelling rules and grammar from the story (homophones, hyphens and adverbials). They will use what they have learned to help them to create atmosphere and impact.

1: Sir Gawain and the Green Knight

Expected outcomes
● All children can plan a story, with support where necessary, and use words to link paragraphs.
● Most children can do this independently.
● Some children can do this using a greater range of linking words.

Curriculum objectives
● To participate in discussions about books that are read to them and those they can read themselves, building on their own and others' ideas and challenging views courteously.
● To continue to read and discuss an increasingly wide range of fiction.

Resources
Sir Gawain and the Green Knight by Michael Morpurgo; at least two different versions (print or online) of the legend of 'Sir Gawain and the Green Knight' that the children can read for themselves, according to reading ability

Introduction
● Ask the class to name some of King Arthur's knights. Write up the names of the knights they mention. Ask: *Who is your favourite knight? Why?*
● Tell them that Michael Morpurgo said about Gawain: *Of all the tales of the Knights of the Round Table, his is the most magical and the one I most love to tell.* Remind them that he also wrote about Sir Gawain and the Green Knight in *Arthur High King of Britain* and ask what they remember about the tale.
● Ask: *Why do you think Michael Morpurgo thinks this is the most magical tale?* Encourage them to describe the magical events they remember from it.

Group work
● Give each group a different version of 'Sir Gawain and the Green Knight'. Ask them to read the first part – up to where Gawain takes up the Green Knight's challenge. Ask them to make notes to answer these questions (or to say if they can't, and why) and give evidence from the story.
  ● *At what time of year did the Green Knight come to Camelot?*
  ● *What was the weather like?*
  ● *What was the atmosphere like at Camelot before the Green Knight came?*
  ● *How did the atmosphere change when the Green Knight arrived?*
  ● *What did Arthur and his knights do?*
  ● *What was the Green Knight like?*
  ● *What personal qualities did Gawain have?*
  ● *What magical events happened in the story? Where?*
  ● *Why did Gawain choose to combat the Green Knight?*
  ● *What was the atmosphere like when Gawain went to the Green Castle?*

Differentiation
● Ensure that children who need support work with others who can read the story and that they have an illustrated version, or provide a version written in simpler language. Each group could decide among its members who should read the story aloud (or take turns). They should be able to read loudly enough for their group to hear without disturbing the others.

Review
● Ask the children to swap answers with another group and to notice any differences between these and their own. Ask for reasons. Discuss how different authors present different views of events and characters. The children should continue reading the story between lessons.

Curriculum objectives
● To continue to distinguish between homophones and other words that are often confused.
● To use knowledge of morphology and etymology in spelling and understand that the spelling of some words needs to be learned specifically, as listed in Appendix 1.
● To use dictionaries to check the spelling and meaning of words.

Resources
Photocopiable page 47 'Homophone roots'; dictionaries; etymological dictionaries (if possible, one per group)

2: Homophones

Introduction
● Ask: *Which word in the story title can be spelled in a different way, with a different meaning?* (*Knight/night*.) What do we call these words? (Homophones – meaning same sound, from Greek *homo* [same] and *phone* [sound].) Explain that English has many homophones and tricky spellings because it has words from many different languages. Explain that *knight* and *night* come from different words from the past: *knight* comes from the Old English *cniht*; *night* comes from more than one language, including Old English (*niht*).

Whole-class work
● Ask for other words from the story that have homophones and ask the children to look up their meanings and the words they come from, for example: *court* (king's court – Old French *cort*, Anglian *curt*), *caught* (Old English *cachte*, *cauhte*).

Paired work
● Provide photocopiable page 47 'Homophone roots' and demonstrate how to complete the first example. Ask two children to take turns to explain the different origins of the pairs of words. They should continue working in pairs in this way.

Differentiation
● Some children could, instead, match up pairs of homophones, written on cards, and check their meanings in a dictionary: *deer/dear, pair/pear, for/four, ring/wring*.

Review
● Ask the children what they have learned. For homework they could make up their own homophone-matching game (match each word to its meaning).

Curriculum objectives
● To use dictionaries to check the spelling and meaning of words.
● To use the first three or four letters of a word to check spelling, meaning or both of these in a dictionary.

Resources
Sir Gawain and the Green Knight by Michael Morpurgo or another version of the story; dictionaries

3: Dictionary work

Introduction
● Read part of *Sir Gawain and the Green Knight* with the class. Ask: *Were there any words you didn't know?* Write these up and ask if anyone knows their meanings. Examples might be: *crescent, incredulous, integrity, chivalry, intricately, exquisitely, aspire*.

Whole-class work
● Give out dictionaries and ask the class to look up the first word on the list. Remind them to look at the second or third letter, if needed. Ask for the definition. Ask how many dictionary definitions there are for it. If there is more than one, ask how to choose the correct one. Remind them to read the sentence containing the word to check which definition makes sense.

Differentiation
● Where necessary, help the children to choose an appropriate part of the dictionary (near the beginning, middle, end, or which quartile – considering alphabetical order) and how to use the first two, three or four letters to find it.

Group work
● Ask the children to share the task of looking up the difficult words from the story and to make a glossary for them.

Review
● Ask: *What kinds of books usually have glossaries?* (Non-fiction/information.) What do authors of fiction and poetry usually do instead to help readers with difficult words? (They put asterisks or small numbers after the words and add footnotes.) Show them some examples of footnotes.

■SCHOLASTIC

Curriculum objectives
- To use hyphens to avoid ambiguity.

Resources
Sir Gawain and the Green Knight by Michael Morpurgo or another version of the story; photocopiable page 'Hyphen game' from the CD-ROM – print each page on different-coloured card (a set per group) and ask some of the class to cut them out

4: Hyphens

Introduction
- In the text, show a hyphen and a dash. Point out that the hyphen is half the length of a dash. Explain that it is used to join words so that they act as one. For example, in *fur-lined cape* it links a noun and an adjective to act as an adjective, describing the cape.

Whole-class work
- Display sentences or phrases from the story that contain hyphenated words, for example:
  - *five-pointed star*
  - *fire-belching dragon*
  - *No knight...was more well-loved...*
  - *This weapon was a real head-cruncher...a hideous widow-maker*
- Invite volunteers to explain the hyphen links and how they work.

Group work
- Give each group three sets of cards made from the photocopiable page 'Hyphen game' from the CD-ROM. Demonstrate how to play: turn over all the cards then take turns to pick up one of each colour and arrange them to make sense, for example: *birds/fish/eating* could make *fish eating birds* – meaning *fish (are) eating birds*. Add a hyphen – *fish-eating birds* – and you have birds that eat fish. Once all the cards have been picked up ask the children to copy the phrases they made, with and without a hyphen, and explain their meanings.

Review
- Ask the children if they made up anything funny: for example: *man eating tiger, baby changing room, gas heating engineer*. They could make up more for fun.

Curriculum objectives
- To note and develop initial ideas, drawing on reading and research where necessary.
- To select appropriate grammar and vocabulary, understanding how such choices can change and enhance meaning.
- To use a wide range of devices to build cohesion within and across paragraphs.
- To perform their own compositions, using appropriate intonation, volume and movement so that meaning if clear.
- To use and understand the grammatical terminology in Appendix 2 accurately and appropriately in discussing their writing and reading.

Resources
Various versions of 'Sir Gawain and the Green Knight' for reference; dictionaries

5: A knight's adventure

Introduction
- Remind the class of the personal qualities required of knights: honesty, truth, kindness, chivalry and bravery. Ask for examples of each quality. Ask: *Which qualities did Sir Gawain show in his quest? How?*

Independent work
- Tell the children that they are going to invent their own knight and make up a magical quest for him. Provide headings to help them to plan each paragraph and to think about characters, objects, places and magic.
  - Name of knight (always *Sir...*)
  - How the quest begins, and where (ask how other quests begin, for example: a search for something or someone, a challenge, a competition)
  - How the knight responds
  - What he has to do
  - Where he has to go
  - Problems he faces and how he overcomes them
  - Characters who help
  - Magical objects that help
- Allow about ten minutes, then ask the children to think about how to link the events in their story. Remind them of useful words for cohesion, for example: *because of this, afterwards, before, meanwhile, all through the night*.

Review
- Ask the children to read their stories, thinking about how to read them aloud to sound interesting. Invite volunteers to read out their stories.

Curriculum objectives
• To continue to read and discuss an increasingly wide range of poetry.
• To check that the book makes sense to them, discussing their understanding and exploring the meanings of words in context.
• To apply their growing knowledge of root words, prefixes and suffixes (morphology and etymology), as listed in Appendix 1, both to read aloud and to understand the meaning of new words that they meet.
• To use dictionaries to check the meanings of words.

Resources
Photocopiable page 'The Lady of Shalott' from the CD-ROM; media resource 'Painting of the Lady of Shalott' on the CD-ROM; dictionaries; photocopiable page 'Narrative poem storyboard' from the CD-ROM

Week 6 lesson plans

This week's lessons are based on the classic narrative poem 'The Lady of Shalott' by Alfred, Lord Tennyson. The children take part in a discussion of the poem and how it is linked to the legend of King Arthur and his knights. They learn to recognise and describe the features of a narrative poem and about poetic language and how poets use devices such as metaphor, simile, imagery, analogy, half-rhyme and assonance to create effects (although not all of these terms need be learned). They learn a verse of the poem and try writing in a similar style.

1: 'The Lady of Shalott'

Introduction
• Tell the children that they are going to read a poem by a famous poet named Alfred, Lord Tennyson, written in 1832. The poem is about one of the stories from the legend of King Arthur, which was very popular then, and the poem inspired many artists to paint pictures of the story. Show the children the media resource 'The Lady of Shalott' on the CD-ROM, a painting based on the poem and tell them its title. Ask: *Which character from the legend do you think she is?* Discuss their ideas and note that it will be easier to tell who it is when they read the poem.

Whole-class work
• Give out photocopiable page 'The Lady of Shalott' from the CD-ROM, and read it to the class while they follow. Ask: *What is the poem about? How does the poet bring our attention to her throughout the poem?* (He repeats *Shalott* in the last line of each verse). Ask them to name the place where the lady is (a castle on the island of Shalott) and to describe the scene outside. *Which place from the legend of King Arthur is farther down the river?* (Camelot.) *How does the poet remind us of Camelot through the poem?* (He repeats *Camelot* in the fifth line of each verse.)
• Ask: *What is strange about the way she looks at the scene through the window?* (She looks at its reflection in a mirror – Tennyson says *shadows* but, technically, they are reflections – otherwise an unknown curse will fall on her.) *Who do they now think she is?* (Lady Elaine.) *What happened to her in Arthur High King of Britain? What happens in the poem?* The children should be able to give an outline of the story even if they do not understand every word. Ask: *What do we call a poem that tells a story?* (A narrative poem.)

Paired work
• Ask the children to complete photocopiable page 'Narrative poem storyboard' from the CD-ROM for the poem, giving headings for the scene and any action, as if it were a film, for example:

Verse	Scene	Characters	Sounds	Actions
I	Countryside, river, fields, road, island of Shalott	People	Almost silent	People go back and forth along road

Differentiation
• Where appropriate, re-read the verse with the children, explaining or helping them to look up words as necessary. Ask: *What would you see/hear?*

Review
• Ask different children to contribute to telling the story of the poem.

Curriculum objectives
● To continue to read and discuss an increasingly wide range of poetry.
● To learn a wider range of poetry by heart.

Resources
Photocopiable page 'The Lady of Shalott' from the CD-ROM; dictionaries

2: The mood and atmosphere of a poem

Introduction
● Ask the class what they remember about the poem from the previous lesson. Re-read verse 1 to them and ask: *Is this scene pleasant or unpleasant? Which words create this atmosphere?*

Paired work
● Provide photocopiable page 'The Lady of Shalott' from the CD-ROM. Allocate a verse to each pair and ask them to discuss and describe its atmosphere and mood, and how the poet uses words to paint a picture. Encourage them to use dictionaries to look up words they do not know – and add footnotes. The children could then work with a partner to memorise the verse.

> **Differentiation**
> ● Re-read the verse with the children, helping them to look up words. Ask: *Is it calm, lively, cheerful, gloomy, sad, happy, threatening, menacing?* Ask them to draw the scene, using colours to match the mood, and label it with words from the poem.

Review
● Invite the children who worked on verse 1 to recite their verse and describe the atmosphere. Repeat for further verses, as time allows. Ask: *When does the mood change from pleasant to menacing?* (Part II, verse 1.) Ask: *What do you think the lines 'A curse is on her if she stay/To look down to Camelot/She knows not what the curse may be' mean?* Between lessons, try to find time for the children to recite their verses.

Curriculum objectives
● To continue to read and discuss an increasingly wide range of poetry.

Resources
Photocopiable page 'The Lady of Shalott' from the CD-ROM

3: Similes

Introduction
● Recap on the language the poet used to create atmosphere. Tell the children that they are going to look at poetic language, beginning with similes. Remind them that a simile compares things, using words such as *like* or *as*, and give some examples: *as red as blood, as cold as a stone, run like the wind.* Point out that these are used so often that they have become clichés (expressions used without much thought), so we should try not to use them.

Whole-class work
● Provide copies of the poem. Ask the children to read Part III, verse 2 and look for a simile (*Like to some branch of stars we see*). Ask: *What does this describe?* (The knight's horse's bridle.) Ask: *What does it tell us about the bridle?* (It has jewels on it that sparkle like stars.)

Paired work
● Ask the children to underline other similes in the poem and to make notes about what they describe and the effects they create. Examples: *Burn'd like one burning flame, Like some bold seer in a trance.*

> **Differentiation**
> ● Help the children to find the simile. Ask: *What is like this? What picture does it make you see in your head?*

Review
● Ask how the similes in the poem compare with the clichés (Introduction). What makes these better?

Curriculum objectives
● To continue to read and discuss an increasingly wide range of poetry.
● To prepare poems to read aloud and perform, showing understanding through intonation, tone and volume so that the meaning is clear to an audience.

Resources
Photocopiable page 'The Lady of Shalott' from the CD-ROM

4: Contrasts in the poem

Introduction

● Demonstrate the effect of contrast by showing the class a picture of, say, a very small dog such as a chihuahua beside a Great Dane or other huge dog. Ask: *What effect does the contrast have?* Tell them that Tennyson used contrasts in 'The Lady of Shalott' and that the first of these is in verse 2.

Whole-class work

● Ask the children to read verse 2 of the poem and to look for contrasts between places. Ask them how each place is different from the others. There is gentle quivering movement of the wind along the river bank – created by rhyme such as *quiver/shiver*, repeated /s/ sounds (alliteration). Then comes a sudden contrast of heavy thuds of one-syllable words in line 6, then the silence of the isle created by assonance of the long /igh/ and /ow/ sounds in *silent isle* and rhyming *flowers/embowers.*

Independent work

● Ask the children to re-read the poem to find other contrasts in atmosphere or mood. The contrast could be created by sound, colour or speed, for example (in verse 3), slow, heavy barges and horses contrasted with fast shallop (*flitteth silken-sailed*).

> **Differentiation**
> ● Read sections of the poem with the children. Point out contrasting parts of a verse and ask how one is different from the other.

Review

● Read out some of the contrasts noted by the class and ask why they think the poet uses contrast.

Curriculum objectives
● To perform their own compositions, using appropriate intonation, volume, and movement so that meaning is clear.

Resources
Photocopiable page 'The Lady of Shalott' from the CD-ROM

5: Prequel to the poem

Introduction

● Ask the children to imagine how and why the Lady of Shalott came to be in the castle with a curse on her that she would die if she looked directly at Camelot. Encourage them to share their ideas with the class and to develop one another's ideas.

Paired work

● Encourage the children to explore their ideas with a partner, to invent characters or include others from the King Arthur legend and suggest what parts they might have played in the story. Tell them that their part of the story should be very short – short enough to be one verse of the poem. Challenge them to write in the style of the poem: a verse of nine lines and, if possible, to use lines that include *Camelot* (line 5) and *Shalott* (line 9). It need not rhyme. Also point out that verses begin with a line or two about the scene. They could begin with the scene where the lady is captured/runs away/gets lost for example.
● Ask the children to practise reading their verse and to think about how it sounds – whether they could change any of the words for a different effect.

Review

● Invite volunteers to read out their verses. After the lesson they could save them on a computer for the others to read and comment.

Curriculum objectives
● To use hyphens to avoid ambiguity.

Resources
Interactive whiteboard; photocopiable page 'Ambiguous sentences' from the CD-ROM

Grammar and punctuation: Hyphens

Revise

● Use the starter activity 1 'Hyphens'.
● Next, display the following sentence on the whiteboard: *In the orchard were three hundred year old trees.*
● Ask: *What was in the orchard?* Invite a volunteer to add hyphens to make the meaning clear (for example: *In the orchard were three hundred year-old trees* meaning that there were three hundred trees in the orchard that were a year old).
● Ask: *What other meaning could the sentence have?* (The orchard contained trees that were three-hundred years old but we are not told how many: *In the orchard were three-hundred-year-old trees*, or the orchard contained three trees that were one-hundred years old: *In the orchard were three hundred-year-old trees.*)

Assess

● Hand out photocopiable page 'Ambiguous sentences' from the CD-ROM and ask the children to add hyphens to create different meanings.

Further practice

● Collect examples of hyphenated words from reading. The children could add these to a class dictionary of hyphenated words. (Use a table in Word, so that words can be added at the end of the list and then sorted in alphabetical order – or , for extra practice in understanding alphabetical order, ask the children to find the correct place for each word.)

Curriculum objectives
● To continue to distinguish between homophones and other words that are often confused.

Resources
Photocopiable page 'Homophone bank' from the CD-ROM; photocopiable page 'Holiday homophone letter' from the CD-ROM

Spelling: Homophones

Revise

● Give the children a list of words that have alternative spellings and meanings or use the photocopiable page 'Homophone bank' from the CD-ROM. Ask them to write two sentences to show the meanings of the homophone pairs, for example:
  ● reeds/reads
  There were reeds growing by the river.
  Hasanna reads two books per month.
  ● week/weak
  There are seven days in a week.
  He was so weak that he could hardly walk.

Assess

● Give out photocopiable page 'Holiday homophone letter' from the CD-ROM. Ask the children to read the story and underline any words that are spelled wrongly. They should then write the correct spelling in the space provided.

Further practice

● From reading, collect examples of words that sound like other words. Spell the homophones. Explain their meanings. Use them in sentences. Where appropriate, provide sentences with the wrong spelling for the children to illustrate and correct, for example:
  ● *He bought two pears of shoes.*
  ● *Look – the Queen's thrown!*
● Use starter activity 2 'Homophones'.

Curriculum objectives
● To continue to read and discuss an increasingly wide range of fiction.
● To increase their familiarity with a wide range of books, including myths, legends, traditional stories and fiction from our literary heritage.
● To discuss and evaluate how authors use language, including figurative language, considering the impact on the reader.

Resources
Photocopiable page 'William Tell' from the CD-ROM; highlighter pens; planning sheet; internet access; a selection of fiction books, including legends and history books (factual) – and/or ebooks; photocopiable page 'Gelert' from the CD-ROM

Reading: Legends

Revise
● Give photocopiable page 'William Tell' from the CD-ROM and a highlighter pen to each child. Allow time for them to read the story. If an adult helper is not available you could pair children who need more support with able readers who could read with them. Ask: *What kind of text is this?* They should be able to identify it as a legend. Ask how they can tell. They should recognise that it has some apparently historical facts (which could be checked) and some parts that are likely to be fiction.
● Ask the children to highlight any parts of the story that might be facts that can be checked. They should note, for example: the names of places (Switzerland, Austria, Bürglen, Altdorf), people (William Tell, Gessler), whether Altdorf is near a lake, whether Austria ruled Switzerland about 700 years ago, and so on.
● Invite feedback and discuss how the facts can be checked. If there is time, the children could do so – or they could do this in another lesson.
● Discuss the events of the story and what words help to create the scene for each part of the story, for example: *skipped* (suggesting a happy carefree walk); other choices of verbs, such as *murmured, barked; Even the birds were silent* (to build suspense); *The colour ran out of William's face* (fear/anxiety), contrasted with *a dark red colour crept over Gessler's face* (anger).
● Also ask the children about the use of contrast, for example:
  ● the father and child chatting happily contrasting with *Suddenly their path was blocked*
  ● the silly-looking hat *but William didn't laugh*
  ● the murmuring crowd, then the silence, then the clattering of hooves.
● Ask the children to find any moments of suspense in the story, for example: when William pulls out the arrows, sets up his bow and fires. (Everything is very slow: *...he took a deep breath and stepped forward. He took another deep breath....* After he fired the shot the reader can't be sure for a moment whether the cry was one of shock and misery that the boy was injured or killed, then *...a cheer from the crowd* makes it clear that he wasn't.)

Assess
● Give out photocopiable page 'Gelert' from the CD-ROM. Provide a sheet of questions and, if possible, a planning sheet for the second part of the assessment.
● Ask questions.
  ● *What kind of story is this?*
  ● *How can you tell?*
  ● *Which parts do you think might be true? Why?*
  ● *How can you find out?*
  ● *Which parts do you think must be fiction. Why?*
● Check, research, report.
  ● Find out as much as you can to check your answers. Write notes about this.
  ● Write a report about whether Prince Llewelyn, his wife Joan, their son and Gelert were real, what you found out about Beddgelert and about the events of the story.

Further practice
● If possible, take the children to a library, or use the school or class library (or a selection of books brought in for this task). Working in groups, ask the children to look at the books and discuss them, and to pick out any they think are legends. They should agree as to why they think this and make a note of their selection and notes about their reasons.

Curriculum objectives

● In narratives, to describe characters, settings and atmosphere and integrate dialogue to convey character and advance action.

Resources

Media resource 'Painting of the Lady of Shalott' on the CD-ROM

Writing: Creating a character and setting in a story

Revise

● Ask the children to imagine the scene as part of the story of the Lady of Shalott (you could use the media resource on the CD-ROM). Ask for a sentence to start telling the story of this scene – in the past tense, beginning with just the facts, for example, *A lady sat in a little boat floating down the river.* Write the sentence on the board.

● Ask: *How did the lady feel?* Help the children to change the words to show the lady's sadness, loneliness and fear, for example: *Alone in a boat with haunted eyes she sat.* Help them to continue this sentence by asking: *What was she doing/what happened as she sat?*
Alone in a boat with haunted eyes she sat, her dress trailing in the waves as the boat floated downstream.

● Each time they add words, ask them to consider others and choose the ones that best create the atmosphere they want. They could add what the lady was thinking, what people thought or said as she floated by, where the boat stopped and what happened to her.

● Ask them to work with a partner to describe the character, write the story and create the atmosphere of the picture.

Assess

● Provide a passage from a story with some words removed. Ask the children to fill the gaps with suitable words.

Further practice

● Provide a passage from a story that describes a character, with words highlighted for the children to change to create a completely different character. For example, they could change descriptions of some of Dickens' characters, such as Miss Havisham in *Great Expectations* (making her young, healthy, joyful and full of life and hope), Mr Gradgrind in *Hard Times* (making him kind and likeable), Uriah Heep in *David Copperfield* (making him a sensible, likeable clerk). You could reduce the level of the activity by providing words to choose from for each highlighted word or increase its level by highlighting additional words. The children could then read one another's altered passages and compare the new characters they have created.

Name: _____   Date: _____

Character scales

■ Choose a character from a story. Decide how good or evil the character is on a scale from 0 (very evil) to 5 (very good). On the first scale, draw an arrow above the number, like this:

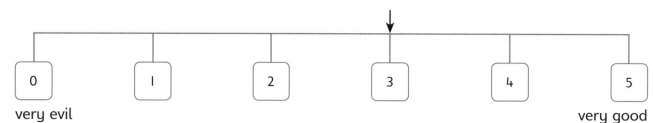

very evil   very good

■ Write your own words on the blank scales, then add arrows to describe your character.

Character's name _____

very evil   very good

I can describe a character in a story.

How did you do?

PHOTOCOPIABLE   ■SCHOLASTIC
                                                                    www.scholastic.co.uk

Ends with /shus/

- Read the words and look up their meanings.
- Write each word in the correct set.

anxious	cautious	conscious	fictitious
gracious	infectious	malicious	obnoxious
precious	spacious	suspicious	vicious

cious

scious

tious

xious

- Choose four words from the list and write the root words they come from or other words from the same root that will help you to spell them.
- Circle the part of the word that helps.

Word	Root word or word from the same root word

I can spell words with endings that sound like /shus/.

How did you do?

Arthur's wedding

- Read the passages and think about which words create the atmosphere.

Passage 1

You should have been there the day Guinevere came to Camelot to be my queen. As she rode up towards the castle, the people came running out of their houses to welcome her. They threw flowers in her path, they cheered, they clapped. I remember, she caught a flower, a foxglove it was, and waved it at them, and they cheered her all the more. They loved her already. We rode out together whenever we could. It was the only way to be alone, for Camelot was fuller every day as the guests gathered from all over the land.

What is the atmosphere like in this passage? _____
- Underline the words that create this atmosphere.
- Rewrite the passage. Change some of the words to make it sound threatening.

_____

_____

_____

Passage 2

I met Merlin on the ramparts. He was looking out over the mist-covered marshes. There were three horses plodding slowly along the causeway, legless in the mist. "Look," said Merlin sadly. "They have come. I feared they might."

What is the atmosphere like in this passage? _____
- Underline the words that create this atmosphere.
- Rewrite the passage. Change some of the words to make it sound joyful.

_____

_____

_____

I can describe the setting and atmosphere of a passage of text.

How did you do?

PHOTOCOPIABLE   **SCHOLASTIC** www.scholastic.co.uk

Words ending '-able' and '-ible'

- Read each adjective. Take off the suffix '-able' or '-ible'. Write the root word. Is this a real word in English? (✓ or ✗)
- Note: The endings of some root words might have been changed.

Adjective	Root word	Real word?	Adjective	Root word	Real word?
acceptable			audible		
bearable			credible		
disposable			divisible		
drinkable			edible		
eatable			flexible		
enjoyable			horrible		
likeable			invincible		
notable			legible		
readable			possible		
reliable			responsible		
suitable			sensible		
usable			terrible		
washable			visible		

- What difference do you notice between the '-able' and '-ible' adjectives?

- Write a rule for adding '-able'.

_____

_____

I can spell some words ending '-able' or '-ible'.

How did you do?

Describing a scene

- Use this table to help you to describe a scene from a story.
Give the scene a heading.

Story title	Scene heading
Atmosphere	**Useful words (or use your own)**
	scary romantic creepy
	mysterious peaceful secure
	exciting terrifying cheerful
	happy lively frightening
	tense carefree joyful
	brutal

How the author creates this atmosphere

Powerful words from the text

Words for actions

Words that describe

Other words

I can describe how an author creates the atmosphere of a scene.

How did you do?

Name: _____   Date: _____

Playscript planner

- Use the headings in the table to help you plan a playscript.

Scene		Where? Time of day? Atmosphere? Weather, if outdoors?
Characters		
Props		

Script

Character	Stage directions	Dialogue

- Continue on the back of this page.

I can plan a playscript.

How did you do?

Suffixes

- Use a suffix to change the words in bold type so that they make sense.
- Read the sentences to check that they make sense.

> - Choose from these suffixes
> ance   ancy   ence   ency

1. I could see the mountains in the **distant** _____ .

2. The shopkeeper said there was a **vacant** _____ for a salesperson.

3. The **brilliant** _____ of the jewels dazzled me.

4. The rose has a lovely **fragrant** _____ .

5. She must have a lot of **confident** _____ to wear that hat.

6. Dad's friend said, "Come when you can. There's no **urgent** _____ ."

7. My sister is having a baby. It is her first **pregnant** _____ .

8. In science we tested the **absorbent** _____ of dishcloths.

9. I couldn't see any **different** _____ between the twins.

10. She showed her **annoy** _____ by shouting at us.

- Write some rules for using each suffix.

To change an adjective ending '-ant' to a noun _____

If the adjective ends '-ant' _____

If the adjective ends '-ent' _____

- Choose suffixes from the box above to change these nouns into different nouns. Then write sentences for each of these and the new nouns on the back of this sheet.

> agent   assistant   infant

> I can change the meanings of words by adding a suffix '-ence', '-ency', '-ance' or '-ancy'.
>
> How did you do?

PHOTOCOPIABLE

Homophone roots

- Choose a pair of homophones. Look them up in a dictionary.
- Write the homophones and their definitions next to the old words they come from.
- Take turns to explain to a partner why these two words that sound the same might have different spellings.

die	hart	hoarse	hole	peace
dye	heart	horse	whole	piece

Homophones	Definitions	Old words they come from
		Old Norse *deyja* (to lose life)
		Old English *deagian* (to colour)
		Old English *heorte* (heart)
		Old Norse *hjortr* (horned beast)
		Old Norse *hars* (rough of voice)
		Old English *hors* (horse)
		Old English *hol* (deep place)
		Old English *gehal* (complete)
		Old French *pais*, Latin *pax* or *pac* (peace).
		Old French *pièce* (part)

I can spell some homophones and I know where some of their spellings come from.

How did you do?

The Railway Children

These lessons are based on *The Railway Children* by E Nesbit. Children investigate the historical setting and discuss the lifestyle of the family at the centre of the story. They take a close look at the characters and the differences in their speech. This provides an opportunity to look at the differences between written and spoken language, including dialect, and how language changes. Children use what they have learned to write a modern version of part of the story, as well as a newspaper report based on an event in the book. They also explore railways and write an explanation text about how steam engines work. Continuing the railway theme, the children read a selection of poems about trains – including 'Night Mail' by WH Auden – and discuss the structure, style, effect and language.

Expected prior learning
- Can identify the features of an adventure story opening.
- Know how we can infer what is not said in a story.
- Can discuss a range of themes they have identified in reading.
- Can discuss the features of a report.
- Can talk about the impact of setting on a story.
- Can state a preference about poems.
- Can use the first three letters of words to locate them in a dictionary.

Overview of progression
- By reading and responding to fiction from our literacy heritage, children will practise and develop the skills of inference and deduction and learn the importance of using evidence from the text to justify opinions.
- They will develop a better understanding of the difference between spoken and written language and the place of Standard English.
- They will develop the skills of note-taking and summarising as well as retrieving, recording and presenting information from non-fiction.
- Children will continue to read and discuss poetry. They will write their own poems and be given opportunities to prepare poems to read aloud.

Creative context
- This work can be linked with geography (connecting ourselves to the world; transport/railways; mapwork).
- The work can be extended into art and design by looking at works of art featuring railways and landscapes, and painting your own.
- In PSHE, you could work in groups to discuss 'Peter's coal-mine' (Chapter 2, *The Railway Children*). Discuss whether stealing is ever justified and why.

Preparation
The main text in this chapter is *The Railway Children* by E Nesbit which is out of copyright and as such there are many different versions widely available.

You will also need:
The Railway Children by E Nesbit; dictionaries; if possible a dictionary including idioms/sayings; internet access; information books about British railways and canals from the past and steam engines; a working model steam engine (optional); A3 paper; felt-tipped pens; audio recordings of informal spoken language; individual whiteboards; highlighter pens; a display-sized simple skeleton outline; small arrows and postcard-sized cards; Blu-Tack®; sticky notes; poems about trains (see week 6); a recording of a factual programme.

On the CD-ROM you will find:
Media resources 'Railway company letters', 'How a steam engine works', 'Railways and canals', 'Britain's railway map', 'Train'; interactive activities 'Relative clauses', 'It's all relative'; photocopiable pages 'Night Mail', *The Railway Children* Chapter 2', 'Flying high for science week', 'Young *MasterChefs* cook to impress', 'Words with /ee/ after 'c'', 'The first railway'

■SCHOLASTIC

Chapter at a glance

An overview of the chapter. For curriculum objective codes, please see pages 8–10.

Week	Lesson	Curriculum objectives	Summary of activities	Outcomes
1	1	RC: 1, 3, 11, 20 WT: 5, 6	Read Chapter 1 of *The Railway Children*, figuring out what has happened that the reader is not told.	• Can engage with a story by asking pertinent questions.
	2	RC: 9	Continue the story. Read and understand new words, checking words in dictionaries.	• Can read, understand and spell new words. • Can use knowledge of phonics, context and other, similar words.
	3	RC: 9, 19	Compare the language spoken by the children in the story with their own and convert it to modern language.	• Can identify changes in language over time.
	4	RC: 5, 20 WC: 12	Compare the language of the formal letter in the story with speech and with the children's informal letter. Convert formal language to informal.	• Can distinguish between formal and informal language.
	5	WC: 12	Read passages of non-standard English and compare with the language of speech and writing. Explore dialect words.	• Can recognise double negatives, dialect words and expressions and abbreviations as a result of accent or dialect.
2	1	RC: 17 WC: 2	Find out about canals and railways from the story.	• Can ask pertinent questions to help them to find information.
	2	RC: 17, 14 WC: 2, 7	Use non-fiction texts and other sources to find information and write a report about railways or canals in the past.	• Can scan and skim a text to locate information. • Can write a report using headings and subheadings, organising it into paragraphs.
	3	RC: 17 WC: 2, 7, 8, 27	Re-read about Peter's steam engine in the story. Research and write an explanation of how a steam engine works.	• Can write an explanation text.
	4	WC: 20, 28	Revise clauses and identify relative clauses in the story. Revise relative pronouns and write relative clauses.	• Can locate relative clauses in texts, write relative clauses and correctly punctuate them.
	5	WC: 22, 28	Read long sentences from the story, punctuated by commas. Use commas in sentences to clarify or change the meaning.	• Can use commas to change or clarify the meaning of a sentence.
3	1	RC: 5, 13, 18, 21	Identify themes in *The Railway Children*. Find and discuss examples.	• Can debate themes related to a story.
	2	RC: 13, 18, 21	Continue to research a theme in the story. Share the task of research with a group then write individual reports.	• Can identify a theme in a story and write a report about it.
	3	RC: 11, 21 WC: 5	Use a mind map to record information and ideas about a character in the story.	• Can plan a character profile.
	4	RC: 21 WC: 5, 20, 22, 28	Referring to the mind map from the previous lesson, write a character profile.	• Can write a character profile.
	5	WC: 5, 12	Investigate how the author shows the reader how characters speak. Read passages of dialogue in the voices of the characters.	• Can identify subject/verb agreement (and non-agreement in dialogue). • Can recognise how authors help readers to 'hear' how characters speak.
4	1	RWR: 1 WC: 21	Play a game: identify verbs from nouns or adjectives (in story) with prefixes/suffixes. Change nouns/adjectives into verbs.	• Can turn nouns and adjectives into verbs.
	2	RC: 1, 11 WT: 4	Read a selection of newspaper cuttings and identify the features of newspaper. Write and the questions news reports answer.	• Can identify features that help a reader to know what a report is about at a glance.
	3	RC: 14 WC: 1, 4	Read news reports more closely to learn about the structure and features of news reports – purpose of each paragraph/sentence.	• Can identify features of newspaper.
	4	RC: 11 WT: 4	Read about a news report in *The Railway Children*. Write a 'newspaper report' about an event in the story.	• Can write a report text in the style of a newspaper.
	5	WT: 4	Spell words with 'ei' for /ee/ after 'c'. Sort words with /ee/ after 'c' into sets. Learning the 'ei' words.	• Can spell /ee/ with 'ei' after 'c'.

Chapter at a glance

Week	Lesson	Curriculum objectives	Summary of activities	Outcomes
5	1	RC: 13	Write a flow chart to represent the plot of *The Railway Children*.	• Can identify the key events in the plot of a story.
	2	WC: 3, 6, 9, 10, 13	Write a précis of *The Railway Children* using flow charts from previous lesson.	• Can write a précis.
	3	WC: 9, 10, 13	Identify parts of the story that would change if the setting were modern.	• Can identify details of a setting.
	4	WC: 1, 4, 5	Write a draft for a modern version of *The Railway Children*. Share ideas for this.	• Can write a draft for a new version of a story, retaining the same theme.
	5	WC: 1, 4, 5, 13	Refine and write a final version of modern *Railway Children*. Proofread.	• Can write a new version of a story, retaining the same theme.
6	1	RC: 1, 15	Read and discuss 'Night Mail' by WH Auden. Watch the film it was written for, listening to the poem.	• Can identify and describe the rhythm and pace of a poem and tell its story.
	2	RC: 1, 15	Read aloud other poems about trains, comparing with 'Night Mail'. Describe their atmosphere and effect and how this was created.	• Can identify and describe the atmosphere and effect of a poem and how they are created.
	3	RC: 1, 15	Continue to read train poems. Identify similes and analogy in the poems.	• Can identify similes and analogy in a poem and their effects.
	4	RC: 8	Choose their favourite train poem and practise reading it aloud in a group.	• Can read a poem rhythmically.
	5	WC: 1, 4	Watch and listen to a film clip of a train. Write poems about trains with a 'train' rhythm.	• Can write a poem with a distinct rhythm.

Background knowledge

Accent: The way in which someone speaks in a region.

Analogy: Presenting something as having the qualities of something else, for example, the train in 'Night Mail' has human traits: shoulders, 'black-eyed' coaches.

Clause: Part of a sentence that could act as a sentence. A clause must have a verb.

Contrast: A contrast is an object, description, place, quality or idea that is the opposite to another that is mentioned close by.

Dialect: The words, expressions and grammar of a region.

Etymology: A word's etymology is its history: its origins in earlier forms of English or other languages, and how its form and meaning have changed.

Metaphor: A figure of speech that describes something as if it were something else.

Paragraph: A distinct passage of text dealing with one pint of a subject or a distinct idea.

Relative clause: A subordinate clause that modifies a noun by including it in a clause, for example: *There was an old lady **who swallowed a fly***.

Relative pronoun: A pronoun used in the construction of relative clauses.

Rhythm: The 'beat' of a poem.

Standard English: English that has correct grammar and no dialect words or expressions.

Style: A characteristic way of writing.

Week 1 lesson plans

In this week's lessons, the children read the opening chapters of *The Railway Children* and look for clues about the setting. They explore unfamiliar words in the text and use them to establish the book's historical setting. They identify words that are no longer used and rewrite parts of the text in modern language. They also look at dialect in the story and examine the differences between the language of speech and writing.

1: *The Railway Children*

Expected outcomes
- All children can engage with a story by asking questions; with support, they can find meanings of words in a dictionary; locate relative clauses; punctuate these in structured examples; write a simple explanation.
- Most children will also be able to ask questions to consider what is not said in a story; locate words in a dictionary using the first four letters; locate relative clauses in example texts; add these to sentences and punctuate them; write an explanation.
- Some children will also be able to recognise subtle clues about what is not said; locate word in a dictionary efficiently; recognise relative clauses in texts; write and punctuate their own examples; write an explanation with a clear structure.

Curriculum objectives
- To continue to read and discuss an increasingly wide range of fiction.
- To increase their familiarity with a wide range of books, including fiction from our literary heritage.
- To ask questions to improve their understanding of what they have read.
- To draw inferences, justifying these with evidence from the text.
- To use dictionaries to check the spelling and meaning of words.
- To use the first three or four letters of a word to check spelling, meaning or both of these in a dictionary.

Resources
The Railway Children by E Nesbit

Introduction
- Read the opening paragraph of *The Railway Children*. Ask the children if they have any questions about what they have read so far. Was there anything they didn't understand? For example, they might not have heard of Madame Tussaud's or Maskelyne and Cook's. (The latter was a popular conjuring entertainment arcade in London.) Ask: *When is this story set? How can we tell that it is not a modern story?* Point out clues, such as the language used: *Zoological Gardens* rather than *zoo, electric bells* (the children might think of a front-door bell but point out that this is plural). Explain that many families had a maid – or more than one – as well as a cook and a nursemaid to look after the children, and would use bells to ring for a servant. Ask them to look out for more clues to the time setting as they read on, for example, *gruel, pigeon pie, nursemaid, cook, Peter's birthday present – the Engine* (a model steam engine), *the girls' pinafores.*

Whole-class work
- Read the rest of Chapter 1. Ask: *Is the family rich, poor, in the middle or very rich? How can you tell?* Point out that when the story was set (the beginning of the 20th century) many families had servants such as a cook, a couple of maids and a nursemaid to look after the children if they were reasonably well-off but not necessarily very rich. This family was quite well-off. Ask: *What kind of life did the children have?* (Secure, happy, problem-free, until the evening of the Visit.) What might change this?

Group work
- Ask the children to discuss what happened during the night of the Visit, looking up any new words. Remind them about alphabetical order and using the first three or four letters of a word. They should list the facts they can find, then their ideas about why the children's father suddenly disappears, where he might have gone and who the visitors were. Ask them to justify their explanations using what they read in the story.

Differentiation
- Group together children who need more support and read the chapter with them. Ask: *What happened that made things change for the family? How was their new life different?* Draw out the contrasts: small house without the comforts of home (cold, dark, only essential items, no servants). Stop at the point where Ruth gives a clue about what has happened: *If you don't mend your ways you'll go where your precious Father's gone.* Ask: *What did she mean? What happened to her? Why?*

Review
- Invite a group to present their explanation of the Visit, what happened, where Father went, and why they think that. Ask: *How can you tell it was something very serious?* They should have noticed Mother's response (acting bravely, reassuring the children) – this is how we know she was very upset.

Curriculum objectives
● To check that the book makes sense to them, discussing their understanding and exploring the meanings of words in context.

Resources
Photocopiable page 'The Railway Children Chapter 2' from the CD-ROM; dictionaries (and if possible, a dictionary of idioms/sayings); computer and internet access

2: New words in the story

Introduction
● Recap the story and ask if the children remember any new words. Point out that some were new to them because they are no longer used: *dripping-pan*, *gruel*, *eau-de-cologne*.

Paired work
● Give out photocopiable page 'The Railway Children Chapter 2' from the CD-ROM. Ask the children to read it and highlight any new words or parts they do not understand, for example: *whitening, she might have had to be a Roman martyr..., wreaths*.

Group work
● When pairs complete the activity, group them to share their findings. One child should act as scribe, entering the words in the first column of a table.

Word, group of words or sentence	What we think it means	Where we can find out	Meaning

● Ask the children to take turns to read out a highlighted word. Once they have made a list, they should discuss and note down what the words mean (leaving this blank if they have no idea) and making a note of where to check (dictionary, encyclopedia, internet search engine).

Review
● Read some of the words listed and ask the class what they mean. Ask if they already knew, guessed or looked them up. Ask: *Which of these words/groups of words were difficult because we no longer use them?*

Curriculum objectives
● To check that the book makes sense to them, discussing their understanding and exploring the meanings of words in context.
● To explain and discuss their understanding of what they have read, including through formal presentations and debates, maintaining a focus on the topic and using notes where necessary.

Resources
The Railway Children by E Nesbit; photocopiable page 72 'Language from the past'

3: Our changing language

Introduction
● In advance of the lesson, ask the children to read the next two chapters. Ask the children what they noticed about the way in which characters speak. How is it different from modern speech? Give some examples from the book: *Don't let's be horrid to each other; We won't quarrel. Indeed we won't; I say*. Ask: *What would you say instead?*

Whole-class work
● Challenge the class to find other short examples of speech that are different from modern speech. Allow about ten minutes for this. Then play a game: throw a soft ball to a child, who reads out an example, then throws the ball to another, who 'translates' it into modern language.

Independent work
● Give out photocopiable page 72 'Language from the past', which requires the children to 'translate' a passage of dialogue from the story into modern speech.

Review
● Ask the children to give their translation to a partner to comment on and make suggestions. Keep these for reference for later work on a modern version of the story (week 5).

■SCHOLASTIC

Curriculum objectives
● To identify and discuss themes and conventions in and across a wide range of writing.
● To ask questions to improve their understanding of what they have read.
● To ensure correct subject and verb agreement when using singular and plural, distinguishing between the language of speech and writing and choose the appropriate register.

Resources
The Railway Children by E Nesbit; dictionaries; media resource 'Railway company letters' on the CD-ROM

4: A formal letter

Introduction
● Read the first part of Chapter 7 of *The Railway Children* to the class, including the letter from the Secretary of the Great Northern and Southern Railway Company, which they can follow on the media resource 'Railway company letters' on the CD-ROM. Ask: *Who is this letter from? Who is it to? What is it about? What is going to happen? Why?* They will probably understand the gist of the letter without understanding every word.

Whole-class work
● With the class, read the children's reply to the letter (on screen 2). Ask: *Which word did they spell wrongly?* (Affectionate – affecate.) *How is the language different?* (It is simpler and less formal.) *What do you think about the type of language used in the Secretary's letter?* (As well as being old fashioned, it is formal.) Ask: *Which words show that it is formal?* Explain that an abbreviation is a short form of a word. Look for abbreviations in the text and discuss what they mean.

Independent work
● Ask the children to look up any difficult words in the letter and to rewrite it in an informal style, using simpler words.

Review
● Read some of the children's versions of the letter. Ask the class: *What differences did you notice between these letters? Do they mean the same as the one in the book?*

Curriculum objectives
● To ensure correct subject and verb agreement when using singular and plural, distinguishing between the language of speech and writing and choose the appropriate register.

Resources
The Railway Children by E Nesbit; Photocopiable page 73 'The language of speech'

5: The language of speech

Introduction
● Ask the class to recap the story so far. With the children, read the part of Chapter 8 where the bargee tells Peter that he can't fish in the canal. Ask: *How is his language different from the narrative part? Why there are apostrophes in words like 'ave and 'ere?* Point out double negatives in *ain't no right* and *not to say nothing*. Ask what is meant by: *Who are you a-shoving of?* Also discuss any non-standard English used in dialects in your locality and note that many of us use non-standard English when speaking but not in formal writing.

Group work
● Give each group photocopiable page 73 'The language of speech'. Ask them to read the dialogue in groups, using the author's spelling and punctuation to help with pronunciation, then underline the parts that are in non-standard English.

Independent work
● Ask the children to rewrite the dialogue in the kind of language used in writing and compare it with the original. Some children could also highlight different types of non-standard English in different colours: missing letters that change pronunciation, double negatives, dialect words.

> **Differentiation**
> ● Where necessary, read the dialogue with the children and ask how the author has changed some words to show how to pronounce them.

Review
● Invite volunteers to read out parts of their corrected dialogue. Ask: *What has been lost?* (We can no longer tell how the people speak.)

Week 2 lesson plans

This week the children will continue to read *The Railway Children* by E Nesbit, but the focus will be on the setting. They will also investigate the railways and canals of the Victorian age, which just preceded the book (first published in serialised form in 1905) and in which the author grew up.

1: Transport in the past

Expected outcomes
● All children can write an explanation text with support, identify relative clauses and add their own to sentences, beginning with words provided.
● Most children can write an explanation text, identify, write and punctuate relative clauses.
● Some children can write and punctuate a wider range of relative clauses.

Curriculum objectives
● To note and develop initial ideas, drawing on reading and research where necessary.
● To retrieve, record and present information from non-fiction.

Resources
The Railway Children by E Nesbit

Introduction
● Invite the children to recap the story so far. Ask: *What types of transport are important in the story?* (Railways and canals.) *What have you found out about road transport from the story?* (The children and their mother travelled by train from home to the local station and then by cart to the house.) Tell them that railways were important at the time for passengers because, although a few cars had been made, hardly anyone had them. Also, both railways and canals were important for transporting goods, especially heavy goods such as coal, iron and steel. Point out that we can find out a lot of facts from fiction books because authors research these.

Group work
● Ask the children to re-read parts of the book that tell them about trains, stations, railways and canals and the work people do on them. Different members of the group could read different parts and make notes.
● Relevant sections include: Chapter 3, where Mr Perks tells them the names of parts of a train and what they are for; Chapter 4, where Bobbie gets into the engine and meets the fireman and the engineer; Chapter 5, the waiting room; Chapter 6, where the children prevent a train crash; Chapter 8, the bargeman and his family: Chapter 11, the railway workers/railway safety; Chapter 12, the signal box.
● Remind the children that their notes should be about the information they find about railways, canals and people's work, and not about the story or its characters.

Review
● Ask the class what they have found out about railways and canals from the time, and the people who worked on them. Ask them to think what else they would like to know and to write some questions to help them to find out. They should keep their notes and questions for the next lesson.

Curriculum objectives
● To identify how language, structure and presentation contribute to meaning.
● To note and develop initial ideas, drawing on reading and research where necessary.
● To use a range of devices to build cohesion within and across paragraphs.
● To retrieve, record and present information from non-fiction.

Resources
The Railway Children by E Nesbit; media resource 'Railways and canals' on the CD-ROM; the children's notes and questions from lesson 1; information books about British railways and canals from the past; photocopiable page 74 'Report planner'

2: Railways and canals

Introduction
● Ask the children to read out some of the questions they wrote at the end of the previous lesson. Ask where they could find the answers. Show them information books about railways or canals and ask how they will know if a book will help them. Review scanning skills (chapter headings, illustrations and captions, index). Invite a volunteer who thinks the book will help to find a page that looks useful and to skim the page to find out what it could tell him/her. Also show them the photographs and paintings from media resource 'Railways and canals' on the CD-ROM.

Group work
● Ask the children to work in groups to find the answers to different questions. Remind them to make notes rather than copying pieces of text: noting important facts or details, missing out unimportant words, using abbreviations and so on.

Differentiation
● The children could work in pairs within their groups: more proficient readers helping others who might find this difficult.

Independent work
● The children could share the information they found and use it to write a report about railways or canals at the time *The Railway Children* was written. Ask them to think about headings, subheadings and paragraphs, photocopiable page 74 'Report planner' will help.

Review
● Read some of the reports and discuss how the paragraphs are organised. The children could read a partner's report and notice how ideas within a paragraph are linked. Ask them for any useful words they noticed.

Curriculum objectives
● To note and develop initial ideas, drawing on reading and research where necessary.
● To use further organisational and presentational devices to structure text and to guide the reader.
● To use a range of devices to build cohesion within and across paragraphs.
● To retrieve, record and present information from non-fiction.
● To punctuate bullet points consistently.

Resources
The Railway Children by E Nesbit; if possible, a model steam engine (stationary or wheeled); information books on steam engines; internet access; media resource 'How a steam engine works' on the CD-ROM; photocopiable page 75 'Steam engine explanation'

3: How a steam engine works

Introduction
● Re-read the parts of the story concerning Peter's engine (in Chapters 1, 4 and 5). Ask: *What happened to Peter's engine? What made it go off with a bang?*

Whole-class work
● Show the media resource 'How a steam engine works' on the CD-ROM. Let the children examine it and discuss how it works. Invite them to explain this. Where necessary, suggest words to help, such as *first, next, then, after that.*

Independent work
● Give each child photocopiable page 75 'Steam engine explanation'. Ask them to use information books or websites to research and plan an explanation for children of their own age who know nothing about steam engines. Remind them that pictures and diagrams will help. They should spend about 15 minutes planning and making notes.

Differentiation
● Where necessary, provide a bank of useful words for support.

Review
● Read some explanations and select sections to read out as examples of clear explanatory writing and good use of structural devices such as subheadings, bullet points or numbers and underlining. The children could complete their writing during a later lesson.

Curriculum objectives
● To use relative clauses beginning with *who, which where, why, that* or with an implied (omitted) relative pronoun.
● To use and understand the grammatical terminology in Appendix 2 accurately and appropriately in discussing their writing and reading.

Resources
The Railway Children by E Nesbit; photocopiable page 76 'Relative clauses'; interactive activity 'Relative clauses' on the CD-ROM

4: Clauses

Introduction

● Read the following sentence from Chapter 1 to the class: *They had a father who was just perfect.* Ask: *What does the sentence tell you?* (The children had a father. He was just perfect.) Explain that two sentences have been joined to make one. Ask: *Which word is used to join the two pieces of information?* (Who.) Explain that *who was just perfect* is a clause that adds information about the children's father. Ask them to add a clause to this sentence to say what the children's mother did: *The children had a mother...* (Examples: *The children had a mother who played with them. The children had a mother who wrote stories.*)

Independent work

● Give each child photocopiable page 76 'Relative clauses' (or the interactive version from the CD-ROM) and demonstrate how to complete the first example. They can then complete the activity and, if there is time, write some sentences of their own that contain relative clauses.

> **Differentiation**
> ● For part B of the activity, provide a relative pronoun for some sentences, as necessary, and ask the children to complete it.

Review

● Write some of the children's completed sentences from part B on the board and ask them to underline the word that links the two clauses. Introduce the term *relative pronoun*. Ask for other examples of relative pronouns. As they continue to read the story they could look for examples.

Curriculum objectives
● To use commas to clarify meaning or avoid ambiguity in writing.
● To use and understand the grammatical terminology in Appendix 2 accurately and appropriately in discussing their writing and reading.

Resources
The Railway Children by E Nesbit; photocopiable page 77 'Clarity with commas'; examples of long sentences from the story containing commas used for clarity, for example: Chapter 11, where the children climb the hill to watch the paper-chase, beginning *Phyllis consented to stick to it...* and a few pages farther on *And now, slowly and gradually, the tail lights grew smaller...*

5: Commas for clarity

Introduction

● Display a long sentence from the story that contains commas used for clarity. Invite a competent reader to read the sentence aloud. Ask: *What helped you to make sense of it?* Draw attention to the commas. Display another sentence, without the commas and read it in different ways. Read it with the intended meaning and invite volunteers to come out and put commas in the correct places.

Whole-class work

● Explain that you are going to read some more sentences from the story that contain commas to help readers make sense of them. Ask the children to write them, putting commas in the correct places.

Independent work

● Give out photocopiable page 77 'Clarity with commas' for the children to complete. Explain that the pairs of identical sentences on it could have different meanings, depending on where you put the commas. Model how to complete the first example. Introduce and explain the term *ambiguity*.

> **Differentiation**
> ● Read the sentences on the photocopiable sheet aloud to the children so that they can hear where the commas belong. Ask them to put up a hand when you come to a part that needs a comma.

Review

● Invite volunteers to read the funniest versions of the sentences aloud. They could try writing some ambiguous sentences of their own and punctuating them with commas in different ways.
● Use starter activity 15 'Commas for clarity'.

ⓂSCHOLASTIC

Week 3 lesson plans

Expected outcomes
● All children, with support, can discuss issues raised by a story and, following a structure, write a character profile.
● Most children can do this independently.
● Some children can discuss issues with greater clarity and write a character profile with greater insight.

This week's lessons are about themes and characters in *The Railway Children* by E Nesbit. They begin by recapping themes from the last book they read – *Arthur, High King of Britain* by Michael Morpurgo – and then naming some of the themes in *The Railway Children*. They look for evidence of these, and other, themes and discuss what the author is saying about them before writing a report about their chosen theme.

Also discussed are the characters in the story: the children say what they think of some of the characters and give reasons before using a mind map to help them to plan a character profile, in which they use evidence from the story to support their views.

Linked with the work on themes and characters, the children's attention is drawn to how the characters speak, and the differences between them. They investigate how the author portrays her characters' ways of speaking and compare the different characters' speech. This provides an opportunity to learn about Standard English and regional accents and dialect.

1: Themes in *The Railway Children*

Introduction
● Tell the children that this lesson is about the themes of *The Railway Children*. Remind them about the last book they read (*Arthur High King of Britain* by Michael Morpurgo). Some of its themes were: magic, bravery, chivalry and honour. Ask: *What themes have you noticed in The Railway Children that are connected with the children and their family?* (Poverty, right and wrong, caring for others.) *What themes are there connected with other characters and events in the book?* (Kindness, honesty, politeness, forgiveness.) Discuss what each of these means and present at least one passage from the book that exemplifies it.

Curriculum objectives
● To summarise the main ideas from more than one paragraph, identifying key details that support the main ideas.
● To participate in discussions about books that are read to them and those they can read for themselves, building on their own and others' ideas and challenging views courteously.
● To provide reasoned justifications for their views.
● To identify and discuss themes and conventions across a range of writing.

Resources
The Railway Children by E Nesbit

Group work
● Allocate a theme from the book to each group and ask them to share the task of making notes about where they notice the theme. They could each re-read a different chapter (more proficient readers could read more than one). Allow time for this, then ask them to share their notes with their group and decide what the author is saying about poverty, right and wrong, caring for others, kindness or honesty.

> **Differentiation**
> ● Identify passages connected with the themes in question and help the children to contribute to a discussion of the theme, for example: poverty. Ask: *Who is poor in the story? How can you tell? Was the children's family always poor? How do we know that Mr Perks is quite poor?*

Review
● Allow time for discussion and then ask if the children notice any contrasts that make the theme more noticeable, for example: poverty compared with wealth (the children, the Russian gentleman, Perks and the barge family compared with the old man on the train, the children's life before the Visit); right and wrong (stealing coal, asking people to give presents for Perks, asking the man on the train for things for Mother); caring for others (Bobbie's concern for her mother, looking after the Russian, stopping the train to avert the crash, rescuing the baby and dog from the fire); kindness (Mr Perks' birthday surprise, the roses for Mrs Ransome); honesty (Bobbie owning up that it was her fault that Peter hurt his foot). Keep the notes for the next lesson.

Curriculum objectives
- To summarise the main ideas from more than one paragraph, identifying key details that support the main ideas.
- To participate in discussions about books that are read to them and those they can read for themselves, building on their own and others' ideas and challenging views courteously.
- To provide reasoned justifications for their views.

Resources
The Railway Children by E Nesbit; the children's notes from lesson 1

2: Report about a theme

Introduction
- Recap on the themes discussed in the previous lesson and how they link with the characters.

Group work
- Ask the children to continue to look for evidence of the theme they discussed in the previous lesson. Suggest that they share this task by each re-reading different chapters. Remind them that others should be able to read and understand their notes and that they should record where in the text they found the evidence (page number and which paragraph).

Independent work
- Ask the children to write their reports. The title should be the theme. Provide subheadings to help: *Scenes, Characters, Contrasts, What the author is saying.*

Review
- Invite a volunteer to read their report to the class. Ask if they agree and why/why not. Acknowledge examples of courtesy during the discussion. Ask them to think about one of the characters connected with one of these themes as they continue to read the story.

Curriculum objectives
- In narratives, to describe settings, characters and atmosphere and integrating dialogue to convey character and advance the action.
- To provide reasoned justifications for their views.
- To draw inferences, justifying these with evidence from the text.

Resources
The Railway Children by E Nesbit; for each group of four children: a sheet of A3 paper with the name of a key character from the story, circled, in the centre: Bobbie, Phyllis, Peter, Mother, Mr Perks, the old man on the train, the barge man, the bargeman's wife; felt-tipped pens in different colours

3: Characters in the story

Introduction
- Ask the class to take turns to name a character from *The Railway Children*. List these on the board. Tell them that they are going to work in groups to create character profiles.

Whole-class work
- Give each group a character sheet (see Resources). Show or recap how to create a mind map to help sort out ideas about a character.

Group work
- Ask the children to work as shown below, writing information and words to describe the character in ovals, and the evidence along lines linking them.

Differentiation
- Begin with a character allocated to a group who will benefit from extra help. Ask the class to say something about him/her, for example:

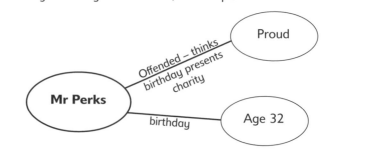

Review
- Invite volunteers from each group to share the information on their mind maps, supporting it with evidence. Invite comments/questions from the others. Encourage them to speak in sentences, for example: *Our character is Mr Perks, the Station Master and Porter. The children meet him in Chapter 3 at the station but it doesn't say his name until later.* Keep the mind maps, and make a note of some of the children's sentences, for the next lesson.

Curriculum objectives

- In narratives, to describe settings, characters and atmosphere and integrating dialogue to convey character and advance the action.
- To provide reasoned justifications for their views.
- To use and understand the grammatical terminology in Appendix 2 accurately and appropriately in discussing their writing and reading.
- To use relative clauses beginning with *who, which where, why, that* or with an implied (omitted) relative pronoun.
- To use commas to clarify meaning or avoid ambiguity in writing.

Resources

The Railway Children by E Nesbit; children's mind maps from lesson 3

4: Writing a character profile

Introduction

- Recap the previous lesson, including some of the sentences the children gave to describe the characters. Tell the class that they are going to use the mind maps to help them to write a character profile. Ask for ideas to introduce the character, for example: *Bobbie is the eldest of three children. She is 11 years old at the start of the story. We know this because she has her twelfth birthday after the move to Three Chimneys.*
- Remind them about relative clauses and relative pronouns (also where to use commas), for example: *Bobbie, who is the eldest of three children, is 11 years old at the start of the story.* If they introduce ideas about Bobbie's character, remind them to start a new paragraph.

Independent work

- Seat the children in groups as in the previous lesson, to share the notes they wrote, but ask them to write their own character profile.

Differentiation

- If necessary, provide some paragraph starters to help the children structure their writing, for example: Mr Perks is the...; He was... years old at the start of the story; We know this because...; He is very... because...

Review

- Read some of the character profiles to the class and ask if they can think of anything to add.

Curriculum objectives

- In narratives, to describe settings, characters and atmosphere and integrating dialogue to convey character and advance the action.
- To ensure correct subject and verb agreement when using singular and plural, distinguishing between the language of speech and writing and choosing the appropriate register.

Resources

The Railway Children by E Nesbit; audio recordings of informal spoken language – these could be recordings made by the children during discussions, or sound recordings from television or radio programmes, or from the British Library database of regional dialects and accents

5: Talking characters

Introduction

- Remind the children of their previous work on the language of speech (week 1, lesson 5). Read what Bobbie says to her mother and her reply (Chapter 9): *Because it's Mr Perks's birthday...he's got other things to keep...the kids and the missus; You mean his wife and children; Yes...It's the same thing.*
- Ask: *Is it the same thing? Why did Bobbie's mother say what she did? Was it Bobbie's normal way of talking?*

Whole-class work

- Play a few short passages of spoken English and ask the children to listen and notice anything they wouldn't use when writing. Ask: *How would Bobbie's mother have corrected her if she said this?*

Group work

- Give each group a passage from *The Railway Children* to read aloud in their groups. Ask them to notice how E Nesbit helps readers to hear how different characters speak. Ask them to underline the parts that help them to speak as the characters did.

Independent work

- Ask the children to rewrite the speech of one character to sound like another character, for example, change the bargeman's speech to make it sound like the old gentleman from the train, or vice versa.

Review

- Read out some of the extracts and the children's conversions to other characters' speech. Ask which character was speaking at first and who they think it was changed to? How can they tell?

Week 4 lesson plans

This week's lessons are based on non-fiction (newspapers), linked with the newspaper article Bobbie reads in *The Railway Children*. The children will examine the use of language in newspaper reports, including the use of headlines, subheadings, quotations, opening sentences that orientate the reader, images and captions. They will examine nouns and adjectives derived from the same root words as verbs and develop their knowledge of suffixes to convert nouns and adjectives into verbs. They will use what they have learned to help them to write their own newspaper-style article about an event in *The Railway Children*. Opportunities will arise to practise reading spelling words containing /ee/ spelled with 'ei' after 'c'.

1: Nouns and adjectives to verbs

Introduction
● Recap verbs and write up some formed from adjectives: *straighten, solidify*; also verbs from nouns: *encircle, befriend*. Ask: *How can you tell it is a verb? Which word does it come from? What kind of word is this? How can you tell?* Ask: *How do we form the verb?*

Whole-class work
● Play a game in which you read out a sentence from *The Railway Children* and ask a child to identify the verb. He or she names another child, who gives a noun or adjective from the same root; this child names another child, who writes the word on a whiteboard. The others should check whether it is correct.

Independent work
● Give each child photocopiable page 78 'Making verbs (1)' and ask them to change the words in brackets to verbs so that the sentences make sense. They should look up these verbs in a dictionary to check the spellings.

> **Differentiation**
> ● For a less-demanding activity, provide fewer sentences and complete an example.

Review
● Ask: *What suffixes and prefixes can turn adjectives or nouns into verbs? What rules can you write for adding these?* Examples include verbs made by adding the suffixes '-en', '-ise', '-ate' or '-fy' to a noun or adjective; sometimes the ending needs to be modified. For example: *flatten, energise, hyphenate, purify*. Note that many verbs formed from nouns have a prefix rather than a suffix.

Curriculum objectives

- To continue to read and discuss an increasingly wide range of non-fiction.
- To draw inferences and justify these with evidence from the text.
- To apply their growing knowledge of root words, prefixes and suffixes (morphology and etymology), as listed in Appendix 1, both to read aloud and to understand the meaning of new words that they meet.

Resources

Photocopiable page 'Flying high for science week' from the CD-ROM and/or your own selection of newspaper reports

2: In the news

Introduction

- Tell the class that they are going to read a different type of text – newspaper reports. Give out photocopiable page 'Flying high for science week' from the CD-ROM. Ask: *How can you tell at a glance what this report is about?* Explain that we call this 'orientating readers' – telling readers what a report is about before they read it.

Whole-class work

- Tell the class that a newspaper should answer the questions *What? When? Who?* and *Where?* (and sometimes *How?* and *Why?*). They can find out *who* it is about quite quickly from the first sentence, which gives the school and the children's names. The second sentence tells them *where* the event took place. Read the report with them and ask: *Which other questions does it answer? What are the answers?*

Paired work

- Give each pair a newspaper report. Ask them first to make a note of what they find out from a quick scan, and where they find this information. Then ask them to read it to answer the questions *What? When? Who? Where?* and, if possible, *How?* and *Why?*

Differentiation

- Select articles that are shorter or longer and use more, or less, complex language, as necessary.

Review

- Ask: *Which questions did your report answer? If it didn't answer all the questions, why not?* (Maybe they were not important.)

Curriculum objectives

- To select appropriate grammar and vocabulary, understanding how such choices can change and enhance meaning.
- To identify how language, structure and presentation contribute to meaning.
- To identify the audience and purpose of the writing, selecting the appropriate form and using other similar writing as models for their own.

Resources

Photocopiable page 'Young *MasterChefs* cook to impress' from the CD-ROM; highlighter pens

3: Newspaper language

Introduction

- Tell the class that they are going to look more closely at how newspaper reports are written and how this suits the audience, purpose and context (where, when and how they are read). Ask: *Who is the audience?* (Local people – a local newspaper.) *What is the purpose?* (To tell local news.) *Where might it be read, when and how?* (Perhaps on a journey, while eating, during a break.)

Whole-class work

- Read the headline and the first two paragraphs of photocopiable page 'Young *MasterChefs* cook to impress' from the CD-ROM while the class follow. Ask: *What facts do we know?* Ask them to read the next paragraph then ask: *What else do we now know?* Repeat this for the next two paragraphs. (Note that it doesn't answer the question *When?* Ask: *How much does this matter? Why?*)
- After they have read the final two paragraphs ask: *What is the purpose of these paragraphs?* (To add details and a comment.)

Group work

- Give each group copies of the report and ask them to take turns to read parts aloud, and to think about the language it uses to describe the event. Ask them to highlight the interesting words.

Review

- Ask: *What interesting words did you find in the report? How do they help?*

Curriculum objectives
● To draw inferences and justify these with evidence from the text.
● To apply their growing knowledge of root words, prefixes and suffixes (morphology and etymology), as listed in Appendix 1, both to read aloud and to understand the meaning of new words that they meet.

Resources
The Railway Children by E Nesbit; photocopiable page 79 'Newspaper report planner'; a copy of the passage at the end of Chapter 10 where Bobbie reads the newspaper article about her father, beginning *And idly she looked at the printing on the paper...*

4: Bobbie's news

Introduction
● Tell the class that they are going to read *about* a newspaper report in *The Railway Children*. Ask: *What questions should the report answer?* (*Who? What? When? Where? – perhaps Why? How?*)

Whole-class work
● Explain that Bobbie has just collected some papers from Mr Perks for Peter to read while he is ill. Read the first three paragraphs of the passage at the end of Chapter 10, beginning *"You're a dear," said Bobbie*. Ask: *Is it good or bad news? How can you tell? What is it about?*
● Read the rest of the passage. Ask: *Who? What? When? Where?* (Bobbie's father has been found guilty and sentenced to five years' penal servitude – ask the children to look up and explain this. We don't know exactly when but the report would say. In court – but we don't know where. The report would say.)

Independent work
● Ask the children to use what they have learned about newspaper reports to help them to write a report about an event in the story: the landslip, the fire, the Russian man finding his family or Parr's rescue from the tunnel. Photocopiable page 79 'Newspaper report planner' will help.

Review
● Ask the children to check that readers can quickly see what their report is about and that it answers important questions. Select a report to read out as an example of this as well as interesting language, use of quotations. Ask: *Could it be written more briefly? How?*

Curriculum objectives
● To use knowledge of morphology and etymology in spelling and understand that the spelling of some words needs to be learned specifically, as listed in Appendix 1.

Resources
Photocopiable page 'Words with /ee/ after 'c'' from the CD-ROM; a list of words with 'cei' spellings (can be selected from the photocopiable sheet above); individual whiteboards and pens

5: Words with 'ei' after 'c'

Introduction
● Give out individual whiteboards and pens. Explain that you are going to say a word that has /ee/ following 'c' (/s/). Remind them that there are different ways of spelling /ee/. They should try to spell the word. Say: *It doesn't matter if you get it wrong. We learn by investigating.* Ask: *Which ways do you know of spelling this sound?*

Whole-class work
● Say the first word (*ceiling*), allowing the children time to write it and then hold up their whiteboards. Group the children according to how they have spelled /ee/. Give praise for using any plausible graphemes and tell them that this is a tricky spelling, especially after 'c'. Point out the correct spelling. Repeat this for: *conceit, conceive, deceit, deceive, perceive, receive*.

Paired work
● Give each pair photocopiable page 'Words with /ee/ after 'c'' from the CD-ROM.
● Ask them to look closely at the spelling of the /ee/ sound in each word and to sort them into sets. Point out that there are few spelling rules to help here, but they should look for any that might help.

Review
● Ask: *How did you sort the words into sets?* Check that they noticed the five different ways of spelling the /ee/ sound. Ask what rules could help. To learn the spellings, ask them to read each word, say it, cover it and then try to write it.

Week 5 lesson plans

During this week's lessons the children will summarise the plot of *The Railway Children* by E Nesbit and then write their own, modern version of the story, keeping the basic plot but changing anything that would be different – not only the technology that has changed, but also the ways in which modern people would behave (not playing on railways, going into railway tunnels, making contact with strangers on trains); what we mean by poverty; people's work; how people speak to one another and modern vocabulary, especially for children.

1: Plot

Introduction
● Tell the class that they are going to think about the plot of *The Railway Children* during this lesson. Ask: *What is meant by* plot? (The main idea of a story and the other parts that fit in around it.) Ask: *What is the main idea or plot of* The Railway Children? (The father of three children is arrested and found guilty of something he didn't do: the story is about how his family cope while he is imprisoned and how he eventually comes back.)

Whole-class work
● Ask: *How does the story begin?*
Write this in note form on a flow chart.
● Ask: *What happens next?*
Add some events to the flow chart.

> A quite wealthy, happy family of parents and three children. Father is suddenly taken away. Go to live cheaply in the country.

> Too poor to buy much coal. Peter caught stealing coal from station.

> Mother ill. Children ask man on train for help.

Group work
● Provide copies of the story in whatever forms are available, for reference. Ask the children to copy the first part of the flow chart onto their group's paper and then to discuss and agree what comes next and to continue the flow chart until they have the entire plot of the book on it.

> **Differentiation**
> ● Where necessary, point out the chapter headings in the book and help the children to skim-read to remind themselves of what happens. Ask them which words they can miss out to write notes quickly. Ask them to read their notes to make sure they can't be shortened even more and that they make sense.

Review
● Explain that the plot is like the skeleton of the story: all the parts that make up the plot fit into it. Show them the display-sized skeleton and invite children from each group to write a summary of part of the plot on a card and fix it to the skeleton. Work down from the head, adding arrows to show the sequence. Ask: *Are the events in the right order? They* should move any that are out of sequence. Keep the skeleton and flow chart for the next lesson.

Curriculum objectives

● In writing narratives, to consider how authors have developed characters and settings in what they have read, listened to or seen performed.
● To assess the effectiveness of their own and others' writing.
● To proofread for spelling and punctuation errors.
● To propose changes to vocabulary, grammar and punctuation to enhance effects and clarify meaning.
● To précis longer passages.

Resources

The Railway Children by E Nesbit; skeleton and flow charts from the previous lesson

2: Writing a précis

Introduction

● Return to the skeleton from the previous lesson. Explain that a *précis* means a short summary. Ask the children to use the skeleton to help them to take turns to give parts of a précis of *The Railway Children*. The others should listen and look out for any mistakes or parts that are too detailed. They can help by correcting mistakes and finding ways to get rid of unnecessary detail.

Independent work

● The children should now write their own précis, based on the skeleton, flow charts and the oral précis the class has compiled. If possible, these should be word-processed and printed for the class or school library, so that others can read about books before choosing what to read.

Differentiation
● Remind the children to use what they and their group wrote on their flow chart and the notes on the skeleton. Help them to convert some of the notes into sentences to get started.

Review

● Ask the children to print their work and swap with a partner or to look at a partner's work on screen. Demonstrate how to edit it and ask them to edit one another's work, marking in a different colour any editing changes they suggest. Keep the skeleton, flow charts and précis for the next lesson.

Curriculum objectives

● To assess the effectiveness of their own and others' writing.
● To propose changes to grammar, vocabulary and punctuation to enhance effects and clarify meaning.
● To proofread for spelling and punctuation errors.

Resources

The Railway Children by E Nesbit; skeleton, flow charts and précis from the previous lesson

3: A modern version

Introduction

● Read out a précis from the previous lesson. Ask: *Can we tell that the story is from just over 100 years ago?* Without the details we just have the plot. We can change the details to make the setting modern.

Whole-class work

● Ask: *How would the journey to Three Chimneys be different today?* (The family might go by train but what kind? They wouldn't get to the cottage by horse-cart.) *Would their mother expect someone to have supper ready? What might they do instead?*

Group work

● Divide the chapters to between groups (some could work on more than one). Ask them to highlight any parts that would need to change if it had a modern setting (they don't need to make the changes yet). Tell them just to think about the main actions; they can focus on details, such as the language people use, later.

Differentiation
● For children who need more support, use their chapter as an example. Point out, for example, that a small station today wouldn't have a porter's room with lamps or a pile of coal for Peter to steal. Suggest that they highlight this part to find out more later on. (Ask: *Could there be something else useful for Peter to steal to help his mother?*)

Review

● Ask each group, working in chronological order, to say what would have to change in their chapters. Ask the class: *How would this change other parts of the story?* Keep the highlighted printouts for the next lesson.

Curriculum objectives
- To identify the audience for and purpose of the writing, selecting the appropriate form and using other similar writing as models for their own.
- In narrative, to describe settings, characters and atmosphere and integrate dialogue to convey character and advance the action.
- To select appropriate grammar and vocabulary and understand how such choices can change and enhance meaning.

Resources
Notes from lesson 3, week 1; chapter from the previous lesson, with parts highlighted for change

4: The Modern Railway Children

Introduction
- Tell the class that they are going to use ideas from the previous lesson and earlier work on language changes to help write a modern version of *The Railway Children*. Remind them of the main themes to keep in the story (lesson 1, week 3): poverty, right and wrong, caring for others, kindness, honesty, politeness, forgiveness.

Whole-class work
- Plan changes to the first chapter with the class. Ask for ideas to introduce the family and their home. Key in the suggested text, save, and display it on the screen/whiteboard as you progress. Ask: *What shall we write about mother?* (Instead of *calls from dull ladies/chatting to boring women*.) There wouldn't be servants, but perhaps a cleaner. They would answer the door for themselves. Ask: *What about Peter's present?* (Something Bobbie can get fixed later, for example: a toy car.)

Group work
- Ask the children to work in their groups, continuing the text that has been keyed in. Point out that this is a first draft; it can be changed later.

> ### Differentiation
> - Children who need more support could work with more proficient writers. Remind the groups that everyone's views and ideas must be considered.

Review
- Ask the children to save their work and move to another group's computer to read theirs. Ask: *What ideas have you found that will help you?* They could leave messages about this for groups whose work they read.

Curriculum objectives
- To identify the audience for and purpose of the writing, selecting the appropriate form and using other similar writing as models for their own.
- In narrative, to describe settings, characters and atmosphere and integrate dialogue to convey character and advance the action.
- To select appropriate grammar and vocabulary and understand how such choices can change and enhance meaning.
- To proofread for spelling and punctuation errors.

Resources
Computers; flow charts and skeleton (lesson 2); drafts of *The Modern Railway Children* from the previous lesson

5: Drafting and refining

Introduction
- Tell the class that, rather than draft an entire story of *The Modern Railway Children*, which would take a very long time, they are going to read through their drafts for Chapter 1 and check for possible improvements, for example: making the speech match the characters, making the dialogue modern and, of course, checking spellings and punctuation.

Group work
- Ask the children to work in the same groups as in the previous lesson, reading the first draft of their story and finding ways of improving it. Remind them about points of grammar they have learned, such as adding relative clauses to sentences (using *who, which, that* and so on), for example: *They peeped through the window of the ticket office where the cashier was chatting on his mobile phone.*
- This is an opportunity to work on dialogue – deciding which characters should have local accents/use local dialect and which should not – and also how the dialogue shows what the characters are like and how they feel. They could then take turns to read parts aloud and check that they sound right.

Review
- Ask members of different groups to read parts of their chapters aloud. The others should listen and check that the main themes of the story are kept. Ask them to listen to how the characters speak. What kind of accent might they have?

Week 6 lesson plans

The lessons this week link with the steam trains in *The Railway Children*, and are based on WH Auden's poem 'Night Mail', commissioned in 1936 for a GPO documentary about the London to Glasgow mail train. For comparison, other poems about trains are suggested, and having explored rhythm, the children write their own train-rhythm poems.

1: 'Night Mail'

Introduction
● Introduce the title of poem 'Night Mail' and tell the class the name of the poet. Read the poem to the class from the photocopiable sheet from the CD-ROM.

Whole-class work
● Give the children an opportunity to respond to the poem by encouraging as many as possible to say something about it. If necessary, ask: *What is it about? What type of train? What is it carrying? From where? To where? What pictures do you see in your mind? What is the story of the poem?*
● Explain that the Post Office asked WH Auden to write the poem for a documentary about the steam train that travelled every night to take the mail from London to Glasgow. Show them the route on media resource 'Britain's railway map' on the CD-ROM.
● Re-read parts of the poem and ask: *What is the atmosphere like?* Discuss the sound of the train and how it affects places it passes through. Parts of the poem suggest that the sound doesn't disturb people (or animals): they don't wake; birds notice it but are not alarmed; the jug shakes *gently*. Ask: *Why doesn't the train disturb anyone?* (Perhaps the people and animals are so used to it that they don't notice.)
● Show the final few minutes of the 1936 documentary film *Night Mail* featuring WH Auden's poem, available online. (You could watch all of the 25-minute film if you have time.) Ask: *Are the pictures and sounds as you imagined from the poem? What do you notice about the rhythm of the poem?* They could tap the rhythm with a finger on a table top as you re-read parts of it.

Paired work
● Give each pair photocopiable page 'Night Mail' from the CD-ROM and felt-tipped pens or highlighters. Explain that the pace of a poem means the speed at which the poet intends it to be read. Ask them to read the poem together and to mark where the speed seems to change. They should make notes about how this matches the story of the poem.
● As the children complete the first part of the activity, ask them to mark sets of rhyming words and make notes about the rhyme pattern and how it helps to create the rhythm. Ask them to make a note of places where the rhyme pattern changes and to notice changes in pace and what happens in the story.

> **Differentiation**
> ● Re-read sections of the poem with the children. Ask them to mark sets of rhyming words in different colours and then to read the poem together and to mark places where it seems to speed up and slow down.

Review
● Ask each pair where they marked changes of speed. Compare with others. Ask how the changes match the story. (It is almost as if the train 'stops for breath' at the top of the hill – after *the climb is done* – and then picks up speed as it goes downhill, then slows to a stop in Glasgow.)

2: Other train poems

Curriculum objectives
• To continue to read and discuss an increasingly wide range of poetry.
• To discuss and evaluate how authors use language, including figurative language, considering the impact on the reader.

Resources
Poems about trains, for example: 'From a Railway Carriage' by RL Stevenson (*The Works*, Macmillan), 'The Song the Train Sang' by Neil Adams (*Poems for 7 year-olds*, Puffin), 'Victoria' by Eleanor Farjeon (*Welcome to the Party*, BBC), 'The Train' by Clive Sansom (*The Works 2*, Macmillan), 'Casey Jones' by Wallace Saunders – traditional folk-song, available online

Introduction
• Tell the class that they are going to read and discuss different poems about trains. Ask them what they might look for when reading a poem: atmosphere, pace, rhyme and rhythm; language (simile, metaphor).

Group work
• Give each group a poem to read and discuss. Suggest that they take turns to read aloud. They should begin by discussing what the poet says about the train or journey and what they like about it, before making notes about the atmosphere and effect of the poem and how the poet creates these with rhyme, rhythm and language. Visit each group and ask if they have found any special kinds of language: similes, metaphors and so on. Point out any they have missed. Ask about the rhyme pattern and other effects of sounds, such as alliteration. Ask: *How do these affect the way you read the poem aloud?* Also ask about the pace of the poem and whether this changes.
• Allow about five to ten minutes then provide another poem for each group.

Differentiation
• Provide poems that are easier to read: 'The Song the Train Sang' and 'The Train'.

Review
• Ask each group which poem they liked the best, and why. Ask: *What was the atmosphere like? How did the poet create this? What rhythm did it have? How did the poet create this?*

3: Poetic language

Curriculum objectives
• To continue to read and discuss an increasingly wide range of poetry.
• To discuss and evaluate how authors use language, including figurative language, considering the impact on the reader.

Resources
Poems about trains, for example: 'From a Railway Carriage' by R L Stevenson (*The Works*, Macmillan), 'The Song the Train Sang' by Neil Adams (*Poems for 7 year-olds*, Puffin), 'Victoria' by Eleanor Farjeon (*Welcome to the Party*, BBC), 'The Train' by Clive Sansom (*The Works 2*, Macmillan), 'Casey Jones' by Wallace Saunders – traditional folk-song, available online

Introduction
• Tell the class that they are going to continue reading poems about trains and to notice poetic language. Recap simile (comparing things using words such as *like*, *than* and *as*: *eyes like grey pebbles, as still as a painting*). Also recap analogy (giving something the characteristic of something else, for example, *the building glared down at us* – like a human).

Group work
• Give out photocopiable page 'Night Mail' from the CD-ROM and/or other train-themed poems containing similes of analogy such as 'From a Railway Carriage'. Ask the children to make a note of any similes they find and to write what is being compared with what. There are several in 'From a Railway Carriage'. They should also look for analogy in 'Night Mail': the engine and coaches are made to seem human or like another animal (*white steam over her shoulder, snorting noisily, blank-faced coaches*); the tugs have an animal analogy: *yelping down the glades of cranes*. Ask them to discuss the effect of each simile and analogy and how effective it is.

Differentiation
• Remind the children to look for words like *as*, *than* and *like* to find similes.

Review
• Ask each group to choose someone to report back to the class. Ask the first for examples of similes and their effects. The others could comment and add their ideas. Ask if anyone found the analogy in 'Night Mail'.

Curriculum objectives
• To prepare poems to read aloud and to perform, showing understanding through intonation, tone and volume, so that the meaning is clear to an audience.

Resources
Poems about trains, for example: 'From a Railway Carriage' by RL Stevenson (*The Works*, Macmillan), 'The Song the Train Sang' by Neil Adams (*Poems for 7 year-olds*, Puffin), 'Victoria' by Eleanor Farjeon (*Welcome to the Party*, BBC), 'The Train' by Clive Sansom (*The Works 2*, Macmillan), 'Casey Jones' by Wallace Saunders – traditional folk-song, available online

4: Reading aloud

Introduction
• Ask if anyone has a favourite train poem, and why they like it. Tell them that they can choose their favourite for this lesson.

Paired or group work
• Arrange children who have chosen the same poem in pairs or groups and ask them first to practise reading it silently to themselves and then to take turns to read it aloud to their group. The others should listen and help with any difficult words. Ask them to say what each reader did well, for example: reading clearly; reading the rhythm; giving an impression of the atmosphere; volume (loud or quiet in the right places); pace (and changing pace).

> **Differentiation**
> • Practise reading the children's chosen poems with them before the lesson. Perhaps another adult or a friend who is a proficient reader could help.

Review
• Ask each group to choose a representative to read their poem to the class. Make a note of what they did well: other members of the class could comment on this, too.

Curriculum objectives
• To identify the audience and purpose of their writing, selecting the appropriate form and using other similar writing as models for their own.
• To select appropriate grammar and vocabulary, understanding how such choices can change and enhance meaning.

Resources
Media resource 'Train' on the CD-ROM

5: Writing a poem with rhythm

Introduction
• Show the class the media resource 'Train' on the CD-ROM. Repeat this and ask them to watch and listen again and to tap the rhythm, including any changes in pace. Invite volunteers to describe the train journey. Ask: *Can you describe it to the rhythm of the train?* Let them try.

Whole-class work
• Go round the class, asking each child to say something about the train using a train rhythm. Write these on a board and ask the class to join in a reading of them all, in a train rhythm.
• As a shared planning activity, arrange these in a suitable order to form a skeleton structure for a poem. Invite them to suggest changes to the words to create a more powerful effect: verbs such as *thundering, clattering, charging, rattling, whirring* and *flashing* suggest different qualities of movement. Also consider descriptions of the scene. Ask: *Is it night or day? What season? What is the weather like? Do you want the atmosphere to be holiday time, stressful, scary, powerful – or something else?* Suggest some words to help with this.

Independent work
• As the children to use the plan to help them to write their own poem that has the rhythm of a train. They could re-read the poems from previous lessons to help with ideas. Remind them to think about poetic language such as similes and analogy.

Review
• Listen to volunteers reading their poems. Ask the class to say what they like and what they think works well for each poem.

Curriculum objectives
● To use relative clauses beginning with *who, which, where, why, whose* or *that* or with an implied (omitted) relative pronoun.

Resources
Interactive activity 'It's all relative' on the CD-ROM

Grammar and punctuation: Relative clauses

Revise
● Begin with starter activity 3 'Relative pronouns'.
● Next, display the sentences below on the whiteboard, and ask the children (verbally) to add relative clauses to give more information, as suggested.
  ● *I gave the book to the teacher.* (Add that the teacher was looking rather stern.)
  ● *There were two houses in the road.* (Add that the road led to the moors.)
  ● *We found a very good spot to put up the tent.* (Add that the tent would be sheltered from the wind in that spot.)
● Ask: *Which pronouns linked the new clause to the first sentence?* Point out the relative pronouns and remind the children that pronouns link to nouns. Ask which noun each pronoun relates (links) to.

Assess
● Give the children a set of sentences and ask them to add a relative clause to give extra information, and then to underline the relative pronouns in each. Provide hints about what information could be added in brackets. The suggestions below can be found on interactive activity 'It's all relative' on the CD-ROM.
  ● *Ellie entered her Labradoodle, Jim, in the dog show.* (Where was the dog show?)
  ● *We sat in the waiting room.* (What was the waiting room like?)
  ● *Four girls were playing football on the field.* (Which field?)
  ● *There were two men in the alley behind the house.* (What did they look like? What were they doing?)
  ● *Maya crept into the garage.* (What did she see in the garage?)
  ● *They had a new neighbour.* (What were the neighbours' children like?)

Further practice
● Collect examples of relative clauses from reading.

Curriculum objectives
● To use knowledge of morphology and etymology in spelling and understand that the spelling of some words needs to be learned specifically, as listed in Appendix 1.

Spelling: Words with 'ei' for /ee/ after 'c'

Revise
● Begin with starter activity 4 'Spelling words with 'ei' for /ee/ after 'c''.
● Next, ask the children to spell *ceiling* (also ask if they can spell its homophone *sealing*). To overcome any confusion, ask about the root word that *sealing* comes from (*seal*), ask them to use *seal*, and then *sealing*, in a sentence. Also ask them to use *ceiling* in a sentence.
● Ask the children to try to spell these words, which they will have used during week 4 lesson 5: *conceit, conceive, deceit, deceive, perceive, receipt* (point out the silent 'p'), *receive*.

Assess
● Provide dictionary definitions of 'cei' words and ask the children to write the correct word for each definition.

Further practice
● From reading, collect examples of words beginning with 'c' followed by /ee/. Challenge the children to find any that have /ee/ after 'c' spelled in a different way, for example: *cede, recede, obscene, scene, scenery, cease, deceased, cereal, conceal, fancy, lacy, excellency, icy, exceed, proceed, succeed.* Ask if they can find any rules to help. If not, they could invent ways to help them to remember the spellings, for example: silly sentences, funny pictures and so on.
● Use starter activity 14 'Spelling bee'.

Curriculum objectives
● To summarise the main ideas drawn from more than one paragraph, identifying key details that support the main ideas.

Resources
Photocopiable page 'The first railway' from the CD-ROM; a recording of a factual television programme, for example, a wildlife or scientific programme, a news item, a history or geography programme (it could be relevant to work in another subject); individual whiteboards and pens

Reading: Making notes

Revise
● Give out photocopiable page 'The first railway' from the CD-ROM. Ask the children to highlight the key facts and ideas. Invite feedback. Ask them to check to see if they missed anything important. Point out any non-essential parts they noted, and explain why they are not necessary. Ask them to make notes about the first paragraph on their whiteboards. Allow a few minutes for this, checking what different children have written. Invite those who wrote accurate, concise, legible notes to show theirs as examples. Discuss why these are good notes. (They should contain all the key facts and make sense, but be as short as possible.) Ask: *could we shorten these notes even more?* Let them try. Ask: *Do the notes still make sense?*

Assess
● Tell the children that they are going to watch a television programme that gives information (or an explanation) about something (say what it is) and make notes about it. Remind them that they should make a note of the main ideas, facts or events, people, dates and so on; notes should be quick but legible; they can check spellings later. Keep these notes to use during the assessment of writing.

Further practice
● Practise note-taking from books, websites, television programmes, radio programmes, films and so on, connected with different subjects. Emphasise that by making notes and then writing from their notes, they can write in their own words, rather than copying from a text.

Writing: Writing a report

Revise

Curriculum objectives
● To use further organisational and presentational devices to structure text and guide the reader.

Resources
Children's notes from the reading assessment on note-making; dictionaries

● Give the children their notes from the reading assessment.
● Ask: *What are your notes about?* Ask them to write a heading for this. Tell them that they are going to use their notes to help them to plan a report about the topic of the programme they watched for other children of their own age, who have not seen the programme and know very little about the topic.
● Ask: *What will be the purpose of the first paragraph?* (To introduce the topic and encourage readers to be interested.) *What will the other paragraphs be about? What will be the purpose of the final paragraph?* (A conclusion, such as a comment about the importance of the topic, how it affects us, animals, the environment, or whatever is appropriate.)
● Record their ideas in a diagram.

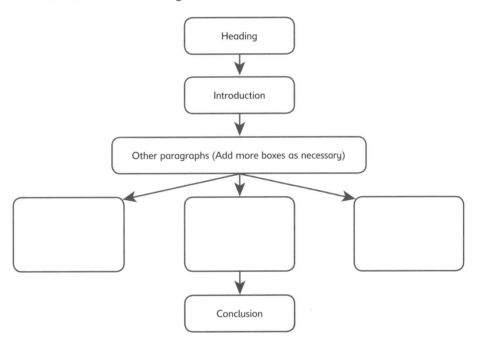

● Discuss useful words for the report, especially for linking ideas within and between paragraphs.

Assess

● Ask how the children use their notes and the diagram to help them to plan their report. Provide dictionaries.

Further practice

● Use this process of note-taking and using a planning diagram for writing reports for work across the curriculum.

Language from the past

- Rewrite this passage from *The Railway Children* in modern language on a separate piece of paper. (Peter and his mother are talking about Jim – the injured boy.)

'You see,' Peter went on, 'of course the girls are all right and all that – I'm not saying anything against *them*. But I should like it if I had another chap to talk to sometimes.'

'Yes,' said Mother, 'I know it's dull for you, dear. But I can't help it. Next year perhaps I can send you to school – you'd like that, wouldn't you?'

'I do miss the other chaps, rather,' Peter confessed; 'but if Jim could stay after his leg was well, we could have awful larks.'

'I've no doubt of it,' said Mother. 'Well – perhaps he could, but you know, dear, we're not rich. I can't afford to get him everything he'll want. And he must have a nurse.'

'Can't you nurse him, Mother? You do nurse people so beautifully.'

'That's a pretty compliment, Pete – but I can't do nursing and my writing as well. That's the worst of it.'

'Then you *must* send the letter to his grandfather?'

'Of course – and to his schoolmaster, too. We telegraphed them both, but I must write as well. They'll be most dreadfully anxious.'

'I say, Mother, why can't his grandfather pay for a nurse?' Peter suggested. 'That would be ripping. I expect the old boy's rolling in money. Grandfathers in books always are.'

From *The Railway Children* by E Nesbit

I can rewrite English from the past as modern English.

How did you do?

The language of speech

■ Fill in the chart to show how the people's speech is different from Standard English.

"Ee, it's clarty in the park after all that rain an' the builders' trucks," said Izzy as she met Asma on the way to school. "Look at me shoes – covered in clarts."

"Aye," said Asma. "I got wrong from me mam yesterday for traipsing clarts onto the carpet. There's the builders. Shall we ask them to leave it clean?"

"Ee, no," said Izzy. "They'll just say we should've went on the path…Oh, no – I forgetten' me bait box. I haven't got no lunch. I've got no money, neither."

"You can share mine," said Asma, "I've got a massive cheese stottie…Look!… Ee, no, I've forgettin' mine, too. But I've got £10. We can gan to the baker's."

Verb doesn't match subject	Double negative	Spelling changed to show pronunciation	Dialect words or expressions (What does it mean?)
			clarty clarts

■ Write the words on the chart in Standard English.
■ What would be lost if the writer had 'corrected' these?

_____

_____

I can spot the differences between spoken and written language: agreement between verbs and subjects and no double negatives.   How did you do?

Report planner

■ Use this page to help you to plan a report about canals or railways.

Title _____

Paragraph 1 introduction	Write in note form.
First railways/canals in Britain	
Why built	

| **History** | Who? When? Where? |

Information paragraphs

How did railways or canals change the lives of rich and not so rich people? How did they affect businesses?

| **Conclusion** | How do we use them today? What is the future for them? |

I can plan a report.

How did you do?

Name: _____ Date: _____

Steam engine explanation

- Use the labelled diagram and other sources to help you write an explanation about how a steam engine works.

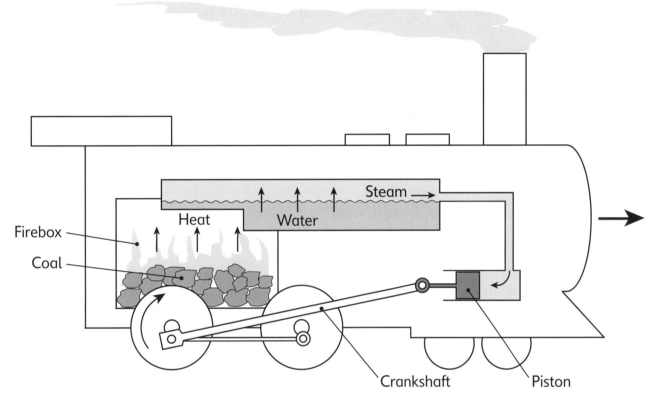

_____
_____
_____
_____
_____
_____
_____
_____
_____
_____
_____
_____
_____

I can write an explanation about a steam engine.

How did you do?

Relative clauses

■ Join each pair of sentences using a relative pronoun (who, which, where, that, when). Remember to use commas for sense.

1. Cinderella had two sisters. They made her do all the housework.

Cinderella had two sisters, who _____

_____

2. One day she opened a letter. It was addressed to 'the young ladies of the house'.

_____

_____

3. She opened the envelope. It contained an invitation to the Prince's ball.

_____

_____

4. Cinderella showed it to her sisters. They said it was for them, not for her.

_____

_____

5. She washed and ironed their gowns. They put them on, and set off for the ball.

_____

_____

6. Cinderella was sitting alone at home. Her fairy godmother suddenly appeared.

_____

_____

■ Add your own relative clauses to these sentences.

1. She waved a magic wand _____ .

2. Cinderella looked at her dress _____ .

3. The fairy godmother waved her wand at the dress _____ .

I can write relative clauses and punctuate them.

How did you do?

PHOTOCOPIABLE   **SCHOLASTIC**
www.scholastic.co.uk

Name: _____ Date: _____

Clarity with commas

■ Read the sentences. Add or change the commas to give them different meanings. Read the new sentences.

	**1.** Coming down the road was a little boy carrying a teddy bear and four large girls with dolls. **1.** Coming down the road was a little boy carrying a teddy bear and four large girls with dolls.
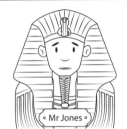	**2.** In the Egyptian room we could see Mr Jones a four thousand-year-old mummy and an Egyptian god. **2.** In the Egyptian room we could see Mr Jones a four thousand-year-old mummy and an Egyptian god.
	**3.** I tell you Richard James will not eat cabbage. **3.** I tell you Richard James will not eat cabbage.
	**4.** On the way home Dad bought some petrol a packet of felt tips and some sweets and a nice piece of steak from the butcher. **4.** On the way home Dad bought some petrol a packet of felt tips and some sweets and a nice piece of steak from the butcher.
	**5.** The girl bought presents for her parents, two dogs Alan and Sara. **5.** The girl bought presents for her parents, two dogs Alan and Sara.

■ Write some sentences of your own with commas on a separate piece of paper. Rewrite them with commas in different places to change their meanings.

I can use commas to make meanings clear.

How did you do?

Making verbs (1)

- Add a prefix or suffix to the adjective or noun in brackets to make a verb.
- Read the sentence to check that it makes sense.

1. No ghost can (fright) _____ me.

2. The BBC will (television) _____ the football match.

3. We painted the walls white to (bright) _____ the room.

4. When you say you are sorry you (apology) _____.

5. The police closed the road so that the spilled petrol would not (danger) _____ people.

6. If you press hard on a piece of dough, you can (flat) _____ it.

7. She put on some make-up to (beauty) _____ herself.

8. If someone faints, you should (loose) _____ any tight clothes they are wearing.

9. If you stroke a pin with a magnet, you can (magnet) _____ it.

10. If you open a door, it will (active) _____ the burglar alarm.

11. It is illegal to (slave) _____ people.

12. See if you can (memory) _____ the poem.

- Write other verbs made in the same ways on the chart.

Prefix 'en-'	Suffix '-en'	Suffix '-ise'	Suffix '-ate'	Suffix '-fy'

- Tell a partner what you notice about most of the words that the verbs in each set are made from.

I can form verbs from adjectives and nouns.

How did you do?

PHOTOCOPIABLE   ■SCHOLASTIC
www.scholastic.co.uk

Newspaper report planner

- Plan a newspaper report about an event in *The Railway Children*.
- Imagine you could interview characters from the story.
- Include some quotations from them.

| A catchy headline attracts attention and says what the story is about. |

Headline _____

Introduction _____

_____

_____

| The introduction says, briefly, what happened. If it is about a person, say who. |

The facts _____

_____

| Who? What? Where? When? |

Characters interviewed

| Who? Member of the family, neighbour, passer-by? Occupation? Age? |

Name and details	What they said

Summary

| What were the consequences? How did it affect others? |

_____

_____

I can plan a newspaper report.

How did you do?

Other cultures and traditions

During this half term the children will read texts connected with China, India and Japan. They will read a traditional Chinese story and make links between this and Chinese culture. Further work will feature plays and traditional stories from the Indian tradition and non-fiction (newspaper reports) about the death of Mohandas Gandhi. They will read haikus and relate them to Japanese culture, learning about their structure and rhythm. Opportunities arise to focus on relative clauses, adverbials and other paragraph linkers and punctuation (commas and inverted commas).

Expected prior learning
- Can make notes from a text they have read.
- Can use commas to separate clauses.
- Can use relative clauses beginning with *who, which* and other relative pronouns.
- Know the features of playscripts.
- Know the features of a newspaper report.
- Can recite an atmospheric poem.

Overview of progression
- Children will increase their familiarity with books and poetry from other cultures and traditions. They will discuss themes and conventions and learn some poetry by heart. They will develop skills in retrieving information from non-fiction, and practise preparing and making presentations.
- Spelling skills will develop as they apply knowledge of root words and affixes.
- To support the development of writing skills children will use other similar writing as models, identifying the audience and selecting the appropriate form. As they write, they will learn to describe settings, characters and atmosphere, and integrate dialogue to convey character and advance the action.
- They will have opportunities to prepare plays to perform and to perform their own compositions, using intonation, volume and movement, to make the meaning clear to an audience.

Creative context
- The ideas in this chapter could be linked to work on Hinduism, Islam, and the religions and traditions of China and Japan.
- There are opportunities to support map work in geography (locating countries, cities, key geographical features), and China, Japan or India could be the focus of a country study.

Preparation
The lesson focus on India, beginning with traditional stories in *Seasons of Splendour: Tales, Myths and Legends of India* by Madhur Jaffrey. A good alternative to this would be *Haroun and the Sea of Stories* by Salman Rushdie, or you could use other versions of Indian myths and legends.

You will also need:
Maps of China, India and Japan; a globe; Chinese and Japanese artefacts; information books about China, India (including information about the country's independence from Britain) and Japan; dictionaries; timers or stopwatches; a trophy; a selection of news reports about historical events; traditional Japanese pictures; examples of modern and traditional haiku; internet access; individual whiteboards; copy of or picture of Mahabharata; scissors; information books about Gandhi at different reading levels; highlighter pens.

On the CD-ROM you will find:
Media resources 'Hua Mulan', 'Give us a clue', 'Independence day in India', 'Natural world'; interactive activities 'Figuring out new words'; photocopiable pages 'Haikus by Bashō', 'News report: The death of Gandhi', 'Newspaper report planner (2)', 'One Rice Thousand Gold', 'Savitri', 'Story summary: Hua Mulan', 'The story of Hua Mulan'

Chapter at a glance

An overview of the chapter. For curriculum objective codes, please see pages 8–10.

Week	Lesson	Curriculum objectives	Summary of activities	Outcomes
1	1	RC: 17	Talk about what they know about China. Raise questions and find answers using non-fiction sources, making notes of key points.	• Can raise questions to help to find information.
	2	RC: 13, 17, 19	Use notes to write a fascinating fact about an aspect of Chinese history, life or culture.	• Can use notes to plan writing.
	3	RC: 13, 17	Research and make notes for a presentation on an aspect of Chinese history, life or culture.	• Can research a topic and make notes of key points.
	4	RC: 17, 19 WC: 7, 28	Decide which parts of their notes to use for their presentation and write the script for it.	• Can prepare an oral presentation and write the script for it.
	5	RC: 19 WC: 12, 14	Present talks to the class on the topic they have researched.	• Can share findings through an oral presentation. • Can listen with interest and ask appropriate questions afterwards.
2	1	RC: 3	Read and discuss a traditional Chinese story.	• Can discuss the meaning of a traditional story from another culture.
	2	RC: 3, 5, 6	Read and verbally summarise another traditional Chinese story and discuss its message.	• Can explain the message of a story.
	3	RC: 3, 5, 6	Write a summary of another traditional Chinese story and explain what these stories reveal about the culture they are from.	• Can summarise a story and discuss its cultural background.
	4	RC: 8 WC: 5	Improvise on a Chinese story and use this to develop a deeper understanding of the story's message.	• Can improvise on a story, using movement, words and intonation.
	5	WC: 7, 20, 22, 28	Revise pronouns, commas and relative clauses.	• Can write sentences with relative clauses, correctly punctuated with commas.
3	1	RC: 3, 5	Read and discuss a traditional Indian story.	• Can discuss the cultural background to a story.
	2	RWR: 1 WT: 5, 6	Read difficult words by focusing on prefixes and suffixes and through analogy. Check these in a dictionary.	• Can read difficult words using knowledge of word roots, prefixes and suffixes.
	3	WC: 10, 22, 28	Compare a passage of text with and without punctuation. Add to sentences using appropriate punctuation.	• Can use commas to clarify meaning.
	4	WC: 10, 24, 28	Use brackets to separate off part of a sentence so that it does not interfere with the meaning of the main part.	• Can use brackets to separate a parenthesis.
	5	WT: 4	Compare the different sounds represented by the letter string '-ough'.	• Can read and spell words with the letter string '-ough'.
4	1	RC: 3, 18	Read aloud from a playscript based on part of the Hindu poem 'Mahabharata'.	• Can read a given role from a playscript and discuss the feelings shown by the characters.
	2	RC: 3, 8	Practise reading and enacting a play from the script from the previous lesson.	• Can discuss how characters should act and speak, justifying their opinions.
	3	RC: 8	Perform the play they have practised; watch others perform and make notes.	• Can participate in a dramatised reading of a playscript.
	4	RC: 4 WC: 1	Read theatrical reviews and discuss how reviewers express and justify opinions. Write reviews of the performances they made notes about.	• Can argue an opinion, justifying ideas.
	5	RC: 19, 21	Discuss the characters in the play they read and performed.	• Can participate in a class debate about a character.

Chapter at a glance

Week	Lesson	Curriculum objectives	Summary of activities	Outcomes
5	1	RC: 17, 20	Read and discuss a newspaper report about the death of Gandhi.	• Can identify how a news report is matched to the needs of its readers.
	2	WC: 20	Explore clauses in sentences and notice how punctuation is used to make meaning clear.	• Can identify the main clause of a sentence.
	3	RC: 17, 20 WT: 8	Read non-fiction texts to research India's Independence Day.	• Can read to find the answers to questions.
	4	RC: 17 WC: 1, 2	Plan and draft a newspaper report about India's Independence Day.	• Can write in a journalistic style.
	5	WC: 9, 10	Check spelling, punctuation and grammar in the reports they wrote and redraft them.	• Can use techniques to ensure that a final piece of work has no grammatical errors.
6	1	RC: 1	Read traditional haikus translated from Japanese and explore their structure.	• Can describe the structure of the haiku.
	2	RC: 1, 15	Read and discuss modern haikus. Explore how they are different from other poems.	• Can appreciate the craft of the haiku.
	3	RC: 1, 7, 8	Choose their favourite haiku to learn by heart.	• Can learn a short poem by heart and recite it.
	4	WC: 1, 9	Look at pictures of the natural world and write their own haiku about one of them.	• Can write a haiku using the right rhythm and choosing the most appropriate language.
	5	WC: 1, 9, 14	Read and review haikus they have written with a partner to check the syllables and pattern.	• Can evaluate their own poems according to agreed criteria.

Background knowledge

Atmosphere: The overall tone of part or all of the text. It is similar to mood, which is more concerned with feelings.

Bracket: Punctuation mark, used in pairs, to separate a parenthesis from the rest of a sentence.

Epic poem: Long narrative poem.

Haiku: A traditional Japanese poetic form with 17 syllables, arranged in three lines: five, seven, five, that tries to capture the essence of its subject.

Main clause: The most important clause in a sentence.

Pace: Speed. A piece of prose or poetry can be written so that it induces the reader to read it at a particular speed.

Parenthesis: An extra piece of information or detail added to a sentence and separated from the rest of the sentence by punctuation marks such as brackets, dashes or commas.

Prefix: An affix placed at the beginning of a word to change its meaning and make a new word.

Syllable: A unit of pronunciation spoken without interruption that contains a vowel.

Tone: Often interchangeable with atmosphere. The general feeling or impression created by a text, or part of it: *for example, insulting, complaining, sombre.*

Week 1 lesson plans

This week's work features non-fiction texts from China. The children begin by sharing what they know about China and formulating questions they would like to answer in order to find out more about something that inspires their interest. They develop research skills, including locating information by scanning and skimming, making notes and recording sources, so that they can return to them. They will then prepare and present what they have learned to the class using PowerPoint. During this the children will refine their skills in linking paragraphs and in choosing vocabulary for its effect.

1: Amazing things about China

Introduction
● Invite the children to show and talk about anything they have brought in that is connected with China. If time runs short, these could be arranged on a display table and board.
● Point out China on a globe and ask the children what they notice about its size, which continent it is in, its capital city and the seas around it.

Whole-class work
● Give the children time to comment on anything they know or have found out about China and ask them to think about what else they would like to know. Tell them that their questions must be ones they can answer by research. List their questions and discuss where they can find the answers.

Paired work
● Ask each pair to discuss what they know and what they would like to find out about China. They could write their question in the centre of a mind map and then add anything they know connected with it and any ideas they have about it (and the reasons). Their ideas might come from what was shown and talked about at the start of the lesson or from items displayed in the classroom. Possible areas of research include the Great Wall of China, the story of the animals of the Chinese years, the Terracotta Warriors, how silk is made, writing, an invention. Check that each pair has chosen a question they will be able to answer; provide guidance, if necessary, to adjust it.
● Allow an appropriate amount of time, then stop the children and ask them to decide where to look for information to answer their question. Ask how they will be able to tell quickly whether a book, website or other text will help. Remind them to scan headings, pictures, captions and so on.
● They could begin to read and make notes to answer their question. Remind them to make brief notes of facts, ideas and any important words and to note/ bookmark where they found information, including pictures, in case they want to return to it.

> **Differentiation**
> ● Provide reference books at an appropriate interest and presentational level but at a simpler reading level.

Review
● Ask each pair what question they are going to find out about. Ask the others which one, apart from their own, interests them the most. Tell them that they will have more time in the next lesson to find information to show how interesting their own question is. Keep their mind maps and notes for the next lesson.

Expected outcomes
● All children can use texts to find information and make some notes.
● Most children can research a topic, make notes of key points and share findings through an oral presentation.
● Some children can lead their groups in this.

Curriculum objectives
● To retrieve, record and present information from non-fiction.

Resources
Artefacts and information about China – ask children to bring in any they have in preparation for the lesson; information books about the geography, history, culture and religion of China; computer and internet access; The British Museum's site on ancient China: www.ancientchina.co.uk; globe and map of China

---

Curriculum objectives
● To retrieve, record and present information from non-fiction.
● To summarise the main ideas drawn from more than one paragraph, identifying key details that support the main ideas.
● To explain and discuss their understanding of what they have read, including through formal presentations and debates, maintaining focus on the topic and using notes where necessary.

Resources
Information books about the geography, history, culture and religion of China; computer and internet access; globe and map of China; the children's mind maps and notes from the previous lesson

2: Non-fiction – a fascinating fact

Introduction

● Provide some *Did you know?* facts about China to stimulate interest, for example: *Did you know that...the Chinese invented paper more than 2000 years ago; they printed books 600 years before the Europeans; they built the world's biggest wall.*
● Tell the class that they are going to use their notes from the previous lesson to help them to prepare a fascinating fact about China to tell others and that, in a later lesson, they will use this and their notes to help them to write a longer presentation.

Paired work

● Seat the class in groups of four so that they can continue working in their pairs from the previous lesson. Allow time for them to read their notes and find out more information. When the time is almost up, tell them that they should now write a few sentences so that they can tell another pair a fascinating fact.

Group work

● Tell the children that they are going to share their fascinating fact with three other pairs. Arrange this so that half the pairs stay in their places and the others move around in a given direction (for example, clockwise). They should begin by sharing their facts with the pair they are with now.

Review

● Ask the children what they learned from other pairs that most interested them.

Curriculum objectives
● To retrieve, record and present information from non-fiction.
● To summarise the main ideas drawn from more than one paragraph, identifying key details that support the main ideas.

Resources
Information books about the geography, history, culture and religion of China; computer and internet access; globe and map of China; the children's mind maps and notes from lessons 1 and 2; if possible, new resources/artefacts from China to add to the display board and table begun in lesson 1

3: Finding out more about China

Introduction

● Remind the class of the previous lesson and ask some questions related to the classroom display. Tell the children they are going to have a chance to find out more about China to help them to plan a presentation about their topic to the class.

Group work

● Group the children according to the fascinating facts they researched in lessons 1 and 2. Tell them that their task for this lesson is to make sure they have all the information they need to help them to plan a longer presentation about their topic. Ask them to re-read their notes and recap note-taking (see lesson 1). Also ask them to return to the books and websites they used and to copy any pictures, maps and diagrams they can use in their presentation.

> **Differentiation**
> ● Where necessary, direct the children to information books and websites that present information at an appropriate level.

Review

● Remind the class of their task for the lesson and ask: *How well have you achieved this?* They should say whether they have the information, pictures maps and so on that they need. Ask where it is (for example, printed/sketched, written on paper/keyed in). Ask: *Have you saved everything you need on the computer or in a file?*

Curriculum objectives

● To retrieve, record and present information from non-fiction.
● To explain and discuss their understanding of what they have read, including through formal presentations and debates, maintaining focus on the topic and using notes where necessary.
● To use a wide range of devices to build cohesion within and across paragraphs.
● To use and understand the grammatical terminology in Appendix 2 accurately and appropriately in discussing their writing and reading.

Resources

Information books about the geography, history, culture and religion of China; computer and internet access; globe and map of China; dictionaries; the children's mind maps and notes from the previous lesson; photocopiable page 104 'Presentation plan'; timers or stopwatches

Curriculum objectives

● To explain and discuss their understanding of what they have read, including through formal presentations, maintaining a focus on the topic and using notes where necessary.
● To ensure correct subject and verb agreement when using singular and plural, distinguishing between the language of speech and writing and choose the appropriate register.
● To perform their own compositions, using appropriate intonation, volume and movement, so that the meaning is clear.

Resources

The children's scripts from the previous lesson

4: Non-fiction: planning a talk

Introduction

● Tell the class that their task for this lesson is to plan and write a talk for the rest of the class about the question they researched. Give them a time limit (perhaps two to three minutes) for their presentation.

Paired work

● Give each pair photocopiable page 104 'Presentation plan', which will help them to write their presentation. Tell them that their aim is to fascinate the class. They might not need to use all the information they gathered; they should choose the most interesting parts.
● Remind them about what they have learned about words to add cohesion or to add information to sentences and to check their work carefully. The children will also need to time their presentation.
● Give the children time to practise and refine their presentations.

> **Differentiation**
> ● Help the children to group the pieces of information they have found and to select the parts to use.

Review

● Ask the children what they need to think about to make sure their audience will want to listen. List all the points they make and add others, if necessary. Keep their scripts for the next lesson.

5: A presentation about China

Introduction

● In advance of the lesson, arrange the room to facilitate the talks (for example, semicircles). Ensure that the children have their plans/scripts from the previous lesson. Tell them that they are going to present their talk to the class. Ask: *What do you need to think about when giving a talk?* List these on the board and add any they omit: speaking clearly and not too fast/too slowly; using notes but looking at the audience when making important points. Ask: *What should the audience do?* (Listen; pay attention; look at the speaker; keep questions until the end – and smile and applaud at the end to make the speaker feel good!)

Group work

● Decide on an order for the presentations – perhaps by drawing lots. Give the class a last opportunity to move about before settling down to listen. Ask the first pair to come to the front and face the class. Check that the audience is ready. A calm, encouraging atmosphere helps; it is worth spending a little time on this. After each talk, allow time for just one or, perhaps, two questions.

> **Differentiation**
> ● Where necessary, give extra encouragement to both speaker and audience and remind them of anything they should do.

Review

● Encourage the entire class to give one another, and themselves, a clap. Ask what they enjoyed about each talk.

Week 2 lesson plans

This week the children read and discuss traditional Chinese stories and find out what these tell us about Chinese values and customs. They practise reading stories out loud, using intonation, tone and volume to make the meaning of the text clear. They investigate the purpose of traditional stories – and examine a story in detail to see how well it fits its purpose. Children also explore story characters through role play and practise and perform a story. Sentences from the texts provide opportunities for revising relative clauses and the use of commas for clarity.

1: A traditional Chinese story

Introduction

Introduce the story 'One Rice Thousand Gold' and explain that it is a traditional story from China. Ask: *What is meant by a* traditional *story?* (An old story that has been passed on from one generation to another, so the authors of most traditional stories are unknown.)

Whole-class work

● Give out the photocopiable page 'One Rice Thousand Gold' from the CD-ROM. Tell the class that they are going to follow the story while some of them read parts aloud. Ask: *What is important when reading aloud?* (Reading clearly, and loudly enough to be heard, but not too loudly. For some parts this needs to be varied. It will sound more interesting if you change your voice for narrative or dialogue or for different characters.) Ask: *What should the audience do?* (Look at the reader, listen quietly, look as if you are listening.) If they want to show their appreciation of the reading, they should wait until the end.

● Select readers for each paragraph, who should mark where they are to begin and end reading. Arrange the class with the readers facing them and so that they can all see them. They can then start reading. Before they begin, point out the footnotes on pronunciation.

● After reading, ask: *If the story didn't mention China or the name of the emperor, would you be able to tell that it is not a British story? How? What would help you to tell that it is from China?*

● Ask the children for the titles of other traditional stories they know. List these on the board and ask, for each one: *What do you think this story was told for, apart from to entertain?* Ask: *Is there anything similar about the reasons why the stories were told and passed on from generation to generation?* (To teach, pass on the values of the culture, encourage good/wise behaviour, and so on.)

● Ask: *What do you think was the purpose of 'One Rice Thousand Gold'?*

Group work

● Ask the children to spend a couple of minutes discussing what the story tells us about Chinese values and customs and, once they agree, to write this on their individual whiteboard. Warn them when you are about to stop them. They should ensure they have their answer written. It has to be brief to fit on the whiteboard.

Review

● Ask the children to show their whiteboards. Ask: *So, how well did the story fulfil its purpose?* (If the answers are very similar, then it did.) Ask: *What do we call this kind of meaning for a story?* (Moral.)

Curriculum objectives

● To increase their familiarity with a wide range of books, including traditional stories and books from other cultures and traditions.
● To identify and discuss themes and conventions in and across a wide range of writing.
● To make comparisons within and across books.

Resources

Photocopiable page 'The story of Hua Mulan' from the CD-ROM; media resource 'Hua Mulan' on the CD-ROM

2: Other Chinese stories

Introduction

● Show the picture of Hua Mulan (on the CD-ROM) and ask: *What do you think this picture shows?* They should notice the weapons and clothing. Tell them that it is not a soldier, or even a man, but a young girl dressed as a warrior. Tell them her name and that they are going to read an old Chinese story to find out why she is dressed as a soldier.

Paired work

● Give the class photocopiable page 'The story of Hua Mulan' from the CD-ROM to share and read. Ask them to discuss with their partner the message or moral of the story and what they can find out from it about Chinese culture, values and customs.

Differentiation
● Pair children who might find the story difficult to read with other, more confident, readers.

Review

● Ask for a summary of the story. Ask: *Why did Hua Mulan dress up as a warrior? What did you find out from the story about the values and culture of China?* (Honour is important. Boys, but not girls, were brought up to be brave and to be prepared to fight for their country or region.) *What is the message of the story?* (We can achieve difficult targets if we try hard enough.)

Curriculum objectives

● To increase their familiarity with a wide range of books, including traditional stories and books from other cultures and traditions.
● To identify and discuss themes and conventions in and across a wide range of writing.
● To make comparisons within and across books.

Resources

Books or printouts of traditional stories from China; photocopiable page 'Story summary: Hua Mulan' from the CD-ROM; photocopiable page 105 'Story summary'; books, printouts and pictures featuring traditional Chinese stories, added to your China display (encourage the children to read the stories and look at the display before and between lessons)

3: Messages and themes of Chinese stories

Introduction

● Remind the class of 'The story of Hua Mulan'. Ask: *What was the story about?*

Whole-class work

● Display photocopiable page 'Story summary: Hua Mulan' from the CD-ROM and use it to demonstrate how 'The story of Hua Mulan' can be summarised: characters and setting; event that started the action; problem; how the main character solved the problem; the outcome.

Paired work

● Ask the children if they have read any other Chinese stories since those lessons (or even just looked at the pictures or scanned), and to think about their favourites. Pair them with others who chose the same story.
● Ask them to re-read and discuss the story with their partner. Give each pair or group photocopiable page 105 'Story summary' and ask them to use it to help them to write a summary of the story, as you did for 'The story of Hua Mulan'. After an appropriate time, stop the class and tell them that they should complete their summary and answer the questions about the message or moral of the story and what it tells us about Chinese culture.

Differentiation
● Steer children towards stories written at an appropriate level, or even picture stories or those written in a comic strip style.

Review

● Invite each pair to give a brief summary of the story they read. Ask: *What was the message of your story? What did it tell us about Chinese culture?* Keep their completed photocopiable sheets for lessons 4 and 5.

Curriculum objectives

● To prepare plays to read aloud and to perform, showing understanding through intonation, tone and volume so that the meaning is clear to an audience.
● In narratives, to describe settings, characters and atmosphere and integrate dialogue to convey character and advance the action.

Resources

The Chinese traditional stories the children worked on in lesson 3; the titles of the stories the children chose on cards

4: Improvising a story

Introduction

● In advance of the lesson, place cards with story titles on tables around the room. Ask the children to go, with their partner from the previous lesson, to a table that has their story title. Ask them to think about the story and, without talking about it, to imagine it taking place: how the characters behave, speak and move. Give them a few moments to sit in silence, perhaps closing their eyes if they wish, picturing and hearing this.

Group work

● Ask the children to decide in their groups who will take the parts of the characters and narrator and to act the story. Tell them that they can stop, make changes, repeat it and even swap roles if it helps, or to ensure everyone has a chance to take part. Visit each group and remind them to think about how the characters might speak, move or behave, not just what they say or do.

> **Differentiation**
> ● Check that all members of the groups are participating; if not, suggest changes such as role-swapping.

Review

● Ask the children to perform their story for the class. Ask the class: *What was the message of the story? What can we learn about Chinese culture from it?*

Curriculum objectives

● To use a wide range of devices to build cohesion within and across paragraphs.
● To use commas to clarify meaning or avoid ambiguity.
● To use relative clauses beginning with *who*, *which*, *where*, *when*, *whose*, *that* or an implied (omitted) relative pronoun.
● To use and understand the grammatical terminology in Appendix 2 accurately and appropriately in discussing their writing and reading.

Resources

Photocopiable page 'Story summary: Hua Mulan' from the CD-ROM; the stories the children read in lessons 1 to 4; the children's completed photocopiable sheets from lesson 3

5: Pronouns, commas and relative clauses

Introduction

● Tell the children that they are going to read a summary of 'The story of Hua Mulan' and look at how pronouns, relative clauses and commas are used for linking ideas and for shortening sentences. Recap pronouns (including relative pronouns) and relative clauses.

Whole-class work

● Give out photocopiable page 'Story summary: Hua Mulan' from the CD-ROM and display the first sentence on the board.
● Invite a child to read it aloud. Invite another child to come out and underline a pronoun and a third to highlight a relative clause.
● Ask: *Which pronoun does the relative clause begin with?* (Whose.) *Which punctuation mark separates the relative clause from the rest of the sentence and helps to make the sentence clear?* (Comma.)
● Show them how the sentence might be written without pronouns or a relative clause: *This story is about a girl in Ancient China. The girl's father taught the girl to ride a horse and fight with a sword, just like any boy.*

Independent work

● Ask the children to underline the pronouns in the rest of the summary, to highlight any relative clauses and circle the commas that separate them from the rest of the sentence.
● To show how these improve a text, ask the children to write each paragraph without the pronouns or relative clauses.

Review

● Read out examples of changed sentences for comparison. The children could use what they have learned to edit their own story summary.

Week 3 lesson plans

This week's lessons are based on *Seasons of Splendour: Tales, Myths and Legends of India* by Madhur Jaffrey. If preferred, other books of traditional Indian stories could be substituted, for example: *Haroun and the Sea of Stories* by Salman Rushdie or other versions of Indian myths and legends.

1: A story from India

Introduction

● Ask the children what they can find out from the cover of the book *Seasons of Splendour* (Madhur Jaffrey) about the author and where the stories come from. Ask a volunteer to point out India on the globe. Allow a few minutes for the children to share anything they know about India.
● Read the introduction to the story 'The Girl who had Seven Brothers' and ask: *What is the author's religion? Did her mother really believe that her fast would help to keep her husband alive?* Compare it with any traditional beliefs the children and their families follow, or festivals they celebrate, but might not really believe in.
● Point out that many customs linked with religions have been carried from one generation to another for purposes such as helping families to feel togetherness; showing respect for family and so on, and that different cultures do this in different ways.

Whole-class work

● Read 'The Girl who had Seven Brothers' with the class. Allow a minute or so for the children to think about the story. Ask: *Why did the girl fast? Could a fast really help her husband to stay well?* Ask about religious fasts the children know about, and why people with faith keep the fasts – not to achieve anything but to show belief and to remind themselves of their faith.
● Ask: *Do you think the girl in the story used the fast to show her love for her husband?* Tell them that the theme of fasting or other hardship, in order to show love or faith, can be found in other traditional stories.

Group work

● Ask the children to re-read the story (and the Introduction: Karvachauth – the Little Clay Pot) with their group and to discuss the meaning of it and what it tells them about the culture it comes from. It will help to provide some questions to focus their discussion: *What happens at Karvachauth? Why? Why do many modern Hindu women keep the fast? What does the story say about family life? What does it say about brothers and sisters, and about sisters-in-law and about brothers and brothers-in-law? What was the girl's character? What is the message of the story? What does this say about the culture it comes from?*

Review

● Ask a group to give their answer to the questions: *What happens at Karvachauth? Why? Do the others agree?* They could add their thoughts about why. Repeat this for the other questions. Ask what the story says about the culture it comes from. *Could this story have come from Britain?* If there is time, discuss how the story might change but still give the message that a married woman must honour her husband.

Expected outcomes
● All children can add phrases or clauses to a sentence, punctuating them with commas, brackets or dashes.
● Most children can do so using more complex language.
● Some children can do so with greater accuracy.

Curriculum objectives
● To increase their familiarity with a wide range of books, including myths, legends and traditional stories and books from other cultures and traditions.
● To identify and discuss themes and conventions in and across a wide range of writing.

Resources
Copies of *Seasons of Splendour: Tales, Myths and Legends of India* by Madhur Jaffrey or other versions of traditional Indian stories for the class to read; globe or map of the world

Curriculum objectives
● To apply their growing knowledge of root words, prefixes and suffixes (morphology and etymology) both to read aloud and understand the meaning of new words they meet.
● To use dictionaries to check the spelling and meaning of words.
● To use the first three or four letters of a word to check spelling, meaning or both of these in a dictionary.

Resources
Seasons of Splendour: Tales, Myths and Legends of India by Madhur Jaffrey or other versions of traditional Indian stories, as read in lesson 1; dictionaries; photocopiable page 106 'Figuring out new words'; interactive activity 'Figuring out new words' on the CD-ROM

2: Difficult words

Introduction
● Ask the children if they could read and understand every word of the story from the previous lesson, or if they skipped some but could still follow the story. Acknowledge that looking up every new word while reading can spoil the story – look them up afterwards.

Whole-class work
● Write up and read out the word *enshrouded*. Ask: *How can we split this word to help with reading it and to figure out its meaning?* If necessary give the hint *prefix and suffix*. Remove the prefix and suffix and ask what is left. Ask: *What is a shroud?* Let them look it up. Ask: *What kind of word is shroud?* Remind them of verbs made from nouns – so what do they think *enshroud* means?
● Ask how the suffix '-ed' changes a verb.

Independent work
● Give out photocopiable page 106 'Figuring out new words' and ask the children to use their knowledge of suffixes and prefixes to help them to figure out the meanings and functions of the words. (Alternatively, use the interactive version on the CD-ROM.)

> **Differentiation**
> ● Edit the photocopiable sheet, simplifying the example words.

Review
● Ask the children to use one of the new words they have learned in a sentence.

Curriculum objectives
● To use commas to clarify meaning or avoid ambiguity in writing.
● To propose changes to vocabulary, grammar and punctuation to enhance effects and clarify meaning.
● To use and understand the grammatical terminology in Appendix 2 accurately and appropriately in discussing their writing and reading.

Resources
Photocopiable page 107 'Growing sentences'; copies of *Seasons of Splendour* by Madhur Jaffrey

3: Adding to a sentence

Introduction
● In advance of the lesson, ask the children to read the story 'A Special Birthday: The Birth of Krishna, the Blue God' from *Seasons of Splendour*. Ask the children their opinions on the story.

Whole-class work
● Display the third sentence from the introduction to the story (beginning *Not only was I raised...*) with the punctuation omitted.
● Ask the children to compare this with the same sentence in the story. They should notice the use of commas and a dash. Ask how these help the reader to make sense of the sentence.
● Ask them to find another sentence in the introduction where punctuation is important and to say what punctuation marks are used, and why.

Independent work
● Give out photocopiable page 107 'Growing sentences'. Ask the children to read the main sentence each time and then add the information from the bubbles to it, deciding what punctuation will help a reader.

> **Differentiation**
> ● Simplify the photocopiable sheet, for example by deleting some of the additional sentences or simplifying some of the vocabulary, as appropriate.

Review
● Ask the children to swap papers with a partner, to try to read their new sentence and to say how well the punctuation helped. Keep the completed photocopiable sheets for the next lesson.

Curriculum objectives

- To propose changes to vocabulary, grammar and punctuation to enhance effects and clarify meaning.
- To use brackets, dashes or commas to indicate parenthesis.
- To use and understand the grammatical terminology in Appendix 2 accurately and appropriately in discussing their writing and reading.

Resources

Completed photocopiable sheets from lesson 3; photocopiable page 108 'Brackets'

4: Brackets

Introduction

- Recap what was learned in lesson 4. Display some of the children's examples. Point out that, even with commas and dashes, too many pieces of information can make a sentence difficult to read.

Whole-class work

- Ask the class if they can think of a punctuation mark that can be used in pairs to surround an extra bit added to a sentence. (Brackets.) Write up the following sentences:
  - *This story is about Holi (the Hindu spring festival).*
  - *Parvati (the wife of the god Shiva) is the daughter of the Himalaya Mountains.*
- Invite volunteers to read the sentences aloud. Ask: *How did the brackets help?* Explain that brackets are used to surround something added to a sentence, so that it doesn't get in the way of the sense of the sentence.

Paired work

- Give each child photocopiable page 108 'Brackets'. Use the first sentence as an example. Read the sentence (ignoring the brackets). Ask: *Does it make sense?* Read the question and, if the children can't remember the answer, check it in *Seasons of Splendour*. Ask what they could write between the brackets to answer the question.

Review

- Ask the children to compare the use of brackets with commas using the two completed photocopiable sheets. They might find the explanation difficult but be able to select the best punctuation for a sentence provided.

Curriculum objectives

- To use knowledge of morphology and etymology in spelling and understand that the spelling of some words needs to be learned specifically, as listed in Appendix 1.

Resources

A list of words containing the '-ough' letter string collected from the traditional Indian stories the children have read, the words should be presented so that '-ough' is pronounced differently in consecutive words, for example: *drought, enough, bough, dough, thought*; small cards; interactive activity 'Give us a clue' on the CD-ROM

5: Words with '-ough'

Introduction

- Ask the class to listen while you read out some words. As soon as anyone spots a connection between the words, they should raise a hand. Stop and ask for their answer. If incorrect, say so and continue. If correct, read a few more words. Ask the class if they agree with the answer. Tell them that they are going to play a quiz game to help them to learn the spellings of these words.

Whole-class work

- Play a quiz game in which you begin by giving a clue to an '-ough' word, combined with a rhyming word. The children's task is to figure out the word. You can use the interactive activity 'Give us a clue' on the CD-ROM – ask the children to guess the word from the clue then click to reveal the correct answer.

Paired work

- Once the children understand how it works ask them to work with a partner to make up their own clues for the game.

> ### Differentiation
> - Write some rhyming '-ough' words on small cards. Shuffle them and place them face down. The children turn over two cards. If the words rhyme, they keep them. If not, they turn them back. The winner is the one with the most cards. After playing this they could try using what they have learned to help them to write clues for the quiz game.

Review

- Gradually combine pairs of children to form groups to play the quiz game. Remind them that the spellings of some words have to be learned.

● All children can discuss the motivation and feelings of story characters, state an opinion and participate in a dramatised reading of a playscript.
● Most children can also argue their opinion using evidence and describe how a playscript differs from a story.
● Some children can discuss and argue using evidence from the story more convincingly.

Curriculum objectives

● To increase their familiarity with a wide range of books, including myths, legends and traditional stories and books from other cultures and traditions.
● To participate in discussions about books that are read to them and those that they read for themselves, building on their own and others' ideas and challenging views courteously.

Resources

A copy of the 'Mahabharata' (or a picture of it); photocopiable page 'Savitri' from the CD-ROM

Week 4 lesson plans

These lessons are introduced by a play that retells a traditional Indian story. The children read and perform the play. They also discuss the characters' feelings and issues raised in the play.

1: Savitri

Introduction

Show the children a copy (or a picture of) the 'Mahabharata' and tell them that it is an epic poem (a long narrative poem). Ask: *What is a narrative poem?* (A poem that tells a story.) Explain that the 'Mahabharata' is a sacred text for Hindus, first written in the ancient language Sanskrit, and that it dates from before 400BCE. It includes tales of princes, Hindu gods and battles.

Whole-class work

● Provide the playscript 'Savitri' from the CD-ROM and tell them that this is a retelling by a modern writer. Ask: *How is a playscript meant to be read? How is it different from a story?*
● Point out the roles listed at the start of the play and allocate these to members of the class. Ask: *What are narrators for in a play?*
● Before the children begin reading, practise reading the Indian words and names. Then ask the characters to come out, face the class and begin reading.

Paired work

● Ask the children to discuss and make notes about the characters Savitri, Satyavan and Yama, about any strong feelings the characters show at different points, and how they can tell. Also ask them to talk about the themes of the play and make a note of these.

> **Differentiation**
> ● Provide headings to help the children to organise their notes, such as *description*, *personal qualities* and *feelings shown (and when)*. Encourage them to provide evidence from the play.

Review

● Ask each pair to share their notes with another pair and to compare their ideas. Ask: *How did the god Yama feel when he first took Satyavan/when Savitri kept following him?* Ask: *What issues or themes is the story about?* (Loyalty, love, death, suffering, determination.)

■SCHOLASTIC

Curriculum objectives

● To increase their familiarity with a wide range of books, including myths, legends and traditional stories and books from other cultures and traditions.
● To prepare plays to read aloud and to perform, showing understanding through intonation, tone and volume, so that the meaning is clear to an audience.

Resources

Photocopiable page 'Savitri' from the CD-ROM

2: Enacting a play

Introduction

● Ask the class what they remember about the play 'Savitri': *Where does it come from? Which epic poem? What are its main themes or issues? Who are the characters? What feelings do they show? When? What personal qualities do they show? What is the evidence for this?*

Group work

● As there are 11 roles in the play, the children could work in groups of six or seven; if they have a small role, they can take on an additional small role. (As the groups will perform their plays in the next lesson, having slightly larger groups could reduce the number of performances.) Give them a few minutes to discuss the roles in their groups and to use a fair method of choosing who should play each one.
● Ask the groups to read through the play, stopping every now and again to decide which parts are quiet, which are spoken more loudly and how the characters should move/behave. Ask: *Which characters should show feelings? What feelings? How should they show these feelings?* The characters should make notes on their script, for example: sounding impatient, quietly, in tears...

Review

● Read some of the children's notes on the scripts. Ask if others playing those roles have different ideas. Ask: *How should the narrators speak?*
● Allow some time for the children to practise their roles ready to perform the play in the next lesson and, if possible, to memorise the words.

Curriculum objectives

● To prepare plays to read aloud and to perform, showing understanding through intonation, tone and volume, so that the meaning is clear to an audience.

Resources

Photocopiable page 'Savitri' from the CD-ROM; photocopiable page 109 'Drama critics'; scissors; a trophy to present as an award (ideally invite the headteacher or other VIP to present it)

3: Performance

Introduction

● Tell the class that they are going to be the audience for each group's performance of 'Savitri'. Remind them how to behave as an audience: watch, listen quietly, applaud at the end.

Whole-class work

● Give each child photocopiable page 109 'Drama critics' and ask them to use it to review each performance. To help to identify each group, give them a name or number. Ask them to focus on what the performers did well and then to note one way in which they could improve.
● Ask each group, in turn, to perform the play while the others watch and listen. After all the performances, the children should cut out and complete the 'Best Actor nomination' slip.

Review

● Collect the 'Best Actor nomination' slips and quickly check these or, better still, pass them to the 'VIP' guest to select the three with the most nominations. Ask: *What did you see or hear that you think was especially good?* Ask: *Did anyone really convince you that he or she really was the character? How? Could you tell how Yama and Savitri, and other characters, were feeling at different times? How?*
● Ask the VIP to read out the Best Actor nominations, with comments on what they did well, and then to present the trophy to the winner.
● Keep the completed photocopiable sheets for the next lesson.

Curriculum objectives
● To recommend books that they have read to their peers, giving reasons for their choices.
● To identify the audience for their writing, selecting the appropriate form and to use other similar writing as models for their own.

Resources
Completed photocopiable sheets from the previous lesson; a short review of a play from a newspaper; photocopiable page 110 'Play review'

4: Theatre critics

Introduction

● Tell the class that their task will be to use their notes from the previous lesson to help them to write a review of one of the performances they watched, and that to help them they are first going to read a short review from a newspaper.

Whole-class work

● Give out copies of a play review and allow time for the children to read it. Ask: *What must a play review say at the start?* (The name of the play, what it is about, important details, where and when it was performed and the names of key actors.)
● Ask: *What do you notice about how the review begins? What is the reviewer's task?* (To give opinions, supported by evidence, but not to tell the story.)

Independent work

● Ask the children to choose one group's performance to review. They should set out their review in a similar way to the newspaper review, using their notes from the previous lesson to help them remember what the group did well. Ask what heading they should use, for example, 'Savitri' *by Aaron Shepard, performed by [class name] at school on [date].* Give out the photocopiable page 110 'Play review' to help them to organise their writing.

Review

● As the children write, read their work so that you can invite some of them to read theirs aloud as an example.

Curriculum objectives
● To explain and discuss their understanding of what they have read, including through formal presentations and debates, maintaining a focus on the topic and using notes where necessary.
● To provide reasoned justification for their views.

Resources
The Indian stories and play the children have read in this chapter's lessons; strips of paper for the children to write on; a box for their answers

5: Debate

Introduction

● Tell the class that this is their chance to give their opinions about characters in any of the traditional Indian stories they have read, but they should be ready to defend their opinion if challenged! Discuss useful vocabulary to describe characters, for example: *brave, weak, powerful, sly, clever, stupid, kind, mean, selfish, cruel, unkind, loyal.*

Whole-class work

● Ask the children to think about three story characters and to write a sentence to say what they think of each character on separate strips of paper. Ask them to fold their papers, write their name on them and put them into a box.
● Invite a child to pull out a paper, read it out and say whether they agree, and why. If they disagree, the writer could defend what they wrote. Invite others to say why they agree/disagree.
● Ask the child who wrote the first sentence to pull out another paper, read it out and say whether they agree, giving evidence for their view. Continue in this way until a reasonable selection has been read and debated.

> **Differentiation**
> ● If necessary, ask questions to help children to articulate their views, for example: *Can you think of anything brave he/she did? So which word describes him better?*

Review

● Give feedback on any particularly good defences of opinions as examples. Comment on any that were well expressed/persuasive, and say why.

Week 5 lesson plans

Expected outcomes
● All children can write a newspaper report and check for errors.
● Most children can do so using a wider range of techniques and can add relative clauses to sentences, punctuating them with commas.
● Some children can do this consistently.

Curriculum objectives
● To ask questions to improve their understanding of what they have read.
● To retrieve, record and present information from non-fiction.

Resources
Photocopiable page 'News report: The death of Gandhi' from the CD-ROM; computer and internet access; information books about Gandhi, at different reading levels

This week's lessons focus on non-fictional writing (newspaper reports) and begin with a news report about the death of Mohandas Gandhi, known as Mahatma (Great Soul). After reading and discussing this, and researching any questions it does not answer, the children research another significant event in the history of India and write their own newspaper report about it.

The text provides an opportunity for the children to identify relative clauses, practise adding them to sentences and use them in their own reports as necessary. They will edit their writing thoroughly, using techniques such as reading it aloud, to check grammar and punctuation.

There are opportunities to learn about making a report clear and unambiguous, yet brief, to consider structure, openings and ways of linking paragraphs – also choices of vocabulary.

1: News report: The death of Gandhi

Introduction
● Tell the class that they are going to read a newspaper report from 1948 about an important and sad event in the history of India: the assassination of Mohandas Gandhi. Ask: *What do you know about Gandhi?*
● Write up the key points, including: the meaning of the name Mahatma (Great Soul) that was given to Gandhi; that he was a devout Hindu and was one of the politicians who had helped to gain independence for India (explain this).

Group work
● Give out photocopiable page 'News report: The death of Gandhi' from the CD-ROM and, before the children begin reading it in their groups, point out that it mention events, people or places they might not know about. After they have read it, ask them to underline any words they do not know, anything that is mentioned that they know nothing about or anything that makes them want to ask a question (for example, *Birla House, the King, Poona.*) They should then discuss any questions they have, for example: *Why should a Hindu kill Gandhi? What is 'that change of heart for which Gandhi laboured and gave his life'?*
● Ask them to write a summary of what they know, their questions and where they will look for answers. They can then begin to research the answers. They might be able to help one another to answer some of the questions; otherwise they should use information books and the internet to find out more.

> **Differentiation**
> ● Ensure that information books at an appropriate level are available. Read the report with the children and explain any difficult parts.

Review
● Read some questions from one group and ask others if they asked anything different. List these and continue until a good range of questions is listed. Choose a question and ask: *What answer did you find? Where did you find the answer?* Discuss why the report raised questions: people in Britain at the time would have known who the King was and who was President of the USA. They would have known about the struggle for India's independence from British rule and the creation of Pakistan, because these had happened not long before the event.

Curriculum objectives
● To use relative clauses beginning with *who*, *which*, *where*, *why*, *whose*, *that* or with an implied (omitted) relative pronoun.

Resources
Photocopiable page 'News report: The death of Gandhi' from the CD-ROM; highlighter pens in different colours

2: Adding to sentences

Introduction

● Recap the news report from lesson 1. Tell the children that they are going to re-read it, not as last time, to find information, but to examine how the writer adds information to sentences.

Whole-class work

● Give out copies of the report and highlighter pens of different colours. Read aloud the first sentence and ask: *What is the main clause?* (The most important clause in the sentence: Mahatma Gandhi was assassinated by a young Hindu extremist.)
● Ask: *Which questions does this clause answer?* (Who? What?) *Which questions does the rest of the sentence answer?* (Where? When?) *How does the writer add this information to the sentence?* (With a relative clause: walking to his prayer meeting...) Ask: *Which relative pronoun introduces the clause?* (*While.*)

Paired work

● Ask the children to highlight the main clause of each sentence in a given colour and any relative clauses in a different colour. Use the third sentence as an example, and point out that the relative clause splits the main clause. Ask: *How does punctuation help?* (Commas surround the relative clause.) After highlighting, ask the children to try splitting sentences with more than one clause into separate sentences and comparing the effect.

> **Differentiation**
> ● Use a simpler text (for example from previous work on local news). Ask the children to highlight the main part of each sentence (the part that makes sense on its own) and, in a different colour, any other parts added to it.

Review

● Discuss what difference splitting the sentences makes.

Curriculum objectives
● To ask questions to improve their understanding of what they have read.
● To retrieve, record and present information from non-fiction.
● To choose which shape of letter to use when given choices and deciding, as part of their personal style, whether or not to join specific letters.

Resources
Information books and bookmarked online sources about India's independence; media resource 'Independence Day in India' on the CD-ROM

3: Researching a key event in the history of India

Introduction

● Tell the children that they are going to find out about an event in the history of India that made many people happy. Show them pictures of Independence Day 1947 from the CD-ROM and ask: *What do you know about Independence Day in India?* Remind them that since Queen Victoria's time, Britain had ruled most of India.

Group work

● Tell the children that their task is to find out how and when India became independent from Britain, about the Indian and British politicians who agreed it and how ordinary people responded. Ask: *What should you do when you make notes?* Write up their replies on the board as a reminder, ensuring that they remember to: write briefly rather than copying large pieces of text (unless they find an interesting short quotation, perhaps from a speech); write neatly so that they will be able to read it; write any names or place names in full so that they will be able to spell them later; make a note of where they found any information or pictures.

Review

● Ask each group for an interesting fact about India's independence. They should keep their notes for the next lesson, to help them to write a newspaper report.

4: Writing the news

Introduction

Curriculum objectives
• To retrieve, record and present information from non-fiction.
• To note and develop initial ideas, drawing on reading and research, where necessary.
• To identify the audience for and purpose of the writing, selecting the appropriate form and using other similar writing as models for their own.

Resources
The children's notes from the previous lesson, Information books and bookmarked online sources about India's independence; media resource 'Independence Day in India' on the CD-ROM; photocopiable page 'News report: The death of Gandhi' from the CD-ROM; photocopiable page 111 'Newspaper report planner (1)'; newspaper reports about other events in history, as examples

• Tell the class that they are going to use their notes from the previous lesson to help them to write a newspaper report about India's independence for modern readers of their own age in Britain. Ask: *How is this different from writing for people at the time or people in India?* (They might not know about the places and people or what happened in India previously.)

Whole-class work

• Remind the class about their earlier work on newspaper reports (Autumn 2, week 4, lesson 4). Ask: *What questions should the report answer?* (What? Who? When? Where? and, if possible, How? and Why?) *How well did the report about Gandhi's death answer these questions?* Re-read if necessary.

Independent work

• Ask the children to plan and draft a report about India's independence. Provide photocopiable page 111 'Newspaper report planner (1)' to help them. Discuss suitable headlines: this is a momentous event that many people worked hard for, so the headline might reflect a celebratory feel. The quotations might be from politicians and members of the public.
• After about ten minutes encourage the children to move from planning to writing. Ask them to think about the tone of their report: perhaps of celebration of an important event. They could read a selection of other newspaper reports of key events in history for ideas on style and vocabulary.

Review

• Read some of the children's draft reports and ask what kind of tone they want to create; highlight words they could change to create this effect. Keep their drafts for the next lesson.

5: Redrafting a report

Introduction

Curriculum objectives
• To assess the effectiveness of their own and others' writing.
• To propose changes to vocabulary, grammar and punctuation to enhance effects and clarify meaning.

Resources
The children's drafts from lesson 4; information books and bookmarked sources about India's independence; media resource 'Independence Day in India' on the CD-ROM; dictionaries; highlighter pens

• Ensure that the children have their draft reports from lesson 4. Tell them that their task this time is to work on their draft report to write a final version. Ask: *What will you need to check in your report?* On the board, display appropriate responses as a checklist: paragraphs, words to link paragraphs, spelling (use a dictionary), grammar (check that verbs agree), tone (choose the best word), clauses (add details to sentences), sentence length.

Group work

• In groups of three, ask the children to read their draft aloud to the others and, as they do so, to think about how easy it is to read. They should discuss and highlight (but not yet rewrite) any parts they can improve, using the checklist to help. Note that if some sentences were difficult to read they should check the punctuation.

> **Differentiation**
> • Working in threes enables two children working at a higher level to work with one who needs more support, without forfeiting a partner working at their own level.

Independent work

• The children should rewrite their marked-up edited drafts for a final report.

Review

• Invite some children to read out well-written reports. Ask the others why they think these were chosen.

Expected outcomes
● All children can appreciate the craft of, and write, a haiku.
● Most children can describe the syllable pattern of, and choose more appropriate vocabulary for writing, a haiku.
● Some children can do so with greater awareness of the matching of language to subject.

Curriculum objectives
● To continue to read and discuss an increasingly wide range of poetry.

Resources
Globe or map of the world, a map of Japan; traditional Japanese pictures, for example Hokusai's paintings of Mount Fuji, and artefacts; photocopiable page 'Haikus by Bashō' from the CD-ROM

Week 6 lesson plans

Haikus are the focus of this week's lessons. Children begin by listening to, and reading aloud, some traditional haikus by Matsuo Bashō and talking about the atmosphere, rhythm and pace of the poems. They then read some modern haikus, look at the structure of the poem and compare it with other forms of poetry to find out what makes a haiku unique. They learn and recite a haiku of their choice then finally have a go at writing their own haiku, using nature as their inspiration.

1: Poems from Japan

Introduction
● In advance of the lesson, set up a Japanese display that includes a globe or world map, a map of Japan, Japanese writing, art and artefacts such as crockery, and photographs of traditional Japanese buildings. Include the traditional haiku 'Old Pond' by Matsuo Bashō (on the photocopiable sheet), displayed with an appropriate picture, if possible. Allow time for the children to explore the display before the lesson.
● Ask the class what they have learned about Japan from the display. It is also useful to point out that the display is about traditional Japanese culture, not modern life. They are probably well aware of modern Japanese technology.
● Point out the poem, without mentioning that it is a poem, and ask if they read it. Read it aloud. Ask: *Is this a poem?* Remind them that a poem need not rhyme and can be very short. Tell them it is a haiku. Ask what they notice about its atmosphere (calm, gentle, quiet), rhythm (matching the actions: old pond seems still; a frog leaps in, sounds like a gentle splash then stillness) and the pace (slow).

Whole-class work
● To help the children appreciate the rhythm and pace, ask them to stand up and move around the room as they read a haiku. Ask: *How did it make you move? What was the atmosphere like?*

Group work
● Give out photocopiable page 'Haikus by Bashō' from the CD-ROM and ask the children to take turns to read a haiku aloud. They could also read the transliterated Japanese, which is written phonetically. Ask them to discuss the atmosphere or mood of each poem and how it matches any Japanese pictures they have seen. They should consider the best words to describe it. They should also consider the rhythm and pace as they read. Write these words as prompts: *atmosphere, rhythm, pace*.

Review
● Ask: *What is similar about the haikus?* (Subject – nature, number of lines, rhythm, no rhyme, gentle tone.) Talk about how the last line seems to complete the haiku; sometimes it introduces something unexpected.

2: Haikus

Introduction
- Recap haikus. Ask: *What makes a haiku different from other poems? How many lines does it have? How many syllables? How many syllables in each line?* Tell the children that, although the haiku is a very old form of Japanese poem, many modern poets from other cultures also write haikus.

Whole-class work
- Read the following modern haiku to the class:

    drip by drip
    the moonlight lengthens
    in the icicle
          by David Cobb (*The Iron Book of British Haiku*)
- Ask: *How is this like the Japanese haikus you read?* (Discuss atmosphere, rhythm, pace and setting.) *What is special about the last line?* (It is unexpected – a 'twist' at the end.)

Group work
- Give each group some modern haikus to read. Ask them to take turns to read a haiku aloud and then check the number of lines, syllables, and syllables in each line. They could do this by reading a haiku aloud again, with a partner silently counting the syllables of each line and making a note of the pattern.

> ### Differentiation
> - Provide other short poems (such as limericks, jingles and short rhymes) for comparison. Ask the children how haikus are different: apart from the line and syllable structure, they should notice the atmosphere and subject matter.

Review
- Ask the class to contribute to a description of a haiku, for example, by beginning *A haiku is a traditional Japanese poem...*

Curriculum objectives
- To continue to read and discuss an increasingly wide range of poetry.
- To discuss and evaluate how authors use language, including figurative language, considering the impact on the reader.

Resources
A selection of modern haikus (*The Works*, chosen by Paul Cookson, Macmillan, has several)

3: By heart

Introduction
- Ask the children if they have a favourite haiku. Ask: *Can you recite it?* Allow volunteers to try. Others might remember parts of it. They could try reciting in groups.

Paired work
- Ask the children to choose their favourite haiku and learn it by heart. Pair children with others who chose the same one. Ask them to work together to learn and recite the haiku. Tell them that one good way to learn is to take turns to recite it, with the other person acting as prompt.
- Allow time for practice and then ask the children to think about how they recite the haiku, remembering the discussion from previous lessons about tone, atmosphere, rhythm, pace and so on. They should recite it with their partner acting as critic, commenting after they have finished.

Review
- Have the children standing in a large circle and ask them each to recite their haiku, working clockwise round the circle. If they know one another's haikus they could prompt if the child reciting forgets part of it. Ask if they thought anyone recited their haiku especially well. Explore what made it successful.

Curriculum objectives
- To continue to read and discuss an increasingly wide range of poetry.
- To learn a wider range of poetry by heart.
- To prepare poems to read aloud and to perform, showing understanding through intonation, tone and volume, so that the meaning is clear to an audience.

Resources
Traditional and modern haikus

Curriculum objectives
● To identify the audience for and purpose of the writing, selecting the appropriate form and using other similar writing as models for their own.
● To assess the effectiveness of their own and others' writing.

Resources
Media resource 'Natural world' on the CD-ROM; copies of traditional and modern haikus for reference

4: Haiku writer

Introduction
● Recap what the children know about haikus and ask what kind of subject they would choose if asked to write a haiku. Show them pictures from media resource 'Natural world' on the CD-ROM, that could inspire haikus and ask them to vote for the one to write about.

Whole-class work
● Try writing a haiku as a shared writing activity. Ask the children not to think about the number of syllables or lines to begin with, but to suggest sentences about the picture. Write their sentences on the board. Ask them to think about the words. Ask: *Do they create the right atmosphere? What other words could we use?*
● Read parts aloud and ask if the rhythm sounds right. Repeat this and ask if the pace is right. Ask: *How can we slow it down?* Ask them to count the syllables. *Do we need to change anything?* Suggest changes, if necessary.

Independent work
● Ask the children to choose a picture to write a haiku about and to begin by writing sentences, as you did in the shared writing. They should read their sentences quietly to check if the words sound right and then make any changes they think help.

Review
● Read some of the haikus as examples. Ask them to comment on the rhythm, atmosphere and pace.
● They could suggest changes. Keep their writing for lesson 5.

Curriculum objectives
● To identify the audience for and purpose of the writing, selecting the appropriate form and using other similar writing as models for their own.
● To assess the effectiveness of their own and others' writing.
● To perform their own compositions, using appropriate intonation, volume and movement so that meaning is clear.

Resources
The children's haikus from lesson 4; the pictures that inspired their haikus

5: Haiku review and performance

Introduction
● Continue from the Review of lesson 4 by reading some of the children's haikus and highlighting the parts that work well and why, considering rhythm, pace, atmosphere, choice of words.

Paired work
● Ask the children to read their haiku with a partner and to talk about the words they used. They could suggest other words and try them out. They could help one another to alter the haiku in order to arrive at the correct number of syllables: line 1 five, line 2 seven, line 3 five – total 17 syllables.
● Once they are happy with their haiku they can practise reading it to their partner who should say whether they should read it more slowly/quickly, emphasise any words, and so on. Encourage them to try to memorise their haiku.

Review
● Have the children standing in a large circle, as for lesson 3. Ask what they should do to be a good audience: look at the person performing, listen attentively, applaud at the end.
● Ask each of them to read or recite their haiku, working clockwise round the circle. They should show the class the picture they used for inspiration.
● Ask if they thought anyone did this especially well. Ask for an encore from anyone chosen. Ask: *What did they do so very well?*

Grammar and punctuation: Brackets

Curriculum objectives
● To use brackets, dashes or commas to indicate parenthesis.

Resources
Examples of uses of brackets from the children's reading

Revise

● Begin with starter activity 5 'Parenthesis'. Next, display the sentences below on the whiteboard, draw some brackets on the board and ask the children to (verbally) use brackets to add information to the sentences, as follows:
It's a long walk to school. (Add that the distance is two miles.)
It's a long (two mile) walk to school.
● Ask: *Could you put the part in brackets in a different place? Would this change the meaning?* Move the brackets around different words, and compare the way in which they read the sentence each time the brackets are moved.
● Also try moving the entire parenthesis from one position in the sentence to another and compare. Ask: *What difference do the brackets make? What other punctuation marks could you try instead of brackets?* Let them try replacing the brackets with commas or dashes. Ask: *Which works best? Why?* Sometimes dashes or commas can be used equally effectively in separating a parenthesis from the rest of the sentence. (If appropriate, introduce the term *parenthesis* for a word or group or words that need to be separated from the rest of the sentence using punctuation marks in order to make sense.)

Assess

● Provide a set of up to ten sentences, as appropriate, for the children to add extra information in brackets.

Further practice

● Collect examples of uses of brackets from reading.
● Use starter activity 13 'Grammatical terminology'.

Spelling: Words with '-ough'

Curriculum objectives
● To use knowledge of morphology and etymology in spelling and understand that the spelling of some words needs to be learned specifically, as listed in Appendix 1.

Resources
Individual whiteboards and pens

Revise

● Begin with the starter activity 6 'Spelling words with '-ough''
● Next, ask the children to write *enough*. Ask them to show their whiteboards. Let them look at each other's and make any changes needed. Show the correct spelling. Remind them of how you pronounced it during the starter activity and ask: *Which words containing the letters 'ough' sound like /oh/?*
● Repeat the above process for these words: *bough* (of a tree), *cough*, *dough* (for bread), *plough*, *rough*, *though*, *thought*, *through* (going through the woods), *thought*, *wrought* (wrought iron).

Assess

● Provide dictionary definitions of '-ough' words and ask the children to write the correct word for each definition, for example:
  ● *The past tense of buy. (bought)*
  ● *Nothing or zero. (nought)*
  ● *The past tense of fight. (fought)*
  ● *These are like little coughs and are very hard to get rid of. (hiccoughs)*
  ● *A verb you use with another verb. It means should. (ought)*
  ● *Hardwearing. (tough)*
  ● *The opposite of smooth. (rough)*
  ● *A farm tool that a tractor drags to dig a field. (plough)*
  ● *Past tense of think. (thought)*
  ● *A word used in the same was as however or but. (although)*

Further practice

● From reading, collect examples of words with the '-ough' letter string.
Ask the children to write silly sentences or rhymes using '-ough' words.
● Use starter activity 14 'Spelling bee'.

Curriculum objectives
● To summarise the main ideas drawn from more than one paragraph, identifying key details that support the main ideas.

Resources
A news report about an event in history

Reading: Making notes

Revise

● Give out copies of a news report. Ask: *What questions should a news report answer?* (Who? What? When? Where? and perhaps How? and Why?) What are the special features of a news report? (Headline, subheadings, photographs, captions, quotations.)

● Remind the children of the key features of making notes:
  ● write briefly
  ● don't write full sentences
  ● shorten common words
  ● miss out words like *a*, *an*, *the*
  ● use abbreviations such as *st* (street), *rd* (road), *ave* (avenue), *UK* (United Kingdom), *approx.* (approximately), *tho* (though)
  ● make a note of important dates
  ● make a note of where you found information and pictures in case you want to look again.

Assess

● Tell the children that they are going to read a news report about an event in history, to highlight the answers to the questions:
  ● *Who?* (Who is the story about? Who else is affected?)
  ● *What?* (What happened?)
  ● *When?* (When did it happen? What day, date and time? Exact or morning/ afternoon – whatever is needed.)
  ● *Where?* (Where did it happen? If it was in another country, which country? If in another town, which town? If in a small village that isn't local, where is that?)
  ● *How?* (What events led up to it?)
  ● *Why?* (An explanation.)

Further practice

● Read, listen to/watch news websites, television news programmes and radio news programmes; write a headline for each and give the answers to the questions *Who? What? When? Where? How? Why?*

Curriculum objectives
● To retrieve, record and present information from non-fiction.

Resources
A chapter from an information book about an event in history (connected to, but different from, the news report used for assessing reading); photocopiable page 'Newspaper report planner (2)' from the CD-ROM; dictionaries

Writing: Writing a news report

Revise
● Tell the children that they are going to read a non-fiction text (tell them what the subject matter is) and make notes about the key facts so that they can write a newspaper report about it.
● Remind them about the news report they read in the reading assessment and the important questions it answered.
● Ask: *What will be the purpose of the headline?* (To tell readers what the report is about and perhaps set the tone for it.) *Which questions will the first paragraph answer briefly?* (What? and perhaps Who? and When?)
● Ask: *What will the other paragraphs be about? What will be the purpose of the final paragraph?* (A conclusion, such as a comment about the importance of the topic, how it affects different people.)
● Give out copies of photocopiable page 'Newspaper report planner (2)' from the CD-ROM. Discuss useful words for the report, especially for adding information using relative clauses and choosing words for their effect and to create the right tone.

Assess
● Ask the children to use their notes and the photocopiable sheet to help them to plan their report. Provide dictionaries.

Further practice
● Use this procedure for writing about other events in history in connection with other history topics studied.

Name: _____ Date: _____

Presentation plan

■ Write a plan for your presentation to fascinate the class.

My question _____

_____

Information, interesting words	Pictures, maps, diagrams (If you need them)	Actions and how to speak
Introduction		
Part 1		
Part 2		
Part 3		
Conclusion		

I can plan a presentation.

How did you do?

Story summary

■ Write a summary of the story.

A summary of the story _____

_____

The setting _____

_____

This story is about _____

_____

_____

The problem _____

_____

_____

_____

The solution _____

_____

_____

The consequences _____

_____

_____

The message of the story _____

_____

I can write a summary of a story.

How did you do?

Figuring out new words

- Use what you know about other words to help you to figure out the meanings of these words. Write your thoughts in the thought bubbles.
- Then write what you think the word means in the box.

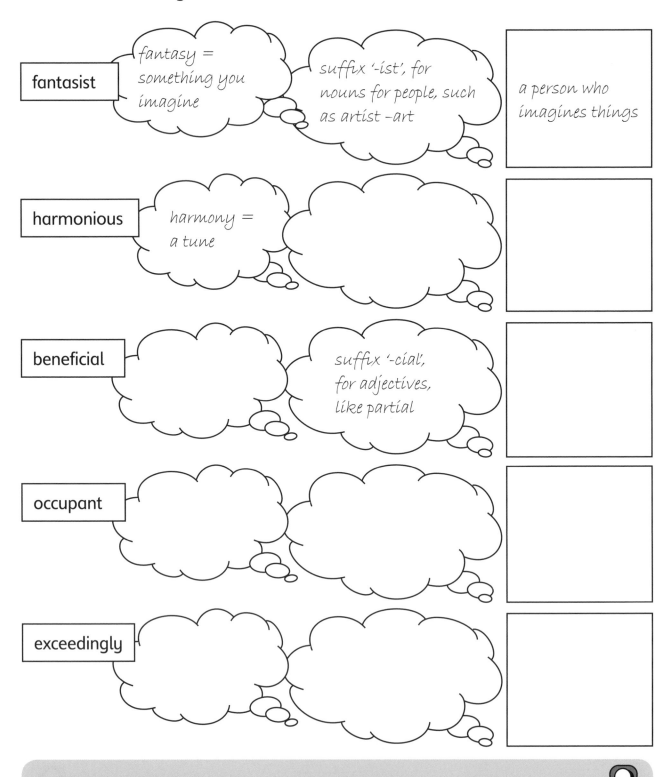

fantasist

fantasy = something you imagine

suffix '-ist', for nouns for people, such as artist –art

a person who imagines things

harmonious

harmony = a tune

beneficial

suffix '-cial', for adjectives, like partial

occupant

exceedingly

I can use what I know about other words to help me to understand new words.

How did you do?

PHOTOCOPIABLE

■SCHOLASTIC
www.scholastic.co.uk

Growing sentences

- Use relative clauses to add the information to the sentences.
- Don't forget the commas.

Dusshera is the Hindu festival of victory.

> Dusshera is when King Ram defeated Ravan, the demon with ten heads.

_____

_____

Most Hindu homes have a family shrine.

> There are statues of gods and goddesses in the shrine.

_____

_____

At Divali, Hindu families light lots of little lamps.

> They put the lamps in the windows of their homes.

_____

_____

Devaki was the sister of the wicked king Kans.

> Devaki was the mother of the god Krishna.

_____

_____

The Nine Days' Festival honours the goddess Parvati.

> Hindus ask Parvati to grant their wishes. The Nine Days' Festival is in March or April.

_____

_____

Holi is the spring festival.

> A model of Princess Holika is burned at Holi. Holika had tried to burn her innocent nephew Prahlad.

_____

_____

_____

I can add clauses to sentences and punctuate them with commas to make the meaning clear.

How did you do?

Brackets

- Read the sentences. In the brackets add some information to answer the question.
- You can find the answers in the author's notes about the stories in *Seasons of Splendour*.

1. Madhur Jaffrey wrote about how her family celebrated

   Divali (_____) in India. | What is Divali? |

2. The goddess Lakshmi (_____) | Which goddess is Lakshmi? |

   is honoured at Divali.

3. Dusshera (_____) is celebrated | What is Dusshera? What is the moon like when it is waxing? |

   on the tenth day of the waxing moon (_____).

4. The night of the wintry full moon (_____) | When is the night of the wintry full moon? What makes it magic? |

   is a night of magic (_____).

5. To make halva, you add sugar, clarified butter and nuts | What might you do to the nuts first? |

   (_____) to roasted semolina.

6. The festival of Holi (_____) is great fun. | Which season is Holi in? |

7. Very dignified older people (_____!) | Add an exclamation about the older people! |

   end up covered with coloured powder at Holi.

8. When the snow melts in her Himalayan home,

   the goddess Parvati (_____) | Whose wife is Parvati? |

   comes down to Earth.

- Write three sentences of your own that use brackets in the same way on a separate sheet of paper.

I can use brackets to provide extra information to a sentence.

How did you do?

PHOTOCOPIABLE   ■SCHOLASTIC www.scholastic.co.uk

Name: _____   Date: _____

Drama critics

- Use this page to assess performances of a play.
- Write what each group did well.
- Think about:
  - clear speech
  - volume and speed – do they vary?
  - movements
  - eye contact – looking at the character being spoken to, or the audience.

Name of play _____

Group	What they did well

✂ --

My nomination for the 'Best Actor' is _____

Because _____

_____

Play review

■ Write a review of the play.

Title _____ by _____

Performed at _____ Date _____

Cast

_____   _____

_____   _____

_____   _____

Introduction

| What was the setting (where, when)? What was it about? Relative clauses will help. |

_____

_____

What you thought of the script, and why.

| What did you think of the language used? Did the script give the actors enough help? |

_____

_____

_____

What the actors did well.

| How well did they speak, move and so on? |

_____

_____

Would you recommend it? Why?

_____

_____

_____

I can review a play.

How did you do?

Name: _____ Date: _____

Newspaper report planner (1)

- Plan a newspaper report about Independence Day in India.
- Read what people at the time said about it.
- Include some quotations from them.

Headline _____

> The headline should say what the story is about and create the atmosphere. You can add this later.

Introduction _____
_____

> The introduction says, briefly, what happened: when and where.

The facts _____

> Who? Why? What had been going on before this date?

_____

_____

_____

What happened in towns and villages across the country?

_____

_____

> Who? Politicians? Ordinary people? People of different religions?

_____

Quotations

Who	What they said

Summary

> What were the consequences? How did it affect ordinary people in the two new countries of Pakistan and India?

_____

_____

I can plan a newspaper report.

How did you do?

Modern fiction

This series of lessons features Michael Morpurgo's books – beginning with *Kensuke's Kingdom*. The children identify themes that interest the author and how he uses language to interest readers. This is linked to non-fiction reading about the plight of orang-utans (researching the topic and writing a persuasive text). The children write an adventure story with an environmental theme, modelled on Michael Morpurgo's writing.

To compare books by Michael Morpurgo, the children read *The Wreck of the Zanzibar*, discuss characterisation and how the diary format helps the structure of the story. The children then write notes for an island adventure story, using the diary format.

Continuing the sea theme, the children read poems about the sea and explore verse forms and poetic styles, expressing preferences and depicting what some of the poems say about the sea. Finally, children watch films of the sea to inspire poetry writing.

Expected prior learning
- Can discuss how an author uses language to influence the reader.
- Can recognise a phrase, a group of words that act together in the same way as a single word.
- Can name a range of different forms of poetry.

Overview of progression
- The children make inferences and compare the settings, characters and themes of a modern children's author (Michael Morpurgo); also story structure, moving between times and places, and use a diary to tell their own shipwreck adventure story.
- They discuss themes that interest the author, leading to a class debate on the protection of orang-utans, and write a persuasive text.
- The children explore how language (including rhyme and alliteration) and structure create different atmospheres and effects in sea poems, and write poems on the sea.
- The texts provide opportunities to study modal verbs, noun phrases, first person and past tense, prefixes and parenthesis.

Creative context
- The texts read in this chapter can provide a springboard into other curricular areas or a cross-curricular topic based on the sea. The settings of Bryher and Sumatra or Borneo could be the focus of an island study or study of an overseas locality in geography. You could also explore the impact of nature on our lives and whether nature has as much effect on us, here, as it did on the people of Bryher around 100 years ago (also links with citizenship and history).
- There are opportunities to link to work on animals in science, for example endangered species or the life cycles of turtles or orang-utans.

Preparation
The main texts featured are *Kensuke's Kingdom* and *The Wreck of the Zanzibar*, both by Michael Morpurgo.

You will also need:
Copies of other books by Michael Morpurgo and other materials to create an author display: promotional posters, photos, information; a globe, atlas or map of the world; a map of Britain or a UK atlas; maps and information about Borneo and Sumatra; maps and information about the Scilly Isles; dictionaries; internet access; rhyming dictionaries; highlighter pens; individual whiteboards.

On the CD-ROM you will find:
Media resources 'The Great Wave', 'Sea'; interactive activities 'Fact or opinion?', 'Dashes'; photocopiable pages 'Recycle now', 'Until I saw the sea', 'Sea Fever', 'Sea Timeless Song', 'Extract from 'The Rime of the Ancient Mariner'', 'How they Brought the Good News from Ghent to Aix'

Chapter at a glance

An overview of the chapter. For curriculum objective codes, please see pages 8–10.

Week	Lesson	Curriculum objectives	Summary of activities	Outcomes
1	1	RC: 1, 3, 4	Discuss a modern children's author (Michael Morpurgo), looking at some of his books and reading openings.	• Can discuss what makes a good opening for a book, giving examples of techniques that create impact.
	2	RC: 1, 3, 12	Discuss what they know/can find out about *Kensuke's Kingdom* from its cover. Predict events. Begin to read the story.	• Can predict what might happen, based on known information.
	3	RC: 1, 3, 6, 12	Continue to read *Kensuke's Kingdom*. Make predictions based on clues in the story. Use modal verbs in making predictions.	• Can use modal verbs in sentences.
	4	RC: 11, 18	Continue to read *Kensuke's Kingdom*. Explain the characters' actions, based on clues in the story.	• Can make inferences.
	5	RWR: 1 WT: 1 WC: 21	Change the meanings of verbs by adding prefixes.	• Can add prefixes to verbs.
2	1	RC: 18	Continue to read *Kensuke's Kingdom*. Discuss the plight of orang-utans – whether money and effort should be spent on saving them.	• Can take part in a discussion about an issue.
	2	RC: 16, 17 WC: 6	Research the answers to questions raised in lesson 1 about orang-utans. Make notes.	• Can make notes from non-fiction sources.
	3	RC: 16, 17, 19 WC: 1, 2, 6	Plan and take part in a debate on *Should orang-utans be saved?*	• Can take part in a debate.
	4	RC: 18, 19 WC: 6	Read a persuasive text and discuss how it persuades the reader.	• Can identify techniques used in a persuasive text.
	5	RC: 19 WC: 1, 2	Use what has been learned in lesson 4 to help to write a persuasive text on saving or not saving orang-utans.	• Can write a persuasive text.
3	1	RC: 16, 18, 19	After finishing *Kensuke's Kingdom*, explore any questions the story raised, such as *Was Kensuke a real person? Was Michael the author?*	• Can ask questions about a story that can be answered by research.
	2	RC: 16	Discuss what they have found out about *Kensuke's Kingdom*. Separate facts from opinions.	• Can separate facts from opinions.
	3	RC: 15	Collect examples of language used for impact in *Kensuke's Kingdom*. Choose the most effective.	• Can identify powerful language and discuss what gives it impact.
	4	WC: 2, 3	Write their own shipwreck adventure.	• Can write an adventure story.
	5	WC: 24, 28	Punctuate parentheses with dashes.	• Can identify a parenthesis and punctuate it with dashes.
4	1	RC: 18	Discuss what can be found out about *The Wreck of the Zanzibar* by Michael Morpurgo from its cover. Start to read.	• Can make predictions based on evidence.
	2	RC: 6, 18	Continue to read *The Wreck of the Zanzibar*. Compare its settings with that of *Kensuke's Kingdom*.	• Can compare the settings of two stories.
	3	RC: 2, 6	Continue to read *The Wreck of the Zanzibar*. Compare its structure with that of *Kensuke's Kingdom*.	• Can compare the structures of two stories.
	4	RC: 6, 11, 18	Continue to read *The Wreck of the Zanzibar*. Discuss which they prefer: this or *Kensuke's Kingdom* – and why.	• Can express and justify a preference for a story.
	5	RC: 12 WC: 18	Consider examples of noun phrases in *The Wreck of the Zanzibar* and discuss their impact. Identify noun phrases in a text.	• Can identify noun phrases.

Chapter at a glance

Week	Lesson	Curriculum objectives	Summary of activities	Outcomes
5	1	RC: 15	Discuss how Michael Morpurgo uses language in *The Wreck of the Zanzibar* to convey feelings and atmosphere.	• Can identify language that expresses feelings or atmosphere.
	2	RC: 5, 13	Identify and discuss themes in *The Wreck of the Zanzibar*. Compare with themes in other stories.	• Can identify and compare the themes of stories.
	3	RC: 13 WC: 3	Research the geographical and historical setting of *The Wreck of the Zanzibar*.	• Can raise questions for research, choose appropriate sources for research, and make notes to help to answer their questions.
	4	RC: 5 WC: 3	Explore the use of diaries in Michael Morpurgo's stories.	• Can identify the features of a diary and discuss its effect as the means for telling a story.
	5	WT: 8, 9 WC: 11, 13	Write a story in the form of a diary.	• Can write a story in diary form.
6	1	RC: 1	Read the poem 'Until I saw the sea' by Lilian Moore. Discuss poetic devices that give an impression of the sea.	• Can identify how a poet creates rhythm in a poem.
	2	RC: 1	Read the poem 'Sea Fever' by John Masefield. Sketch the scene it suggests.	• Can appreciate the picture a poem creates in the reader's mind.
	3	RC: 1, 7, 8	Read the poem 'Sea Timeless Song' by Grace Nichols. Identify language that creates the timeless effect and the feel of the sea.	• Can identify devices used to create an effect in a poem, such as repetition.
	4	RC: 1	Read the poem 'The Rime of the Ancient Mariner' by ST Coleridge. Identify devices used to create effects.	• Can identify alliteration.
	5	WC: 4, 10	Write a poem on the sea, based on films of the sea.	• Can write a poem that conveys an image, feel or sound of the sea.

Background knowledge

Dialogue: Conversation in a book, play or film.

First person: A story written in the first person has the author or main character telling the story as himself/herself; written with *I* or *we*.

Noun phrase: A phrase that acts as a noun. For example: ***Your sister's friend*** is pretty; Fetch me **the box with the flowers on**.

Week 1 lesson plans

This week's lessons focus on Michael Morpurgo's novels. After introducing the author and discussing what the children know about him, and any of his books they have read, there is an opportunity to present their views about these books and present any recommendations before beginning to read *Kensuke's Kingdom*. After reading the opening of *Kensuke's Kingdom* the children discuss its impact and make predictions about what will happen next. Opportunities arise for investigating prefixes for verbs and practising spelling them. Further work focuses on making inferences on characters' thoughts and motivations, and what the dialogue tells us about them.

Expected outcomes
● All children can discuss what makes a good opening for a book.
● Most children can give some examples of techniques that create impact in a book opening.
● Some children can also compare opening techniques used by different authors.

Curriculum objectives
● To continue to read and discuss an increasingly wide range of fiction.
● To increase their familiarity with a wide range of books, including modern fiction.
● To recommend books they have read to their peers, giving reasons for their choices.

Resources
A selection of books by Michael Morpurgo (omitting *Kensuke's Kingdom*); materials for a Michael Morpurgo display: his books, reviews of them, details of films based on them and, if possible, publishers' posters and information (the display should be set up in advance of the lesson); a large graph listing Morpurgo titles on which children can record their preferences

1: Michael Morpurgo

Introduction
● Ask the class if they have looked at the display about Michael Morpurgo. Ask: *What do you know about him? Which of his books have you read?* Remind them about *Arthur High King of Britain* (Autumn 1). Ask: *What type of story is that?* (Historical novel.)
● Tell them a little about the author or ask them to read about him on his website at www.michaelmorpurgo.com. Michael has written more than 120 books and has won many awards, including the Whitbread Children's Book Award *for The Wreck of the Zanzibar* and the Red House Children's Book Award for *Kensuke's Kingdom*. He was Children's Laureate from 2003 to 2005.
● Michael is well known for his charity work. With his wife, Clare, he founded the charity Farms for City Children, which has farms in beautiful countryside with holiday cottages where schools can take groups of children for a holiday. Another charity he supports is Action for Children's Arts, which organises activities for children connected with all kinds of arts. Bag Books is another charity that Michael supports. It is the only organisation in the world that publishes multi-sensory books specifically for people with learning disabilities.

Whole-class work
● Invite volunteers to name any Michael Morpurgo book they have read, saying what type of story it is, and who and what it is about.
● Distribute books from the collection around the class and ask different children to read the opening paragraph of their book aloud. After each reading, ask the class what it tells us about the setting, plot and a character.
● After each book opening has been read, ask: *If you could choose one book from all these, judging by the opening, which would it be?* Show the class the graph that you have prepared and tell the children that you would like them to vote for their favourite opening. Hold up each book in turn, asking the children to raise their hands at the appropriate point. Invite volunteers to enter the number of children choosing each book on the graph.
● On completing the graph, ask: *Which book is the most popular, based on their openings?* Ask children who chose it to explain the reasons for their choice.
● Invite children who have particularly enjoyed any of the books included in the lesson to speak to the class to recommend the book to them. Ask if any want to change their minds about their book choice, and amend the graph.

Review
● Ask: *What most influenced your choice of a book to read – a recommendation or the opening of the book?* Challenge them to find out about other books by Michael Morpurgo.

Curriculum objectives
● To continue to read and discuss an increasingly wide range of fiction.
● To increase their familiarity with a wide range of books, including modern fiction.
● To predict what might happen from details stated and implied.

Resources
Kensuke's Kingdom by Michael Morpurgo; media resource 'The Great Wave' on the CD-ROM; cover of *Kensuke's Kingdom*, added to the display before the lesson

2: *Kensuke's Kingdom*: opening

Introduction
● Show the class the cover of *Kensuke's Kingdom*. Ask what they think the setting is and what they think the story might be about, and why.
● Show them the map at the start of the book and the contents page, and ask if these give any more clues. They should notice the Japanese writing. Also display media resource 'The Great Wave' on the CD-ROM. The cover illustration has a similar style – so the book has some connection with Japan. The name *Kensuke* may also provide same hint.

Whole-class work
● Read the opening sentence of *Kensuke's Kingdom* to the class. Ask: *What do you now know about the story?* (In addition to the link with Japan and the sea, we know it is about a boy who will be 12 once the story starts, that he disappeared but that he must have survived, because he is telling the story.)
● Read the first two chapters of the story to the class and ask: *What do you think is going to happen?*

Independent work
● Ask the children to write a short prediction of what might happen, and to support it with clues they have found in the story so far. They should keep this for the next lesson.

Review
● Read some different predictions about the story and acknowledge why each could be possible at this point or, if not, ask questions to elicit why.

Curriculum objectives
● To continue to read and discuss an increasingly wide range of fiction.
● To increase their familiarity with a wide range of books, including modern fiction.
● To make comparisons within and across books.
● To predict what might happen from details stated and implied.

Resources
Kensuke's Kingdom by Michael Morpurgo

3: Michael falls overboard

Introduction
● Recap the story so far, with different children contributing and talking about their predictions from lesson 2.

Whole-class work
● Read Chapter 3 of *Kensuke's Kingdom* to the class. Ask: *Is Michael going to survive? How do you know? How do you think he will survive?* Give the children time to think about what they know about the story, including other characters, some of whom they have met and some whose names they have been given, and what might happen, then ask for their ideas.

Independent work
● Ask the children to write their predictions and to explain what they are based on. They should include places and characters that might be important. Hints: *Where was the yacht when Michael fell overboard? Which other character has been mentioned who sounds important but that the reader has not yet met? What about Stella? What do you know about the way Michael Morpurgo moves a story from one setting to another?* Remind them how this was done in *Arthur High King of Britain*. (Autumn 1.)

> **Differentiation**
> ● Suggest useful words for expressing reasons and possibilities: *because, so, if, might, could.*

Review
● Invite children to read their predictions aloud as examples of how to use evidence from the book (cover, map and contents, title and the character mentioned in the opening paragraph (Kensuke)). Encourage them to read on, between lessons, at least up to the end of Chapter 4.

■SCHOLASTIC

Curriculum objectives
● To make inferences and justify these with evidence from the text.
● To participate in discussions about books that are read to them and those they can read for themselves, building on their own and others' ideas and challenging views courteously.

Resources
Kensuke's Kingdom by Michael Morpurgo, ideally one copy per group

4: Kensuke's thoughts

Introduction
● Ask who has continued reading the book and invite them to recap Chapter 4. (Remind anyone who has read to the end not to spoil others' enjoyment of the story.)

Whole-class work
● Read Chapter 5 with the class. Ask: *What do we know about Kensuke? What might we be able to figure out about him that we are not told?* (For example, how he ended up alone on the island, why he forbids Michael to light a fire, why he leaves food for Michael and so on.)

Group work
● Ask the children to read Chapter 6 and to look for reasons for Kensuke's actions and behaviour based on what he says and does in Chapters 5 and 6. Ask: *What do you think Kensuke would do if someone came to rescue Michael?* They should say what they think but others should challenge this with courteous questioning. All views should be supported by evidence.

> ### Differentiation
> ● Arrange the children in mixed-attainment groups so that they can all benefit from a good discussion.

Review
● Ask a member of each group to say something about Kensuke. The others should listen and then ask questions or give comments, such as *What if...?*
● Encourage the children to read the rest of the book and, between lessons, discuss whether or not Kensuke was a real person.

Curriculum objectives
● To apply their growing knowledge of root words, prefixes and suffixes (morphology and etymology) both to read aloud and to understand the meaning of new words that they meet.
● To use further prefixes and suffixes and understand the guidelines for adding them.
● To learn the grammar for Year 5 in Appendix 2.

Resources
A list of verbs with prefixes from the first five chapters of *Kensuke's Kingdom*; photocopiable page 136 'Verb prefixes'; dictionaries

5: Verb prefixes

Introduction
● Tell the class that while reading *Kensuke's Kingdom* you noted down certain types of verb. Ask: *What kind of word is a verb?* Read the verbs on your list. What do they notice? Ask: *Where in a word is a prefix added?*

Whole-class work
● Re-read the opening sentence of the book. Ask: *Which word is a verb?* (*Disappeared.*) *What is its prefix? What is the root word? How does the prefix 'dis-' change its meaning? What other verbs can you add 'dis-' in order to make their opposite?* (For example, *disagree, disallow, disapprove*).

Group work
● Give out photocopiable page 136 'Verb prefixes' and ask the children to highlight the verbs that have a prefix, write the meaning, the root word and say how the prefix changes the verb's meaning. They can use a dictionary to check.

> ### Differentiation
> ● Children could highlight the verb that has a prefix and then write another sentence using the same verb.

Review
● Ask: *What prefixes did you find?* List these. Ask what each one means. Ask for another verb with the same prefix. Ask: *Does the root word change when a prefix is added?* (No. Note that when a prefix ends with the same letter as the first letter of a word there will be a double letter: *overreact, dissatisfy, ennoble, re-elect*.)

Expected outcomes
● All children can recognise issues in a text, participate in discussions and, with support, write persuasive texts.
● Most children can also understand these issues and write with less support.
● Some children can also discuss these issues using evidence.

Curriculum objectives
● To participate in discussions about books that are read to them or they can read for themselves, building on their own and others' ideas and challenging views courteously.

Resources
Kensuke's Kingdom by Michael Morpurgo, ideally, one copy per group; internet access and/or leaflets from voluntary organisations such as the Orangutan Foundation (UK) www.orangutan.org.uk

Week 2 lesson plans

These lessons link non-fiction reading with the story *Kensuke's Kingdom*, in which Kensuke and Michael save an island's orang-utans from hunters. The children research the plight of orang-utans in the modern world: how they are endangered and why, and discuss whether scarce resources should be devoted to saving them (or any endangered species). Discussion and debate are followed by an opportunity for persuasive writing on the topic of endangered orang-utans. This includes how to engage the reader's interest and sympathy.

1: Orang-utans

Introduction
● Recap Chapter 9 of *Kensuke's Kingdom*, in which Kensuke enlists Michael's help to keep as many newly hatched turtles as possible safe from birds until they reach the sea. Ask if they think he was right to do this. Ask: *What about the birds?* (They have to eat. Carnivorous birds will eat other animals, too. Should they all be saved?)

Whole-class work
● Tell the class that they are going to listen to/read the next chapter, in which Kensuke and Michael save another type of animal from a different danger. Read Chapter 10 with the class, up to where Kensuke and Michael find Kikanbo. Allow the children time to think about it. After a pause, just a word or two, such as *Well...* or *What do you think?* will encourage them to talk about their responses.

Group work
● Tell the children that orang-utans live only in very small areas of the world and are endangered. Ask them to talk in their groups about what they know about orang-utans, including what they have learned from the story.
● They should list what they know and then discuss what this makes them want to find out. Make a note of their questions. A chart might help, with an added column for notes on the answers they find.

What we know about orang-utans	Our questions	Where to look for answers	Answers
Live in forests Eat fruit Hunted	Which countries do they live in? What fruits do they eat? Why?	Internet search Online encyclopedia	

Differentiation
● Check that the children have listed all they know by asking questions. For each fact, ask: *What else could you find out about this?*

Review
● Ask what we already know about orang-utans and invite each group to share its questions with the class. Add others, as necessary, for example: *Why do people hunt orang-utans? What other dangers face them? What other factors threaten their survival?*
● Keep the children's notes for the next lesson.

Curriculum objectives
● To distinguish between statements of fact and opinion.
● To retrieve, record and present information from non-fiction.
● To précis longer passages.

Resources
Computer and internet access and/or leaflets from voluntary organisations such as the Orangutan Foundation (UK); the children's notes from lesson 1

2: Finding the facts

Introduction
● Recap lesson 1 and tell the children that they are going to look on the internet for answers to the questions they wrote in the previous lesson. Tell them that many websites give opinions as well as facts. Ask: *How can you tell the difference between facts and opinions?* (Facts can be checked.) Remind them that sometimes opinions are expressed as if they were facts, for example: *Newcastle United is the best football team in the world!* or *You can't live without our chocolate.*

Group work
● The children should begin to look for the answers to the questions they raised in lesson 1. Ask them to share the task of making notes of facts. Also ask them to make a note of any opinions they find in the sources they use. They could compare facts given in one website with those given in another in order to check them.

Differentiation
● Where necessary, help the children to find simpler online sources, such as the website of the Sumatran Orangutan Society (www.orangutans-sos.org) and parts of the wildlife section of the BBC website (www.bbc.co.uk/nature).

Review
● Ask the class what facts they have found. For each of these, ask: *Did anyone else find something that disagrees with this?* Ask about any opinions they came across. Ask: *Was it supported by evidence? What evidence?*
● Keep the children's notes for lesson 3.

Curriculum objectives
● To distinguish between statements of fact and opinion.
● To retrieve, record and present information from non-fiction.
● To précis longer passages.
● To identify the audience for and purpose of the writing, selecting the appropriate form and using other similar writing as models for their own.
● To note and develop initial ideas, drawing on reading and research where necessary.
● To explain and discuss their understanding of what they have read, including through formal presentations and debates, maintaining a focus on the topic and using notes where necessary.

3: Should orang-utans be saved?

Introduction
● Recap lesson 2 and ask the children to think about the information and opinions they have read and to consider whether people should spend time and money on saving orang-utans. Tell the children that they are going to work in pairs and use drama to explore the question *Should orang-utans be saved?*

Paired work
● Ask the pairs to decide who will take which role. One child will take the role of television or radio reporter. The other will be the interviewee – either someone who wants to save orang-utans or someone who thinks that funds and time should not be spent on this. Point out that the questioner should think of arguments against the other person's view, so that he or she will use arguments to defend it. Make a note of useful questions and answers from different groups so that they can be presented as examples.

Differentiation
● Where it helps, two children could work together on each role.

Review
● Present any useful questions the reporters asked, and the answers given. Point out that it is useful to consider opposing views when writing a persuasive text.
● Keep the children's notes from lesson 2.

Resources
Computer and internet access and/or leaflets from voluntary organisations such as the Orangutan Foundation (UK); the children's notes from lesson 2

Curriculum objectives
- To explain and discuss their understanding of what they have read, including through formal presentations and debates, maintaining a focus on the topic and using notes where necessary.
- To participate in discussions about books that are read to them or they can read for themselves, building on their own and others' ideas and challenging views courteously.
- To précis longer passages.

Resources
Photocopiable page 'Recycle now' from the CD-ROM

4: How to persuade

Introduction
- Tell the class that they are going to read a persuasive text about recycling to help them to plan their own writing.

Whole-class work
- Give photocopiable page 'Recycle now' from the CD-ROM. Read it with the class. Ask: *Who is the audience for this text?* (Everyone – individuals rather than groups or businesses.)
- Ask: *How does the introduction grab the reader's attention?* (It uses words that shock: *kill* and *killing*.) Mention that another way to start is to ask a question that grabs attention. *How does make readers feel that they are involved or even part of the problem?* (It uses the word *you* and says why you should recycle.) *How do paragraphs six and seven try to involve readers in the solution?* (By answering questions they might use to argue against recycling.) *How does the final paragraph summarise the persuasion?*

Independent work
- Ask the children to write a summary of the article in no more than three sentences. Remind them about adding clauses, including relative clauses, to shorter sentences.

> **Differentiation**
> - Where necessary, ask questions that the children can answer in short sentences, then show them how to link the sentences, as appropriate.

Review
- Ask the children to swap their work with a partner to read. Mention that they should check how it deals with possible arguments against it.

Curriculum objectives
- To identify the audience for and purpose of the writing, selecting the appropriate form and using other similar writing as models for their own.
- To note and develop initial ideas, drawing on reading and research where necessary.
- To explain and discuss their understanding of what they have read, including through formal presentations and debates, maintaining a focus on the topic and using notes where necessary.

Resources
The children's notes from lesson 2; photocopiable page 'Recycle now' from the CD-ROM; photocopiable page 137 'Persuasive writing'

5: Persuasion

Introduction
- Remind the children of the discussions they had in lesson 3. Ask them to use these, and what they have learned from their research, to help them to decide whether orang-utans should be saved. They will then write a persuasive text to encourage others to agree with them.

Whole-class work
- Give out photocopiable page 'Recycle now' from the CD-ROM. Re-read the first sentence and ask: *Which two words are used for their effect on the reader?* (*Kill* and *killing*; they emphasise the damage rubbish is doing; they are more powerful than *harm* or *damage*.) Ask the children to re-read the rest of the text: *Who can find another word used for effect?*

Independent work
- Ask the children who they think should be the audience for their own persuasive writing to help save orang-utans, for example, people who buy exotic pets, woodcutters, oil palm planters or people who use these products.
- Give out photocopiable page 137 'Persuasive writing' and ask the children to use it to help them to write a persuasive leaflet aimed at one of these, thinking carefully about the language they should use.

Review
- Ask the children to swap their work with a partner to read. Mention that they should check how it deals with possible arguments against it.

Week 3 lesson plans

After finishing reading *Kensuke's Kingdom*, the children are encouraged to discuss whether they think any of the characters were real, what might have inspired Michael Morpurgo to write the story and what it tells them about the author. They will also look at how other themes or issues in his books support this. There are opportunities to learn from the vocabulary, grammar and punctuation used effectively in the story and to write their own 'shipwreck' story.

1: Who was Kensuke?

Introduction

● Having finished reading *Kensuke's Kingdom*, ask: *Were you left wondering about anything at the end of the story?* Allow some time for the children to talk about this. Tell them that there are some questions the story doesn't answer but they might be able to infer some answers or even check them. Examples include: *What happened to Michael and his family? Did they continue sailing round the world or did they go back home? What happened to Kensuke? Did he stay on the island alone until he died?* (See also the questions below in Group work.)
● Ask: *What did Michael promise Kensuke at the end of the story? Why? Would this have been a difficult promise to keep? Why?* Mention how Michael would answer questions about what he did on the island and how he survived – what he ate and so on.

Group work

● Ask the children to discuss the following questions in their groups:
  ● *Was Michael right to keep his promise to Kensuke? Would Kensuke be safe as he got older? Should Michael have done anything about this, or was he right to respect Kensuke's choice?*
  ● *Was Kensuke a real person? How can we find out?*
  ● *Was the island a real place and, if so, where? How can we find out?*
  ● *Who was Michael in the story? Could he have been Michael Morpurgo? How can we check?*
● Show them the material available for checking some facts: atlases, websites.
● Remind the children that they should back up what they say with evidence, and encourage them to think of *What if...?* questions to challenge others' views. Also remind them of any class rules for discussions: listening to others, not interrupting (but not talking for too long), giving everyone a chance to speak, encouraging anyone who hasn't said anything, arguing courteously.

Review

● Ask a group for their answer to the first question. They should give a reason. Ask: *Does anyone disagree? Why?* If no one disagrees, offer a challenge, for example: *Should all promises and secrets be kept or are there times when this would not be right? When?* Repeat this procedure for the other questions. Possible challenges: *Could the author have made up the letter in the postscript as part of the story? Have you found the island on an atlas? Did Michael Morpurgo give the character his own first name, Michael, to make you think it was really him?*

Expected outcomes
● All children can distinguish between fact and opinion and, with support, add a parenthesis to a sentence.
● Most children can also explain how to distinguish between fact and opinion and use brackets for parenthesis.
● Some children can write their own sentences with parentheses.

Curriculum objectives
● To participate in discussions about books that are read to them or they can read for themselves, building on their own and others' ideas and challenging views courteously.
● To explain and discuss their understanding of what they have read, including through formal presentations and debates, maintaining a focus on the topic and using notes where necessary.
● To distinguish between statements of fact and opinion.

Resources
Kensuke's Kingdom by Michael Morpurgo; atlases

Curriculum objectives
● To distinguish between statements of fact and opinion.

Resources
Cards with 'F' and 'O' written on them; *Kensuke's Kingdom* by Michael Morpurgo; interactive activity 'Fact or opinion?' on the CD-ROM

2: Fact or opinion?

Introduction

● Tell the class that you are going to make some statements about *Kensuke's Kingdom* and that they should decide whether each is a statement of fact or opinion by holding up a card to show 'F' (fact) or 'O' (opinion).
● You can make up your own statements, or use interactive activity 'Fact or opinion?' on the CD-ROM.

Whole-class work

● Ask the children to write some statements about the story then to read one out. (They should think of more than one statement in case someone else has the same). The others decide whether it is fact or opinion and hold up a card.

Group work

● Make a note of anything that was said to be a fact and, if it hasn't been checked in a previous lesson, ask the children to do so.

> **Differentiation**
> ● Look at the book with the children, where necessary, and ask: *What can we say that is definitely true about the book? What might or might not be true?*

Review

● List some facts and opinions and ask: *What is the difference between these?* Ask for a fact and an opinion about what made Michael Morpurgo write the story.

Curriculum objectives
● To discuss and evaluate how authors use language, including figurative language, considering the impact on the reader.

Resources
Kensuke's Kingdom by Michael Morpurgo

3: Language in the story

Introduction

● Remind the class of the opening of *Kensuke's Kingdom* and point out how the author uses language to create an impact – with interesting phrases, such as *the whole extraordinary story, let sleeping lies sleep on* and *back from the dead*. Also point out how he uses repetition for emphasis, for example *nothing, nothing at all* on the first page.
● Re-read in Chapter 1 the arrival of the letter saying that the brickworks were closing. Ask: *Which phrases have impact?* (For example, *a terrible silence at the breakfast table* – disbelief, everything has suddenly changed; *a creeping misery came over the house* – great sadness and hopelessness.)

Group work

● Allocate a different chapter/passage to each group and ask them to make a note of any language they think has impact – and the effect it creates. Suggested passages include the following:
  ● Chapter 3 – where Michael falls overboard
  ● Chapter 4 – the opening
  ● Chapter 4 – where Michael wakes up on the beach
  ● Chapter 4 – the description of the island (the atmosphere)
  ● Chapter 5 – meeting Kensuke
  ● Chapter 6 – where Michael lights a fire and Kensuke objects violently
  ● Chapter 7 – where Kensuke nurses Michael after the jellyfish sting
  ● Chapter 9 – scaring off the birds and helping the little turtles into the sea
  ● Chapter 10 – rescuing the orang-utans.

Review

● Ask each group for their favourite example of language for creating an effect. Ask what they think makes it effective, for example, repetition, the image it creates in their mind, a feeling it evokes.

4: My shipwreck adventure

Curriculum objectives
● To note and develop initial ideas, drawing on reading and research where necessary.
● In writing narratives, to consider how authors have developed characters and settings in what they have read, listened to or seen performed.

Resources
Kensuke's Kingdom by Michael Morpurgo; dictionaries; computers and internet access

Introduction
● Ask the class for some ideas to summarise the plot of *Kensuke's Kingdom*. Write the main events on a flow chart.

Whole-class work
● Ask the children to imagine their own shipwreck, plane crash or near-drowning adventure, in which they survive and meet someone interesting. If it helps, they could make a flow chart to plan the main events or, like many writers, they could just imagine the story bit by bit as it happens.
● Ask: *Where could your story begin? Where might you end up?* Point out that they will need to research the route and the place if their story is to be realistic.

Independent work
● Ask the children to draft the opening of their story, building up to the shipwreck or other event that they survive. Ask questions as you read what different children have written, to challenge them to check facts online to ensure that their writing is realistic.
● Ask, where appropriate: *What might happen next?* Encourage them to spend time thinking about their story.

Review
● Invite different children to read aloud from their story so far. The others could raise questions that they hope it will answer.

5: Parenthesis

Curriculum objectives
● To use brackets, dashes or commas to indicate parenthesis.
● To use and understand the grammatical terminology in Appendix 2 accurately and appropriately in discussing their writing and reading.

Resources
Photocopiable page 138 'Dashes'; interactive activity 'Dashes' on the CD-ROM

Introduction
● Recap brackets to surround extra ideas or information in a sentence. Explain that an extra bit like this is called *parenthesis*, which can be surrounded by brackets, commas or dashes. Show this example from Chapter 1 of *Kensuke's Kingdom* and discuss how the dashes help:
  ● *Sometimes we'd be the only boat on the reservoir – by the way I was better at fishing than either of them – and Stella Artois would be curled up behind us in the boat...*
  ● *And as for my mother, the truth is – and I admit it – that I didn't know she had it in her.*

Whole-class work
● Write the following sentences, one at a time, on the board and invite volunteers to come out and add a parenthesis, as suggested in brackets.
  ● *I never stopped asking questions about football when my grandfather visited.* (Add that the speaker loved football. Use a relative pronoun.)
  ● *Annoying though she could be Ella was my best friend.* (Add that Ella never put anything back where it belonged. Use a clause that could act as a sentence.)

Independent work
● Ask the children to complete the sentences on photocopiable page 138 'Dashes' (or the interactive version on the CD-ROM).

Differentiation
● Edit the first part of the activity to leave a gap where the parenthesis belongs.

Review
● Read completed examples and discuss how the meaning might change with the parenthesis in a different part of the sentence.

Week 4 lesson plans

These lessons begin with another novel by Michael Morpurgo: *The Wreck of the Zanzibar*. The children compare it with other books by Michael Morpurgo and discuss which they prefer, *The Wreck of the Zanzibar* or *Kensuke's Kingdom*, and why. They research the book's geographical and historical setting, before thinking about why the author writes both books as if he is a character in the story – even using his own name, Michael – and discussing and researching whether the stories are about real events. After enjoying the story there are opportunities to learn about grammar from the author: exploring the use of noun phrases.

1: *The Wreck of the Zanzibar*

Introduction

● Ask the class what the title and front cover tell them about the book. Have they heard of Zanzibar? Tell them that it is the name of part of Tanzania in East Africa and help them to find this on a map.
● Ask: *What is* Zanzibar *in the title of this book?* (A ship.) Ask the children to read the back cover blurb. Ask: *Where is this story set? When? Who is the main character?*
● Read the opening pages, including the letter from Great Aunt Laura, and ask: *What could Great Aunt Laura mean by* Zanzibar *here? The country? The ship? Why do these seem wrong? Does the mystery make you want to find out? Which animal do you think will feature in this book?* (Turtle, because there are turtles on the cover.)

Whole-class work

● Continue reading up to and including February 12th. Ask: *Which island is the setting of the story? What other story do you know that was set partly in the Scilly Isles?* (*Arthur High King of Britain*, by the same author.) The children should be able to locate this area on a map of Britain and look in more detail at the map at the front of the book to find the island where Great Aunt Laura lived (Bryher, pronounced *Briar*).
● Ask the class if they can see any similarities between this book and that of *Kensuke's Kingdom*, even though their settings are nearly 7000 miles apart? (Both are set on islands, and the sea and ships are important in both books.) Ask: *How do we know that Kensuke's Kingdom was set in either Sumatra in Indonesia or Borneo?* (They are the only parts of the world where orang-utans live in the wild. Both Sumatra and Borneo have gibbons, turtles and jellyfish.) There are also turtles in the Scilly Isles. Ask: *What do you think about the character's name?* (Perhaps the author wants readers to believe it to be a true story.)

Independent work

● Ask the children to find out more about Bryher, the setting for *The Wreck of the Zanzibar*, to investigate whether the author had any connection with the Scilly Isles and makes some notes. Ask: *What about the Zanzibar? Was this the name of a real ship?* Ask the children to keep their notes for the next lesson.

Review

● Invite the class to share their ideas and evidence, for example: *Does Michael Morpurgo have a connection with the Scilly Isles?* (He has spent holidays there with his wife and family.) *Were ships wrecked near Bryher?* (Yes. This might have inspired Michael Morpurgo to set the story there.) *Was Zanzibar the real name of a ship wrecked there?* (None appears in any list of real wrecked ships.)

2: Comparing settings

Curriculum objectives
● To participate in discussions about books that are read to them and those they can read for themselves, building on their own and others' ideas and challenging views courteously.
● To make comparisons within and across books.

Resources
The Wreck of the Zanzibar by Michael Morpurgo; *Kensuke's Kingdom* by Michael Morpurgo; maps of the world, globes and atlases; map and information about Borneo and Sumatra; map and information about the Scilly Isles; computer and internet access

Introduction
● Recap the children's findings from the previous lesson about the setting of *The Wreck of the Zanzibar* and make a note of the main points on the board. Tell them that some groups are going to look at the Scilly Isles in more detail, while others will focus on Borneo and Sumatra in South-East Asia – the setting of *Kensuke's Kingdom*.

Group work
● Assign an island setting to each group and ask them to find out more about the geography, wildlife, people, their way of life and their work, so that they can compare them with other groups' findings about the other setting.
● Recap the key elements of note-taking (making note of important words or names, where they found their information, where they came across useful maps or pictures, possibly using headings to organise the notes).

> **Differentiation**
> ● Provide useful headings and ask questions about them, for example: *The land – what is the land like in the Scilly Isles?*

Review
● Ask each group to nominate a spokesperson to report back to the class. Begin with one setting and then move on to the other. Ask the class: *How are the places similar? How are they different?* Note that both areas are important for their wildlife and are destinations for holidays with a wildlife theme. Ask: *What does this tell you about Michael Morpurgo?*

3: Comparing stories

Curriculum objectives
● To read books that are structured in different ways and read for a range of purposes.
● To make comparisons within and across books.

Resources
The Wreck of the Zanzibar by Michael Morpurgo; *Kensuke's Kingdom* by Michael Morpurgo; photocopiable page 139 'Comparing two books'; the children's notes from lesson 2

Introduction
● Read *The Wreck of the Zanzibar* up to and including August 23rd. Ask: *Do you notice any similarities between the openings of this story and Kensuke's Kingdom?* (They begin with a family with someone named Michael and a sad event in each family; both books are connected with the sea and include looking after animals.)
● Ask: *How does the author move from one setting to another (which could be time or place) in each book?* (Michael's near-drowning in *Kensuke's Kingdom* and Great Aunt Laura's letter to Michael, and her diary, in *The Wreck of the Zanzibar.*) *What is similar about the way he tells about the main action in each story?* (It is in a diary.)

Independent work
● Give out photocopiable page 139 'Comparing two books' and ask the children to complete the comparison chart about the two stories. They could also re-read their notes about the settings. Ask them to look for other similarities and differences in addition to those already discussed.

Review
● Read some of the comparisons the children made and ask the class: *What can we tell about Michael Morpurgo from these stories? What have we learned about how he takes the reader into a story?* Ask them to look out for these ideas in other stories by the same author.

Curriculum objectives
● To participate in discussions about books that are read to them and those they can read for themselves, building on their own and others' ideas and challenging views courteously.
● To make comparisons within and across books.
● To draw inferences and justify these with evidence from the text.

Resources
The Wreck of the Zanzibar by Michael Morpurgo; *Kensuke's Kingdom* by Michael Morpurgo

4: Preferences

Introduction
● Recap the story of *The Wreck of the Zanzibar* so far. Read up to and including November 1st. Ask: *How has the atmosphere of the story been changing? How is life for Laura's family changing? How is nature around them changing?* Point out that people's lives used to be more closely linked to the weather and seasons. What do the children expect to happen before long? (A shipwreck – because of the title.)

Independent work
● Ask the children to think about the opening chapters of *Kensuke's Kingdom* and *The Wreck of the Zanzibar* and decide which of the beginnings they like better. Which made them want to read on more, and why? Was it the setting, the main character, the events of the story, any mystery or unanswered questions, anything they hoped might happen?
● Display these ideas and other useful questions on a mind map. Ask the children to create their own version of the mind map, adding their thoughts about each book in response to the questions.
● Then they should say which book they prefer overall.

Review
● Invite volunteers to say which book they like better, and why. Ask the class to vote for the one they prefer so far. Remind them that they haven't yet finished *The Wreck of the Zanzibar*, so it will be interesting to see if they change their mind later.

Curriculum objectives
● To use expanded noun phrases to convey complicated information concisely.
● To predict what might happen from details stated and implied.

Resources
The Wreck of the Zanzibar by Michael Morpurgo; photocopiable page 140 'Noun phrases'

5: Noun phrases

Introduction
● Read November 30th to December 8th, inclusive. Ask the children to predict what will happen soon, and why. Tell the children that we can learn from expert writers such as Michael Morpurgo, and that you are going to look at how the author uses language in ways that tells us a lot in few words.

Paired work
● Recap nouns, using the noun test: if a word makes sense with *a, an, the, his, her, its, our* or *their* before it, it is usually a noun (apart from most names). Explain that a phrase can also act as a noun, for example *mad old stick* (what everyone on the island calls Granny May). Ask what effect this creates. What about the following noun phrases: *twitchy eyebrows, stony silence, eyes like steel, gently smiling mouth*? The children might notice that one of the noun phrases is also a simile.
● Ask the children to complete photocopiable page 140 'Noun phrases', which asks them to underline noun phrases from the story and to describe the effects they create.

> **Differentiation**
> ● Where necessary, help the children to find the first noun phrase, ask them to underline it, and ask: *What does it make you see in your mind?*

Review
● Remind the children of *the noun test* and ask them to test the noun phrases.

Week 5 lesson plans

Continuing to read *The Wreck of the Zanzibar*, the children explore Michael Morpurgo's use of language to create an impact on the reader and examine the themes of the book. They consider how the author knew what life in the Scilly Isles was like at that time, and research it for themselves. The structure of the book, including the use of the diary in the first person, is explored and the children try this for themselves in order to tell the story of another character in the book.

1: Expressive language in *The Wreck of the Zanzibar*

Introduction

● Recap the recent events in the story and ask: *How were Laura, her family (especially Granny May) and their neighbours feeling by December 8th?* Remind them of some of the language the author used to communicate the mood of despair: *The cold of winter has crept into the house*; Granny May's words: *I was born here. I'll die here, I'm not leaving*; *She's disappeared inside herself completely, and I don't think she'll ever come out again.* Ask: *Was the pace of the story fast or slow then?* (Slow – everyone was just waiting, unable to do much apart from search for anything they could find to eat.)

Whole-class work

● Read December 9th and ask: *Where did the atmosphere of the story suddenly change?* (When the wreck was spotted and everyone called out *Wreck! Wreck!*) Ask: *How does the pace of the story change after that?* It had been moving slowly and had almost come to a halt, describing daily life and the seemingly hopeless wait for a change in fortune – and enough to eat – but here the pace suddenly becomes very fast-moving and urgent as everyone is spurred into action by the wreck.

Paired work

● Ask the children to re-read the paragraph following the spotting of the wreck and to look for verbs that create this change of pace: *hauling, leapt, pushed, driven, caught.* Ask: *What gives a feeling of emergency and hurrying?* (The dialogue; the chief shouting commands: *'You take it!', 'You, Laura, you!', 'Come on!', 'Row, you beggars, row!'*)
● Give out photocopiable page 141 'Expressive verbs' and ask them to list these verbs in the chart provided. They should use a dictionary to list others with a similar meaning and then explore how they can change the effect of the text by changing the verbs.

> **Differentiation**
> ● Where it helps, ask the children to enact the scene as a more-confident reader reads it aloud. The reader's task is to act as director, using his/her voice to give meaning to the verbs. This also gives the reader practice in interpreting the atmosphere of a text and expressing this using their voice (changing pace, pitch and volume of his/her voice).

Review

● Ask different pairs to read out one of their altered sentences after reading the original from the story. Ask the class: *What difference does the new verb make?*

Curriculum objectives
● To identify and discuss themes and conventions in and across a wide range of writing.
● To summarise the main ideas drawn from more than one paragraph, identifying key details that support the main ideas.

Resources
The Wreck of the Zanzibar by Michael Morpurgo; photocopiable page 142 'Themes in a story'

2: Themes in *The Wreck of the Zanzibar*

Introduction

● Tell the class that you are going to read to the end of *The Wreck of the Zanzibar*. Ask: *Can you figure out yet who Zanzibar might be? How do you think Laura's story in her diary will end? How will the book end?* (Remind them how it started, if necessary.)

Whole-class work

● Read to the end of the book and allow time for the children to comment freely on it to others around them. Ask: *Which parts were what you expected? Which parts surprised you?*
● Remind the children what is meant by *themes* by referring to the themes of other stories they have read, such as poverty, kindness and caring for others (in *The Railway Children*) and care for animals, the environment and loyalty (in *Kensuke's Kingdom*). Ask: *What themes does* The Wreck of the Zanzibar *have?* (Poverty, hardship, caring for animals, families and links between different generations in a family, community, death.)

Group work

● Allocate a theme to each group. Ask them to share their memories from the book about this theme and then to check these in the book and make a note of the evidence for it using photocopiable page 142 'Themes in a story'. Ask them to discuss how it affects the characters in the story or their families in the future, how characters deal with it, and what the author is saying about the theme.

> **Differentiation**
> ● Suggest chapters to re-read that deal with the theme in question.

Review

● Invite a speaker from each group to report their ideas to the class and ask if the others agree.

Curriculum objectives
● To summarise the main ideas drawn from more than one paragraph, identifying key details that support the main ideas.
● In writing narratives, to consider how authors have developed characters and settings in what they have read, listened to or seen performed.

Resources
The Wreck of the Zanzibar by Michael Morpurgo; computer and internet access; websites that give biographical information about Michael Morpurgo and the Scilly Isles' history (including marine disasters and lifeboats) – bookmarked in preparation for the lesson: www.gibsonsofscilly.co.uk www.scillywebcam.com

3: Life in 19th century Scilly

Introduction

● Ask the class how Michael Morpurgo knew what life was like in the Scilly Isles in the past. If they think he was the Michael in the book and knew from his great aunt's diary, ask how we can check. Invite children to come out and read highlighted sections of text about the author. Ask: *Do you think he was Michael in the story? If not, how did he know about life in the Scilly Isles in the past?*

Group work

● Ask the children to use information texts and websites to find out about life in the Scilly Isles in the 19th century, including lifeboats and shipwrecks. Ask them to look for information about life for poorer people, and about shipwrecks and how the islanders responded.
● Remind them to make brief notes rather than copying chunks of text, and to make a note of where to find any useful pictures.

Review

● Ask: *How did people at the end of the 19th century in the Scilly Isles manage everyday things like cooking; washing themselves, clothes and the dishes; heat, light, getting food, clothes and other things they needed? What about school, work and leisure?*

Curriculum objectives

● To identify and discuss themes and conventions in and across a wide range of writing.
● In writing narratives, to consider how authors have developed characters and settings in what they have read, listened to or seen performed.

Resources

The Wreck of the Zanzibar by Michael Morpurgo

4: Diaries in fiction

Introduction

● Tell the children that their task in this lesson is to explore how Michael Morpurgo uses a diary to tell the story of *The Wreck of the Zanzibar* and to consider the advantages and disadvantages of using one character's diary.

Whole-class work

● Ask: *How does Michael Morpurgo introduce Great Aunt Laura, and then her diary?* (He begins with her funeral and a letter she has left for her great-nephew, Michael.) Point out that many diaries are boring in places if they record many of the same day-to-day activities, and ask: *How does the author avoid this?* (He has the writer of the diary choose the most interesting parts to pass on.) Ask: *What makes a diary a good way to tell a story? What does it miss out?* (The thoughts and actions of other characters that the diary character doesn't know about.)

Group work

● Allocate different parts of Great Aunt Laura's diary in *The Wreck of the Zanzibar* to each group. Ask the children to re-read this part of the diary and to discuss and make notes about what it tells them that other characters wouldn't know, what it *doesn't* tell them, and which characters might have told a different part of the story (and what they might have told).

Review

● Ask the children for their ideas about what Laura's diary doesn't tell.

Curriculum objectives

● To ensure the consistent and correct use of tense throughout a piece of writing.
● To proofread for spelling and punctuation errors.
● To choose which shape of a letter to use when given choices and deciding, as part of their personal style, whether or not to join specific letters.
● To choose the writing implement that is best suited for a task.

Resources

The Wreck of the Zanzibar by Michael Morpurgo; photocopiable page 143 'Diary story'; blank diaries, made by the children in advance of the lesson (if there is time, show them how to make a cover, how to bind it and add a suitable picture)

5: Telling a story through a diary

Introduction

● Tell the children that they are going to use what they have learned from how Michael Morpurgo uses Laura's diary in *The Wreck of the Zanzibar* to tell their own version of part of the story through another character's diary.

Independent work

● Ask the children to choose a character in *The Wreck of the Zanzibar* whose diary they would like to write. Ask: *Which person is a diary written in?* Recap first person. *What tense?* (Mainly past but there could be some present tense.)
● Ask them to make the diary fit in with the dates and events in Laura's diary and to tell what she doesn't, for example: Billy's voyage to America, what Granny May does while she's in her own home and her thoughts in the hard times; what Laura's mother or father are doing and thinking, and any conversations they might have with other people on the island.
● Tell them to write in rough for the first draft on photocopiable page 143 'Diary story' and then to copy it in neat handwriting into their diary.

Paired work

● Ask the children to swap diaries with a partner and to check tenses, use of the first person, spelling and other grammar.

Review

● Read extracts from the diaries. Ask the children to complete them between lessons so that they can be displayed in the class or school library for others to enjoy.

Curriculum objectives
● To continue to read and discuss an increasingly wide range of poetry.

Resources
Photocopiable page 'Until I saw the sea' from the CD-ROM

Week 6 lesson plans

This week's lessons are based on poems about the sea. The children read poems from different times, with different styles and structures, and describe these using their growing vocabulary of poetic terms. They have time to respond to the poems, draw or paint the pictures they make them imagine, discuss which they like, and say why, and choose a poem (or part of one) to learn. After watching and listening to audio-visual recordings of the sea they write their own poem on this theme.

1: 'Until I saw the sea'

Introduction

Ask the class what, in nature, had the greatest effect on the lives of the people in the story *The Wreck of the Zanzibar*. (The sea.) Tell them that the sea has inspired many poems over the centuries and that they are going to read different kinds of sea poems. Ask if any of them know any sea poems.

Whole-class work

● Read 'Until I saw the sea' by Lilian Moore from the photocopiable page 'Until I saw the sea' from the CD-ROM. Ask: *Can we tell from the poem which part of the world, or what kind of place this is?* (No – it could be any sea.) *Do you think this is an old or modern poem? Why?* (The language doesn't sound old.)

● *What is the sea like in this poem?* (The poet doesn't say that the sea is calm but we get the impression that it is.) *How does she create this effect?* Ask them to join in a second reading. Ask: *How do the lengths of the lines affect the way you read it?* (They make the reader read slowly, then pause slightly, then continue.) *How do the sounds of the words affect the way you read it?* (The repeated /s/ and /w/ sounds of the first two verses and the /th/ and /sh/ sounds in the last verse also slow you down.) Introduce or recap the term *alliteration*.

● Ask: *How does the shape of the poem affect how you read it?* (The shape is like the sea going in and out. It makes the reader speak with the rhythm of the sea going in and out gently.)

Paired work

● Recap figurative language and ask the children to discuss and make a note of examples of any different types of figurative language they can find in the poem, for example, simile, metaphor or imagery. Ask them to make a note of the effect each example creates, or the picture or sound it creates in their minds. Also ask them to make a note of any other poetic devices they notice, such as rhyme, and their effects.

> **Differentiation**
> ● The children could begin by drawing the picture each verse creates in their minds and then writing the main words that create the effect. Provide examples of similes, metaphors and imagery, and ask which of these are used in the parts that made them think of these pictures. (Examples: *wrinkle water so, splinter a whole sea of blue, a sea breathes in and out*.)

Review

● Ask: *Does the poem rhyme? What pattern does the rhyme have?* Ask for examples of imagery and ask the children to explain them, for example: *How can the wind wrinkle a sea? How can the sun splinter a sea? How can a sea breathe in and out?*

Curriculum objectives

● To continue to read and discuss an increasingly wide range of poetry.

Resources

Photocopiable page 'Sea Fever' from the CD-ROM; dictionaries

2: 'Sea Fever'

Introduction

● Remind the class of the last sea poem they read and summarise your discussions about it. Tell them that they are going to read another sea poem – 'Sea Fever' by John Masefield. Give out copies of the photocopiable page 'Sea Fever' from the CD-ROM and read the poem aloud.

Whole-class work

● Ask: *Is this poem modern or old? How can you tell? What is the sea like? (A stormy sea or just windy weather?) Which words tell you this? How does the poet feel about the sea? Which words tell you this?* Remind them of analogy, in which something is described as if it is something else. Ask: *What makes the sea seem to be alive? (The sea's face;* the call of the tide is *a wild call and a clear call that may not be denied.)*

● Ask them to re-read the poem and to mark any words they don't know, to look them up and write footnotes.

Independent work

● Ask the children to re-read the poem and to sketch the scene it makes them think of and, around their sketches, to write any words from the poem that made them picture it like this.

Review

● Ask the children to show their pictures to one another and to say what similarities they notice. Ask them to read out the words they wrote. Draw attention to any repeated sounds (alliteration or assonance) and similes.

Curriculum objectives

● To continue to read and discuss an increasingly wide range of poetry.
● To learn a wider range of poetry by heart.
● To prepare poems to read aloud and perform, showing understanding through intonation, tone and volume so that the meaning is clear to an audience.

Resources

Photocopiable page 'Sea Timeless Song' from the CD-ROM; dictionaries

3: 'Sea Timeless Song'

Introduction

● Tell the children that they are going to read another sea poem – 'Sea Timeless Song' by Grace Nichols. Give out copies and read it aloud.

Whole-class work

● Ask: *Is this modern or old? How can you tell? Are there any words you don't know?* (Ask them to look up *hibiscus* in a dictionary.)

● Ask: *How can we tell what kind of place this is?* (Clues: hibiscus grows in the Caribbean, which also has hurricanes and tourists.) *What do you notice about the language? Is it in sentences? Try adding words to make sentences* (for example *The sea is timeless.*) Notice how this changes the effect of the poem. *What makes it a song?* (The chorus. Explain *chorus*, if necessary.)

● Ask: *Is the sea rough or calm? What does* timeless *mean? How does the chorus help to create the timeless effect?* (Repetition.) *Can you find any contrasts that emphasise timelessness?* (Hurricanes, hibiscus flowers and tourists come and go; the sea goes on for ever.)

Paired work

● Ask the children to re-read the poem aloud with a partner, to learn it and to practise reciting it with the rhythm of a calm sea flowing in to the shore and out again.

Review

● Ask half the class to recite the main verses and the others the chorus, and then to swap over.

Curriculum objectives
● To continue to read and discuss an increasingly wide range of poetry.

Resources
Photocopiable page 'Extract from 'The Rime of the Ancient Mariner'' from the CD-ROM; highlighter pens

4: 'The Rime of the Ancient Mariner'

Introduction
● Tell the class that they are going to read part of another, very long, sea poem – 'The Rime of the Ancient Mariner' by Samuel Taylor Coleridge. Give out copies and read the extract aloud.

Whole-class work
● Ask: *Is this poem modern or old? How can you tell? Is it a description of the sea, or more than that?* (It is part of a narrative poem – it tells a story.) *What is the weather like at the start? How does it change? Is this good or bad? Why?* Ask: *What does* all the boards did shrink *mean?*

Paired work
● Ask the children to re-read the poem aloud with a partner and to notice the pace (how fast or slow it seems). Ask them to make a note where it is faster or slower to show how the sounds of the words create these effects. Ask them to underline rhyming words and highlight repeated sounds at the beginnings of words (alliteration); also underline similes – and discuss the effects of the poet's choice of similes, such as *As idle as a painted ship/Upon a painted ocean* and *The water, like a witch's oils.*

Review
● Invite volunteers to talk about what they noticed about the effects of the words used in the poem. Draw attention to alliteration and similes.

Curriculum objectives
● To select appropriate grammar and vocabulary, understanding how such choices can change and enhance meaning.
● To propose changes to vocabulary, grammar and punctuation to enhance effects and clarify meaning.

Resources
Media resource 'Sea' on the CD-ROM; rhyming dictionary

5: Writing a sea poem

Introduction
● Tell the class that they are going to look at short films of the sea and to choose one to write about. Watch the videos on the media resource 'Sea' on the CD-ROM.

Whole-class work
● After showing each film, ask the children to describe it, giving any words that come to mind, for example: *gusts, squall, ripple, wave, rough, roaring*. After the last film ask them to each choose a film to write a poem about.

Group work
● Group the children according to choice of film. Ask them to watch it again together and list the words they think of as they watch. They could take turns to say phrases or short sentences that describe the sea. Ask them to think about the effects of the words and to notice whether they match the sea in the film. If not, encourage them to find others.

Independent work
● Ask the children to use the ideas from their discussion to help them to write their poem. Emphasise that it need not rhyme. If they want to find meaningful rhymes, help them to use a rhyming dictionary and list possible words.

> **Differentiation**
> ● Ask questions such as: *What did you see and hear at the start?* Then: *Write a sentence about it. Change it to sound more like a poem. Think of words that sound like the sea.*

Review
● Invite volunteers to read out their first drafts. Ask the others to comment on any parts that sound like the sea. Allow time for redrafting.

Curriculum objectives
● To use expanded noun phrases to convey complicated information precisely.

Grammar and punctuation: Noun phrases

Revise
● Begin with starter activity 7 'All in a noun phrase'.
● Then display the sentence below on the board and ask the children (verbally) to add a word to the underlined noun to make a noun phrase, then to add another word or more than one word, and so on until the noun becomes an expanded noun phrase. For example:
  ● *Farther along the lane we came to a **house**.*
  ● *Farther along the lane we came to a **dilapidated house**.*
  ● *Farther along the lane we came to a **dilapidated house with bats flitting around the eaves**.*
  ● *Farther along the lane we came to a **dilapidated house with bats flitting around the eaves and creepers covering most of the windows**.*

Assess
● Provide a set of up to ten sentences, as appropriate, for the children to add extra information to a given noun to make it into a noun phrase.

Further practice
● Collect examples of uses of noun phrases from persuasive texts such as advertisements.

Curriculum objectives
● To use further prefixes and suffixes and understand the guidelines for adding them.

Resources
Individual whiteboards and pens

Spelling: Verb prefixes

Revise
● Use starter activity 8 'Make the opposite verb'.
● Tell the children that we can use prefixes to change the meanings of verbs in other ways. Show them an example on the board: write *print* and add the prefix 're-' to make *reprint*.
● Read out a verb. Ask the children to change its meaning using a prefix and this time to write it. Suggested verbs: *play, read, charge, come, balance, sign, act, come, eat, match, behave, fit.*
● Ask them to show their whiteboards. Let them look at one another's whiteboards and make any changes they think they need.
● Ask: *Which prefixes have we used?* Choose a prefix. Ask: *How does this prefix change a verb?*
● Ask: *Did you change the verb before adding the prefix? What happens when the prefix ends with the same letter as the first letter of the verb?* (The verb doesn't change, so there is a double letter.)

Assess
● Give clues for verbs with prefixes and ask the children to write the verb. Examples: *to read again; to play again; to take off a cover; to send goods for sale abroad; to put back in its place; to eat too much; to eat too little; to try again; to hear wrongly; to understand wrongly; to match wrongly.*

Further practice
● From reading, collect examples of verbs with prefixes. Ask the children to use them in sentences.

Curriculum objectives
● To précis longer passages.
● To evaluate and discuss how authors use language, including figurative language, considering the impact on the reader.

Resources
Photocopiable page 'How they Brought the Good News from Ghent to Aix' from the CD-ROM; sheet of instructions; map of Europe; highlighter pens

Reading: Learning a poem

Revise

● Give out photocopiable page 'How they Brought the Good News from Ghent to Aix' from the CD-ROM featuring the poem by Robert Browning.
● Read the first two verses and ask: *What kind of poem is this?* (Narrative.) *What is the story about? What do we know about the journey?* (The riders have a purpose and have to hurry. We know from the title that they are taking good news from Ghent to Aix.) *Which country do you think this is?* (Ghent is in Belgium and Aix – now Aachen – is just over the border, in Germany.) Provide a map of Europe and ask the children to find Belgium, then ask them to find Ghent and Aix (Aachen).
● Ask: *How are the people in the poem travelling? How many people are there? What time is it?* (Night – around midnight.) *What happens in the first verse?* (The riders have to be let through a locked gate – perhaps in a town wall.) *What is the atmosphere of?* Discuss what we would hear if we were there: sounds echoing from the walls, with all else silent. *How does the poet create the sound of the echoes?* (By repeating *speed*.)
● *What is the pace of these verses? Which words help to create a fast pace? How does the poet use repeated sounds (alliteration) to give a feeling of speed?* (He repeats words such as *galloped* and other words with a /t/ sound. Point out the /t/ sound spelled with '-ed' in past-tense verbs such as *galloped*, as well as the other words with 't' and 's': *gate-bolts, postern, abreast, lights, rest, speed, kept, pace, stride, place, saddle, girths, tight, strap, right, whit*. These repeated /t/ and /s/ sounds create a feeling of speed.)
● *What is the rhythm like?* (Galloping horses.) *How does the poet use rhyme and the lengths of words and lines to create this rhythm?*

Assess

● Tell the children that they are going to read the rest of the poem. Provide a sheet of instructions and questions.
  ● *Read the poem to yourself.*
  ● *Write a summary of the story.*
  ● *Make notes in the margin about the pace of each verse.*
  ● *Highlight the words or parts of words that create this effect.*
  ● *List examples of the following poetic devices: rhyme, alliteration, repetition.*
  ● *Write about the atmosphere and the feelings of the riders in verses 1, 2, 6, 8 and 9. Give evidence to support this (just a few words).*

Further practice

● Ask the children to collect examples of poetic devices such as rhyme and alliteration from other poems and to describe their effect.

Curriculum objectives

- To select appropriate grammar and vocabulary, understand how such choices can change and enhance meaning.
- To proofread for spelling and punctuation errors.
- To ensure the consistent use of tense throughout a piece of writing.

Resources

A chapter from a book the children have read; photocopiable page 143 'Diary story'; dictionaries

Writing: Writing a story through a diary

Revise

- With the class, read a chapter of a book that the children know and ask them who the main character is. Ask: *Is the author telling the story from this character's point of view?* Ask them to imagine the events through the viewpoint of one of the other characters. Ask: *How might this character's experience be different? What might he/she see/hear/know that the main character doesn't? What might he/she feel? What if he/she recorded it in a diary?*
- Remind the children of the format of a diary. Ask: *In which person is a diary written?* Ask for an example of a sentence in the first person. Ask: *How would you write in the first person about something you did at break yesterday? What tense should you use?* Elicit that a diary records things that have happened or events that are happening at the time. *Which other tense could it be written in?* (Present, but the same tense all the way through to show whether the writer is recording events as they happen, or afterwards – unless this is a deliberate change, for example, it might be mainly in the present tense but change to the past tense for something that happened earlier. It might include some future tense if it is about something that is going to happen or might happen.)

Assess

- Ask the children to use photocopiable page 143 'Diary story' to help them to plan the diary of a character from the story you read with them. Provide dictionaries. Remind them to read it through, when finished, to check that the tense is correct and they have kept the first person throughout. They should also check other grammar as well as punctuation, including commas, dashes and brackets.

Further practice

- Use this procedure for retelling other stories the children know from a different character's point of view or for moving the setting from one place and time to another – as in *The Wreck of the Zanzibar* by Michael Morpurgo.

Name: _____   Date: _____

Verb prefixes

- Read these sentences from *Kensuke's Kingdom*.
- In each sentence highlight the verb that has a prefix.

1. She could not have foreseen how the letter was going to change our lives.
2. I soon discovered parents were more than just parents.
3. I was encouraged to write in it (the ship's log) every few weeks.
4. It reassured me to hear the sound of my own voice.
5. He had saved my life twice, fed me and befriended me.

- Write the verbs in the chart. Look up and write their meanings.
- Write the root word the verb comes from and how the prefix changes its meaning.

	Verb	Meaning	Root word	Prefix	How the prefix changes its meaning
1					
2					
3					
4					
5					

I can recognise root words and prefixes that make up verbs.

How did you do?

Name: _____   Date: _____

Persuasive writing

- Use this page to help you write a persuasive leaflet.

Title _____

Audience _____

Introduction	Grab the readers' attention. Make them want to read on.
Paragraph 1	Make your first point – giving information.
Paragraph 2	Make your second point – giving more information.
Paragraph 3	Make your third point – giving more information.
Arguments against	Answer possible arguments against these points.
Summary	Sum up. Suggest what readers can do.

I can write a persuasive text.

How did you do?

Dashes

■ These sentences from *Kensuke's Kingdom* had dashes to help readers to make sense of them.

■ Read the sentences. Put in a pair of dashes where they belong in each sentence.

1. Only one of the crew was allowed to be idle Stella Artois and she was always idle.

2. Annoying though she could be she would bring her smelly wetness everywhere we never once regretted bringing her along with us.

3. Stella came over to bother me she wanted to play but I pushed her away.

4. As far as I could tell though I couldn't be sure of it there were only the two of us on this island, the old man and me.

5. I just hoped the typhoon for that was what I was witnessing had passed them by.

6. A boat with some strange red-brown sails I supposed it to be some kind of Chinese junk and not that far out to sea either.

■ Add information to these sentences – in a parenthesis – using dashes.

1. She gave me a bright green jumper _____ for my birthday.

   > Add that you hate bright green.

2. The new teacher _____ looks like Justin Bieber.

   > Add that you should see him!

3. Mrs Grace said it was cold _____ and cold weather made her sad.

   > Add that you know that.

4. We saw the old man _____ at the shops.

   > Add that he was the one who lost his cat.

I can use dashes to separate part of a sentence, so that the sentence makes sense.

How did you do?

Comparing two books

- Use this chart to help you to compare two books.

Title 1 _____

Title 2 _____

	Similarities	Differences
Setting		
How the author moves from one setting to another		
Plot		
Characters		
Themes		
Other		

I can compare two books, thinking about their settings, characters, plot and themes.

How did you do?

PHOTOCOPIABLE

Name: _____ Date: _____

Noun phrases

- Underline the noun phrases in these sentences from *The Wreck of the Zanzibar*.

1. A great curling stormwave broke and came tumbling towards us.
2. She knows every likely cluster of seaweed on Rushy Bay, and everywhere else come to that.
3. I can't make any sense of it but it's a kind of rambling prayer.
4. A witch's brew of wind and tide and current took us and tossed us about at will.
5. By this evening the beach on Rushy Bay was littered with piles of loot.

- Describe the effect each noun phrase creates.

Sentence	Noun phrase	Effect
1		
2		
3		
4		
5		

I can recognise and describe the effects of noun phrases.

How did you do?

Expressive verbs

■ Read this passage from *The Wreck of the Zanzibar* and underline the verbs
the author chose to create effects.

> When we reached the boathouse they were already hauling the gig down into the
> surf. Time and again the crew leapt in and we pushed them out, up to our waists
> in the icy sea, and time and again they were driven back by the waves. In the end
> she was caught broadside on, capsized and everyone was upturned into the sea.
> After that everyone wanted to give up, everyone except the chief.

■ Use a dictionary to find other verbs with similar meanings but different effects.

Verb	Other verbs with similar meanings

■ Rewrite the passage but change the verbs to others with similar meanings.
Make the passage sound calm and peaceful, or as if the people are having fun.

_____

_____

_____

_____

_____

_____

_____

I can use words with similar meanings to create different effects.

How did you do?

Themes in a story

- List the main themes in a book you are reading.
- Make notes of evidence of the theme from the story and what the author seems to be saying about it.

Title of book _____

Author _____

Theme	Evidence	What the author is saying

- What do these themes tell you about the author?

_____

I can recognise the themes of a story and what they say about the author.

How did you do?

Name: _____   Date: _____

Diary story

- Draft your diary story below.

This is the diary of _____ in _____

Date _____   Date _____

Date _____   Date _____

Date _____   Date _____

I can tell a story in a character's diary.

How did you do?

Greek myths

These lessons begin with non-fiction texts about Ancient Greek deities, which the children research and write a factfile on. They read and compare Greek myths and legends, discuss the behaviour of some of the characters in 'Theseus and the Minotaur' and develop an idea for a Minotaur computer game. They go on to explore the language in 'Daedalus and Icarus' (including metaphors such as *flying too close to the sun*) and write a puppet play on it. They read and explore 'Arachne and Athena' as well as translations of Ancient Greek poetry. Additional writing activities include writing a persuasive text (a travel guide to Greece) and writing an ode about the modern Olympics.

Expected prior learning
- Can describe what a myth is.
- Can name some Greek gods, goddesses and heroes.
- Can call upon a range of tales to compare with Greek myths.
- Can name a range of poetic techniques.

Overview of progression
- Throughout the course of this chapter, children continue to read a range of stories and poems. They identify story themes and discuss the behaviour of the characters. They learn how to summarise plots by writing précis; they write a story as a play and write their own narrative poem.
- In non-fiction, they learn how to use organisational devices such as bullet points and practise writing instructional and persuasive texts, remembering to choose an appropriate form of writing for their audience.
- Children explore how to convert nouns and adjectives into verbs using suffixes. There are opportunities to explore the etymology of English words of Greek origin and practise the spellings of words ending in /shus/.

Creative context
- The lessons in this chapter can be linked with history (Ancient Greeks and archaeologists) and geography (natural and built environments of rural Greece and cities, climate, crops, mapping).
- PE lessons could have an Olympics focus and maths skills could be developed in timing races and measuring distances of races, and measuring lengths and heights of jumps.
- Ancient Greek religious beliefs could be explored and how these affected daily life. In citizenship, children could learn about democracy in Ancient Greece and in the UK today.
- Make Daedalus and Icarus puppets for week 4 lesson 3 in D&T.

Preparation
You will need versions of Greek myths: 'Theseus and the Minotaur', 'Daedalus and Icarus' and 'Arachne and Athena'. These are in *Greek Myths* by Marcia Williams but other collected versions are available, including *The Usborne Book of Greek Myths* and *The Orchard Book of Greek Myths*.

You will also need:
Non-fiction books about Ancient Greece, including information about the gods and goddesses; a large wall map of Greece and a European atlas; dictionaries, including standard, biographical, etymological, quotations, idioms; travel guides and films about various locations; film clips and information from the most recent Olympic Games; different versions of the Christian Bible, including the King James Bible; individual whiteboards; highlighter pens; internet access; pictures of Daedalus and Icarus; pictures of Minos in Crete and Sounion in Greece, very simple computer game.

On the CD-ROM you will find:
Media resource 'Minotaur'; interactive activity 'Add an adverb'; photocopiable pages 'Ancient Greek odes', 'Puppet play', 'Words from Greek'

Chapter at a glance

An overview of the chapter. For curriculum objective codes, please see pages 8–10.

Week	Lesson	Curriculum objectives	Summary of activities	Outcomes
1	1	RC: 17	Research Ancient Greek deities, choose one and compile a factfile about him/her.	• Can make notes on information from non-fiction texts.
	2	WC: 6, 8	Contribute to a class dictionary of Ancient Greek deities.	• Can extract key points from non-fiction texts.
	3	WC: 8, 26, 27	Explore different ways of setting out a list and separating the items: commas, colons and bullet points.	• Can use a colon to introduce a list and punctuate bullet points correctly.
	4	WC: 6, 8, 26, 27	Make a set of picture reference cards about Ancient Greek deities.	• Can summarise research findings and present them in an engaging way.
	5	WT: 1 WC: 21, 28	Convert nouns and adjectives to verbs by adding a suffix.	• Can convert a noun or adjective to a verb by adding the correct suffix.
2	1	RC: 1, 3 WC: 6	Read the myth of 'Theseus and the Minotaur', explore meanings of new words and write a summary of the story.	• Can summarise a story.
	2	RC: 19	Discuss the behaviour of characters in 'Theseus and the Minotaur'.	• Can take part in a discussion of a character.
	3	RC: 19 WC: 1	Write a letter to a character in the story of 'Theseus and the Minotaur', explaining what he/she should do.	• Can write a persuasive letter, justifying suggestions.
	4	WC: 1	Use a flowchart to plan a computer game based on 'Theseus and the Minotaur' and write instructions for programmers.	• Can use a flowchart for planning.
	5	WC: 1	Describe and draw screen pictures and instructions for the Minotaur game.	• Can write clear instructions.
3	1	RC: 15, 16	Read travel articles and advertisements, noting their structure and language.	• Can recognise how a writer uses language for its effect on the reader: adverbs, alliteration, rhyme.
	2	RC: 16, 17	Research the locations of the story of the Minotaur.	• Can make succinct notes on information from non-fiction sources.
	3	RC: 17 WC: 1	Plan what to include in a travel guide and how to present it to attract tourists. Review one another's work.	• Can write a draft.
	4	WC: 4, 7, 19	Explore adverbs to enhance the meanings of adjectives. Compare the effects of different adverbs.	• Can use adverbs to enhance the meanings of adjectives.
	5	WC: 4, 8, 19	Write a travel guide, based on previous research and plans.	• Can use language for effect on the reader.
4	1	RC: 1, 18	Read the myth of 'Daedalus and Icarus'. Identify themes in the story.	• Can identify the themes in a story and support this with evidence.
	2	WC: 5, 14	In groups, improvise on the story of 'Daedalus and Icarus'.	• Can improvise on a story, using actions and voice effectively.
	3	RC: 14 WC: 5, 14	Write a puppet play based on the story they have read and enacted.	• Can write a playscript using a conventional format that includes dialogue and some stage directions.
	4	RC: 15	Explore the meanings of common metaphors that have arisen from stories and write their own story for a metaphor.	• Can explain metaphors.
	5	WT: 4	Spell words ending /shus/. Match /shus/ words to meanings.	• Can spell the /shus/ ending in different ways, and use learned spellings to choose the appropriate one.

Chapter at a glance

Week	Lesson	Curriculum objectives	Summary of activities	Outcomes
5	1	RC: 3, 5, 18	Read and discuss motives of characters and identify themes in the myth of 'Arachne and Athena'. Write a character profile.	• Can write a character profile.
	2	RC: 3, 5, 6 WC: 6, 26	Choose a Greek myth to summarise and comment on the characters' behaviour and the themes of the story.	• Can use evidence from a story to support opinions.
	3	RC: 5 WT: 8, 9 WC: 5	Discuss the behaviour of the Greek deities in myths and write newspaper-style headlines to describe this.	• Can summarise in a catchy headline.
	4	WC: 5, 7, 28	Write their own Greek myth about an Ancient Greek deity, based on what they have read.	• Can write a story modelled on others they have read.
	5	WT: 4, 6	Explore English words with Greek roots and explain their meanings.	• Can identify root words, prefixes and suffixes from Greek and explain the meanings of words containing them.
6	1	RC: 1, 5, 14, 15 WT: 5, 6	Read, discuss and explain translations of Ancient Greek poems. Explore their structure.	• Can identify rhythm and other patterns in a poem.
	2	RC: 1, 5, 14, 15	Discuss the style of language used by Ancient Greek poets.	• Can identify powerful language and describe its effect on the reader.
	3	RC: 2, 17, 20	Research the ancient Olympic Games.	• Can summarise research and organise it in a table.
	4	WC: 2, 4	Write their own poems in the style of Ancient Greek poetry, based on films of the Olympic Games.	• Can use language to create effects.
	5	WT: 4	Look up words with Greek roots and make links between these and other words from the same root.	• Can check the meanings of words in a dictionary.

Background knowledge

Imperative: The command form of a verb.

Morphology: A word's morphology is its internal make-up defined in terms of a root word, with changes such as the addition of prefixes and/or suffixes. (*Singing* has the morphological make-up *sing + ing*.)

Myth: A traditional story, wholly or partially fictitious, that explains a belief or something in nature or science; a story about a supernatural person or events.

Prefix: An affix placed at the beginning of a word to change its meaning and make a new word.

Root word: A word that does not contain any smaller root words, prefixes or suffixes. (*Lovable* consists of the root word *love* with the suffix '-able'.)

Rhyme: Correspondence of the terminal sounds of words.

Theme: A topic or idea covered in a story of poem.

Week 1 lesson plans

This week's lessons introduce the Greek myths. The children use non-fiction sources to research the deities of Ancient Greece: the parallel world they were believed to inhabit and the tales of their interactions with one another and with mortals. They learn how the people of Ancient Greece explained many natural and scientific phenomena as the results of the actions of the deities.

1: An introduction to the Greek deities

Introduction

- Tell the children that they are going to read about the gods and goddesses of Ancient Greece, who were believed to live on Mount Olympus. Invite a volunteer to point out Mount Olympus on a large map of Greece.
- Tell them that this is the highest mountain in Greece and was where the Ancient Greeks believed their gods and goddesses lived. Point out that this is not the site of the ancient Olympic Games. The ancient Olympics took place in Olympia in the south-west of Greece, where there were many temples dedicated to the deities. Find Olympia on the map of Greece.
- Ask the children what they know about the Greek gods and goddesses. Write up the names of some of these and ask if they have heard any of these names used for anything else. Examples include the names of planets, groups of stars, ships and spacecraft. Ask: *What do we call stories of the lives of gods and goddesses?* (Myths.)
- Tell the class that the Ancient Greeks had many gods and goddesses and believed that they lived forever but led lives that were similar to those of humans. Introduce the terms *mortal* for humans and *immortal* (with its *opposite* prefix 'im-') for deities.

Independent work

- Allocate a Greek deity to each child and ask them to find out as much as they can about him or her so that they can make a factfile. (Ensure that Athena is included as she features in a lesson in week 5 and children will need to refer to the information about her.)
- If children are going to use the internet as a source, websites with age-appropriate information include the British Museum's Ancient Greece website (www.ancientgreece.co.uk) and the BBC Schools website (www.bbc.co.uk/schools).
- Give each child photocopiable page 168 'Greek god factfile' to help them to organise the information they find.

> **Differentiation**
> - Where appropriate, children could work in pairs and share some of the facts they find.

Review

- Collect information from the class about some of the Greek deities. Keep their factfiles for lesson 3.

Curriculum objectives
● To précis longer passages.
● To use further organisational and presentational devices to structure text and to guide the reader.

Resources
Computers; a biographical dictionary

2: A dictionary of Greek gods and goddesses

Introduction

● In advance of the lesson, set up a two-column table in a Word document to which the children can add the name of the deity they researched and some information.
● Tell the children that they are going to use the information they recorded to make a dictionary of Greek gods and goddesses that others can use. Show them a biographical dictionary and point out the length of the entries about each person. Ask what order the names are in.

Group work

● Ask the children to discuss what kind of information about Greek gods and goddesses they should enter in a dictionary of Greek deities. Remind them that dictionary entries should be short so they should choose the most important information about the god or goddess they have researched.
● Ask them to prepare their entry for the dictionary, then key it into the table (name in the left-hand column and information in the right-hand column).
● For practice, display a list of all the gods and goddesses the class has researched and ask each group to put them in alphabetical order.

Review

● When the children have completed their dictionary entries, ask them to sort them alphabetically or make sure the children have added a line to the table in the appropriate place.

Curriculum objectives
● To use further organisational and presentational devices to structure text and to guide the reader.
● To punctuate bullet points consistently.
● To use a colon to introduce a list.

Resources
Photocopiable page 169 'Bullet points'

3: Bullet points

Introduction

● Display a text that has a list featuring bullet points. Read the text aloud with the children and ask: *Can anyone find a list in this text? What is in the list? How can you tell it is a list?*
● Remind them of other ways of separating items in a list. (Commas for single or two-word items.)
● Ask why they think the items in this list are separated by bullet points instead of commas. (Bullet points make the list stand out and make it easier to read.)
● Ask what other punctuation is used (a colon to show where the list begins and a full stop at the end of the list). No punctuation is needed after each item, although sometimes bullet point lists have a semicolon after each item. These are not necessary.

Whole-class work

● Tell the children that they are going to practise using colons and bullet points in lists because these will be useful in the next lesson when they write up their information about Greek gods and goddesses.

Independent work

● Give out photocopiable page 169 'Bullet points' and ask the children to read each text carefully and then rewrite it, using bullet points to make the list stand out and make it easier to read.

Review

● Ask the children to compare their answers with a partner's and, if any are different, to decide which reads better.

Curriculum objectives
- To précis longer passages.
- To use further organisational and presentational devices to structure text and to guide the reader.
- To punctuate bullet points consistently.
- To use a colon to introduce a list.

Resources
Small cards (slightly larger than playing cards)

4: Presenting information

Introduction
- Tell the children that they are going to use the information they recorded about Greek gods and goddesses to make a set of cards about them.

Whole-class work
- Show the children the cards they are going to write on and tell them that these will be displayed on the picture of Mount Olympus, so they must be written very carefully and neatly. Ask: *Will you be able to fit in all the information from your factfile? What can you do to help?* Tell them that their writing needs to be quite small, but not too small to read, and that they can use headings and bullet points. Remind them how to use bullet points: each point (not a complete sentence) begins on a new line, with no punctuation except a colon to introduce the list and a full stop following the final point.
- Ask: *What can we do to make the cards look like a matching set?* Decide which information to record, for example, name, god/goddess of..., symbol, special powers, special places (this could be where his/her temple is). Display the agreed headings and layout.

Independent work
- Provide the children with cards on which to record the information about their deity, following the layout they agreed.

Review
- As the children complete their cards, ask them to display them on the picture of Mount Olympus. They can then read one another's cards.

Curriculum objectives
- To use further prefixes and suffixes and understand the guidelines for adding them.
- To use and understand grammatical terminology in Appendix 2 accurately and appropriately in their writing and reading.
- To learn the grammar for Year 5 in Appendix 2.

Resources
Photocopiable page 170 'Making verbs (2)'

5: Making verbs

Introduction
- Display some nouns that can be made into verbs by adding a suffix, for example: *motor, memory*. Ask the children to use each word (noun) in a sentence. Ask: *What does this word do in the sentence?* (It names something.)
- Convert one of the words into a verb, for example *motorise*. Ask the children to use it in a sentence. Ask: *What does this word do in the sentence?* (It says what someone or something is doing.) Recap nouns and verbs.
- Display some adjectives that can be made into verbs by adding a suffix and repeat the above process. Examples: *bright, electric, fat*. Recap adjectives.
- Ask: *What can we do to nouns or adjectives to convert them into verbs?* (Add a suffix or prefix.) *When do we have to change then ending of the word first?*
- Recap how the endings of words change when a suffix is added, for example: doubling the last letter; dropping the final 'e' or 'y'; changing 'y' to 'i'.

Independent work
- Give out photocopiable page 170 'Making verbs (2)' and ask the children to look for verbs in the sentences in the first section and to underline the suffixes. In the second section they should think about whether the word endings need to change before adding the suffix.

Differentiation
- Provide alternative sentences with simpler nouns and adjectives, where appropriate.

Review
- Ask: *What suffixes do you know for converting nouns or adjectives into verbs?*

Expected outcomes

● All children can summarise a story, discuss characters and use a flowchart to help plan a letter and instructions.
● Most children can also write more persuasively and clearly, justifying ideas with evidence.
● Some children can also use a greater range of persuasive language.

Curriculum objectives

● To increase their familiarity with a wide range of books, including myths.
● To continue to read and discuss an increasingly wide range of fiction.
● To précis longer passages.

Resources

Map showing the Mediterranean, Greece and Crete; pictures of Minos in Crete and Sounion in Greece; the story of 'Theseus and the Minotaur'; media resource 'Minotaur' on the CD-ROM; dictionaries

Week 2 lesson plans

This week's lessons are based on the myth of 'Theseus and the Minotaur'. A version of the story is available in *Greek Myths* by Marcia Williams but there are many other versions available in print and online. After reading the story the children enact it and discuss the behaviour of the characters and what this says about them. They create their own monster-in-a labyrinth idea for a computer game using precise language for the instructions.

I: The myth 'Theseus and the Minotaur'

Introduction

● Invite a volunteer to point out Greece on a map of Europe, and to look for Crete nearby in the Mediterranean Sea. Show pictures of Minos in Crete and Sounion in Greece and tell them that they are going to read a story set there. Ask: *What do you notice about the places?* Listen to their descriptions and ask: *What kind of story might be set there?*
● Write up the word *labyrinth* and ask: *Can anyone read this word? What does it mean?* Ask the children to look it up and practise spelling it using *Look, Say, Cover, Write, Check.*
● Ask: *Have you ever been into a labyrinth or any other place like that?* (For example, a maze.) Tell them that they are going to read an Ancient Greek myth about a king of Crete who built a huge labyrinth.

Whole-class work

● Read the story of 'Theseus and the Minotaur' with the class and allow a few minutes for them to respond to and comment on the story. Ask: *What kind of story is this?* (A myth.) *How is a myth different from other kinds of story?* (It is usually about events in the lives of gods, goddesses or heroes and might be told to teach or explain something, as a warning or to commemorate a person or deity.)
● Ask: *How do you think the Minotaur got its name?* The children could look this up in an etymological dictionary or online. It comes from the name of the king, Minos, and the Greek word *tauros,* which means bull (as in the zodiac sign Taurus).
● Ask: *Who was Minos? Why did he have the labyrinth built? What was the Minotaur? What do you think it looked like?* Show the children media resource 'Minotaur' on the CD-ROM and ask: *How do you feel towards the Minotaur?* (Glad it was killed, sorry for it, wanting to protect and care for it, scared?)
● Why do the children think Minos hated the people of Athens? *How did he get revenge on them? What happened to stop this revenge? Who helped Theseus to find his way out of the labyrinth? Why did Ariadne do this?*

Paired work

● Ask the children to write a brief summary of the plot of the story in note form, using a flow chart.

Review

● Invite each pair of children to share their flow chart with another pair to help them to check that they included all the main points of the plot – and that they do not have any unnecessary details. Keep the flow charts for lesson 2.

Curriculum objectives

● To explain and discuss their understanding of what they have read, including through formal presentations, maintaining a focus on the topic and using notes where necessary.

Resources

The children's flow charts from lesson 1

2: The characters

Introduction

● Ensure that the children have their flow charts from lesson 1. Recap the story.

Whole-class work

● Ask: *Whose fault was it that the people of Athens had to send children to Crete every nine years for the Minotaur? Why didn't anyone before Theseus try to stop this? Should the families of the children have tried to do something about it? Was Minos right to keep the Minotaur in a labyrinth? Was Theseus right to kill it? Was this creature treated cruelly? What else could have been done?*

Group work

● Remind the class of the summaries they made of the story of 'Theseus and the Minotaur'. Ask them to work with their partner and another pair to discuss the behaviour of the characters. Encourage them to think about whose behaviour was good and whose was bad, and in what ways, giving examples.
● Encourage them to use their flow charts to remind them who did what and to make notes of their discussions.

> **Differentiation**
> ● An adult helper could help with note-taking, by noting the main points of the discussion and helping the group to add anything they have omitted or noted incorrectly.

Review

● Ask each group to choose a speaker to report back to the class. Invite different groups to comment on the behaviour of a different character. Keep their flow charts and notes for lesson 3.

Curriculum objectives

● To explain and discuss their understanding of what they have read, including through formal presentations, maintaining a focus on the topic and using notes where necessary.
● To identify the audience for and the purpose of writing, selecting the appropriate form and using other similar writing as models for their own.

Resources

Story of 'Theseus and the Minotaur'; the children's flow charts from lesson 1 and notes from lesson 2

3: A letter to a character

Introduction

● Remind the children of lesson 2 and tell them that they're going to write a letter to say what should be done about the Minotaur, as if they were a child from Ancient Greece. Ask them to choose a character to write to (King Minos, Theseus, the people of Athens, the leaders of Athens or Ariadne). They should think about what that character might be able to do.
● Recap how to set out a letter and discuss how formal or informal the letter should be (more formal than a text to a friend but not as formal as a business letter).

Independent work

● Ask the children to write a letter to a character in the story. Remind them to begin a new paragraph as they move on to a new part of the latter, for example:
  ● Paragraph 1: Say why you are writing.
  ● Paragraph 2: Describe what they did.
  ● Paragraph 3: Say what you thought was right and wrong.
  ● Paragraph 4: Say what you think they should have done, and why.
  ● Paragraph 5: Conclude the letter with something like: *I hope you will consider my suggestion.*

Review

● Model how to enact the part of a character in the story reading aloud a letter written to him/her and make some comments about what you might/ will not do, and why/why not. Invite volunteers to enact characters' roles in the same way.

Curriculum objectives
● To identify the audience for and the purpose of writing, selecting the appropriate form and using other similar writing as models for their own.

Resources
Computers and a very simple adventure game; large sheet of paper for each group

4: Planning a computer game

Introduction
● Tell the children that they are going to plan a computer adventure game based on the story of 'Theseus and the Minotaur'. First of all they will look at another game to see how it is structured and put together.

Group work
● Give the children an opportunity to try a computer adventure game. Visit each group and ask them to notice what happens on the screen and what sounds they hear at different points. Ask them to think about what instructions the game designer would have to give to the programmer.
● Ask: *What instruction would you give to the programmer for the opening screen?* Show them how to write this on a flow chart on a large sheet of paper. You could draw the first section of the flow chart in an appropriate place on their paper. Ask: *What happens next?* This might depend on what the player does, in which case the flow chart will need to branch. The children should complete as much as possible of the flow chart but the game might be too complex for them to complete more than three or four stages.

> **Differentiation**
> ● Help the children to describe each scene briefly. Ask: *What happens next?* Sketch part of the flow chart for them.

Review
● Ask the children to swap flow charts with another group, who should read it and make a note anywhere they cannot follow the instructions, so that they can question the other group.

Curriculum objectives
● To identify the audience for and the purpose of writing, selecting the appropriate form and using other similar writing as models for their own.

Resources
Story of 'Theseus and the Minotaur'; large sheets of paper

5: Writing the instructions for the game

Introduction
● Remind the children how they wrote flow charts about the computer game they played. Tell them that in this lesson they can make up their own computer adventure game based on the labyrinth in 'Theseus and the Minotaur'.

Paired work
● Ask the children to plan their game with their partner, using a flow chart. Ask them to begin with a labyrinth/maze that the players have to find their way through. They should draw this and then show what happens if they get through the maze and what scary things might happen in there if they take a wrong turn (for example, being caught or chased by the Minotaur). What happens at the end? Will they be rescued?

> **Differentiation**
> ● Guide the children through the process, where necessary, asking: *How does the game start? Draw the labyrinth. What happens if the player gets through it? What happens if they go wrong here? What might jump out and get them? Can they get away from it? How?*

Review
● Invite volunteers to show and explain their plans to the class and give the class time to ask questions.

Week 3 lesson plans

These lessons are based on non-fiction texts about the settings of the two places in the story of 'Theseus and the Minotaur': Athens and Crete. The children research these places and read travel guides to learn about the genre before writing their own guides to encourage fans of the story to visit the places where it all happened. This involves learning more about the structure of the texts (headings, bullet points, pictures, captions, charts for data such as weather statistics) and the type of language to use (direct and personal, using imperative verbs, modal verbs, adverbs).

I: Travel guides

Introduction

● Tell the class that they are going to watch some films about holiday destinations and their task is to notice the language used to make viewers want to go there. Show the films. Pause after the first clip and ask: *What words have you made a note of?* Ask what makes them effective, for example, powerful adjectives, adverbs used to make adjectives more effective, alliteration. Continue without further discussion, until the end, then collect and discuss other examples.

Group work

● Give each group a collection of travel articles and ask them to read them alone or with a partner in their group. Ask them to decide which articles make them want to visit the place.

Whole-class work

● Ask: *Which places did you read about? Did the articles make you want to visit them? What made them sound good to visit?* Write these up, then read out each, one by one, and ask: *Is this a fact?* Underline any facts. Read out the others and ask if each one is an opinion. Ask: *What evidence can you find to support this opinion?*

Paired work

● Ask the children to re-read an article and to highlight any language that makes the place sound good to visit, for example: *at the heart of Umbria, one of Italy's most beautiful regions; an intriguing mixture of wonderfully preserved 13th-century architecture; each evening, it feels like the entire city emerges; an endlessly fascinating display of outdoor theatre; a particularly fine region for food.*
● Use an example to show adverbs enhancing adjectives, superlatives, alliteration, rhyme and similes, such as: *spicy as salsa, volatile as the volcanoes of the central sierra, monumental as the pyramids.* Also ask them to look for catchy headings and subheadings.

Differentiation
● Ask the children to highlight language that makes the place sound inviting. Remind them of previous learning about poetic language.

Review

● Invite different children to read out a short extract (no more than two sentences) from a travel article that they think uses language that invites readers to visit. Ask: *What made this inviting?*

Expected outcomes
● All children can identify effective language and, with support, use it in their writing. They can make notes and write a travel report.
● Most children can also describe how language is effective and use adverbs to modify adjectives.
● Some children can also use a greater range of effective language in their writing.

Curriculum objectives
● To distinguish between statements of fact and opinion.
● To discuss and evaluate how authors use language, including figurative language, considering the impact on the reader.

Resources
Short films about holiday destinations; travel guides from newspapers and online sources about holiday destinations, but excepting Athens and Crete; picture of Minos in Crete and Sounion in Greece; computer and internet access; highlighter pens; useful websites that feature travel information, bookmarked in advance

---

Curriculum objectives
● To distinguish between statements of fact and opinion.
● To retrieve, record and present information from non-fiction.

Resources
Computers and internet access; information books and leaflets; photographs and travel brochures about Minos in Crete and Sounion in Greece; a map of the Mediterranean showing Crete and Greece; atlases of Europe; useful websites for information about Crete and Greece, bookmarked in advance of the lesson (for example www.visit-ancient-greece.com); set up a display area on Minos in Crete and Sounion in Greece, including a map and pictures

2: A trip to Minos in Crete and Sounion in Greece

Introduction

● Remind the class about the story of 'Theseus and the Minotaur'. Ask: *Where was the story set? Which city state did King Minos take revenge on? What for?* Ask if anyone has been to Crete or Greece and, if so, ask them what they remember about it. Ask what they would write about on a postcard if they wanted to encourage others to go there.

Independent work

● Ask the children to find out about Minos in Crete and Sounion in Greece so that they can write a travel guide for tourists who want to see the sites of the story of 'Theseus and the Minotaur'. Ask them to think about what tourists might find interesting (for example, buildings, temples, statues and other art) and what else might attract them (sunshine, scenery, the sea, restaurants).
● They should make notes that include factual information, where they found this, and where to find any pictures they might want to include. Ask them to look for what makes the places special and different from anywhere else. Keep the children's notes for lesson 3.

> **Differentiation**
> ● Begin the Review with children who have not been able to write as much as the others, to give them a chance to contribute.

Review

● Ask different children to report something they have found out. Invite others to add anything that hasn't been mentioned.

Curriculum objectives
● To identify the audience for and purpose of the writing, selecting the appropriate form and using other similar writing as models for their own.
● To retrieve, record and present information from non-fiction.

Resources
Computers and internet access; information books and leaflets; photographs and travel brochures about Crete and Athens; pictures of Minos in Crete and Sounion in Greece; a map of the Mediterranean showing Crete and Athens; atlases of Europe; photocopiable page 171 'Travel guide planner'; the children's notes from lesson 2; useful websites for information about Crete and Greece, bookmarked in advance of the lesson

3: Travel guide planner

Introduction

● Ask the children to think about how to present their travel guide to Minos and Sounion for tourists who are fans of the story of 'Theseus and the Minotaur'. Ask: *What can you do to catch their attention?* (For example, add a picture of a statue of the Minotaur; an eye-catching headline, in colour and perhaps writing that suggests a Greek style.)

Independent work

● Hand out photocopiable page 171 'Travel guide planner' and ask the children to plan what they will include in their guide, describe their main picture and make up a headline. Emphasise that this is a draft – they will be able to create a final version and make it look good in another lesson.

Paired work

● As the children complete their plans, ask them to work in pairs to review one another's work and make other suggestions, where appropriate.

> **Differentiation**
> ● Add notes to the photocopiable sheet to give extra guidance for each paragraph.

Review

● Invite volunteers to describe what their first paragraph will say. Ask the others: How well will this make people want to read on? Why? Would you change anything? How will that help? Keep the children's notes and photocopiable sheets for lesson 5.

Curriculum objectives
- To select appropriate grammar and vocabulary, understanding how such choices can change and enhance meaning.
- To use a wide range of devices to build cohesion within and across paragraphs.
- To use modal verbs or adverbs to indicate degrees of possibility.

Resources
Examples of language from travel guides that includes adverbs and modal verbs, used to enhance meaning; photocopiable page 172 'Add an adverb'; interactive activity 'Add an adverb' on the CD-ROM

4: Dynamic language

Introduction
- Give out copies of passages from travel guides that contain adverbs used to enhance the meanings of other words. Read a sentence with the class and point out the first adverb. Tell them that it is an adverb and that its purpose in this sentence is to give another word a special meaning. Point out the word it modifies and ask how the adverb affects this word, for example:
  - *Stay in delightfully quaint guesthouses.*
  - *Most of the hotels and restaurants and the finest beaches are all conveniently concentrated in the island's south-west corner.*

Paired work
- Ask the children to find more adverbs that help to give meaning to other words and to underline these words (adverbs in one colour and other words in another). Allow about ten minutes before inviting feedback.

Independent work
- Give each child photocopiable page 172 'Add an adverb' (or provide access to the interactive activity on the CD-ROM) and ask them to add their own adverbs in the gaps in the sentences to make the places attractive to tourists.

Review
- Invite a volunteer to read out the first sentence. Ask if anyone used a different adverb. Continue until all variations have been read. Compare the effects of the different adverbs. Repeat this for other sentences if there is time.

Curriculum objectives
- To use modal verbs or adverbs to indicate degrees of possibility.
- To select appropriate grammar and vocabulary, understanding how such choices can change and enhance meaning.
- To choose which shape of a letter to use when given choices and decide, as part of their personal style, whether or not to join specific letters.

Resources
Computers and internet access; information books and leaflets; photographs and travel brochures about Crete and Athens; pictures of Minos in Crete and Sounion in Greece; a map of the Mediterranean showing Crete and Athens; atlases of Europe; the children's notes from lesson 2; useful websites for information about Crete and Greece, bookmarked in advance of the lesson

5: Writing a travel guide to Minos and Sounion

Introduction
- Ensure that the children have their completed photocopiable sheets and their notes from lesson 3. Remind them of the purpose of the photocopiable sheet: to plan a draft travel guide to Minos in Crete and Sounion in Greece for tourists who want to see the sites of the story of 'Theseus and the Minotaur'.

Independent work
- Ask the children to use their draft and notes to help them to write their travel guide. Remind them about what they learned in lesson 4 about how adverbs can help to create effects, and ask them to try to use these in their writing.
- Remind them about an opening sentence to catch readers' imagination. This could be a question or an instruction, such as: *Where else could you..., Come to Sounion to see....* Also remind them that the final version should be written in their best handwriting.

> **Differentiation**
> - Read the children's draft plans and help them to write the first sentence of the final version of their travel guide. Ask them to make readers want to read more.

Review
- Ask the children to check their work for grammar and punctuation errors and then to swap with a partner to check again.

Week 4 lesson plans

These lessons are based around the myth of 'Daedalus and Icarus'. According to Ancient Greek myths, Daedalus, a renowned craftsman, created the labyrinth in which King Minos kept the Minotaur. Minos then had Daedalus imprisoned in a tower with his son Icarus to prevent them from disclosing the route through the labyrinth. Daedalus made wings from birds' feathers fixed together with wax, so that they could fly from the top of the tower and make their escape. After reading the story, the children discuss the behaviour of the characters, compare the feeling of imprisonment in the tower with the freedom of flying through the air and use figurative language to communicate these feelings. The story offers opportunities to explore metaphors, such as *flying too close to the sun* and spelling (words ending /shus/). The children also plan a puppet theatre play based on the story and write the script.

1: The myth 'Daedalus and Icarus'

Introduction
● Remind the class of the story of 'Theseus and the Minotaur'. Ask: *What did King Minos keep the Minotaur in?* Tell them that Minos had asked the best engineer he could find to build the labyrinth; his name was Daedalus (which means *clever worker* in Greek) and his assistant was his son, Icarus.

Whole-class work
● Ask: *How could Daedalus and Icarus become a threat to Minos?* (They might tell others how to find their way through the labyrinth.) *What could he do about this?* Write up the children's ideas and ask what they think he should have done, or whether he needed to do anything.
● Read the story of 'Daedalus and Icarus'. Give the class a minute or two to think about the themes of the story. Ask: *What themes did you notice in the story?* (Fear of attack by others/losing power, adventurousness/common sense, freedom/captivity.) Ask: *Who was afraid of attacks from others?* (Minos.) *How did he protect himself? Did he suspect the right people?* (No – his daughter, Ariadne, betrayed his trust.) *Who or what were in captivity?* (The Minotaur, Daedalus and Icarus.) *Why?* (The Minotaur was dangerous and might harm Minos or his people and, if someone else took it, they might use it to harm Minos. Daedalus and Icarus were imprisoned because Daedalus gave Ariadne the ball of string which helped Theseus survive the labyrinth and defeat the Minotaur.)
● Compare the captivity of Daedalus and Icarus with the feeling of freedom

Captivity	Freedom
shut in	flying
dark	bright
prison	soaring
cramped	free

as they flew through the air. Ask for words connected with captivity and the freedom of flying. List them in a table.

Group work
● Give each group two sheets of paper, headed 'Captivity' and 'Freedom' and ask the children to discuss and write words, phrases and sentences about each, including similes, for example, *fly like a bird, soar over the sea, close to the sun.*
● Ask them each to choose a word, phrase or sentence to copy in large, decorative writing and cut out to display alongside pictures of Icaria, Daedalus and Icarus.

Review
● Allow time for the children to read the displayed text, choosing parts they think work together like a poem.

Expected outcomes
● All children can discuss themes in a story and metaphors, improvise on a story and spell some words with /shus/ endings.
● Most children can also identify themes in stories and use voice and actions effectively in improvisations.
● Some children can also explain metaphors and spell a range of words with /shus/endings.

Curriculum objectives
● To continue to read and discuss an increasingly wide range of fiction.
● To participate in discussions about books that are read to them and those they can read for themselves, building on their own and others' ideas and challenging views courteously.

Resources
The story of 'Daedalus and Icarus' (a version of the story is available in *Greek Myths* by Marcia Williams but there are many other versions available); pictures of Daedalus and Icarus; a map of the Mediterranean area showing the Icarian Sea and the island of Icaria; pictures of Icaria; a display board with a blue background to represent the sea, and a large sun, onto which the pictures, map and the children's writing can be fixed, prepared in advance

■ SCHOLASTIC

2: Acting the story

Introduction

● Recap the story of 'Daedalus and Icarus' and ask the children to imagine the scene in the tower. Ask: *What did Daedalus do? What do you think he and Icarus talked about?* Discuss possible conversations between Daedalus and Icarus, including his final words as they leap from the tower and fly.
● Ask: *What might Daedalus have said? What do you think Icarus replied?* Ask them to imagine the flight, what they saw, how it felt to fly above the land, what Icarus might have said (to Daedalus or to himself) as he flew and what Daedalus said as he saw Icarus flying closer and closer to the sun.

Paired work

● Give the children time to re-read the story, then collect the text so that they will not be able to read from it as they enact the story. Ask them to act the story with their partner, using their voices to show their feelings while they were in their prison and while they were flying away. Visit each pair to help them to refine their role play – making their actions and voices as expressive as possible.

Review

● Ask each pair to join another pair so that they can each watch the others enact their play and give feedback about what was good – and ideas about parts they can improve.
● During design and technology lessons, introduce puppet-making: Daedalus and Icarus could be glove puppets with papier-mâché or paper bag heads fixed onto cardboard tubes.

Curriculum objectives
● In narrative, to describe settings, characters and atmosphere and integrate dialogue to convey character and advance the action.
● To perform their own compositions, using appropriate intonation, volume and movement so that the meaning is clear.

Resources
The story of 'Daedalus and Icarus'

3: Puppet play

Introduction

● Recap lesson 2 and tell the children that their task in this lesson is to use their role play from the previous lesson to help them to create a puppet play of the story of 'Daedalus and Icarus'. Tell them that the audience might know nothing about the story, or why 'Daedalus and Icarus' are imprisoned in the tower – so they will need to use the dialogue to tell them or have a narrator at the start. They should choose which they think is the more effective.

Paired work

● Arrange the pairs as for the previous lesson and give each pair photocopiable page 'Puppet play' from the CD-ROM to help them to plan their puppet play.
● To encourage them to use their own words, do not provide the text of the story, which they will now know.

> **Differentiation**
> ● If necessary, the children could enact the story again using their puppets with an adult helping to transcribe the dialogue.

Review

● Visit each pair and check that the dialogue tells the audience all they need to know. Useful questions: *Have you told the audience why Daedalus and Icarus are in the tower? How can you do this? When should you do this? How will they know that Daedalus is making wings?* (The puppet can't do this but the dialogue can show it.) *How will you show the puppets flying?*

Curriculum objectives
● In narrative, to describe settings, characters and atmosphere and integrate dialogue to convey character and advance the action.
● To identify how language, structure and presentation contribute to meaning.
● To perform their own compositions, using appropriate intonation, volume and movement so that the meaning is clear.

Resources
Daedalus and Icarus puppets (made with the class during design and technology lessons); photocopiable page 'Puppet play' from the CD-ROM

Curriculum objectives
● To discuss and evaluate how authors use language, including figurative language, considering the impact on the reader.

Resources
Dictionaries of quotations, saying and idioms (such as *Brewers Dictionary of Phrase and Fable, Dictionary of Idioms* by Linda and Roger Flavell); computers and internet access; photocopiable page 173 'Metaphors from stories'; useful websites for looking up metaphors and for Aesop's Fables, bookmarked in advance of the lesson

4: Metaphors

Introduction

● Recap *metaphor* and tell the class that many metaphors come from well-known stories, plays and poems, and that the metaphor *flying too close to the sun* comes from the story of 'Daedalus and Icarus'. Ask: *What do you think this metaphor means?*
● Tell them some other metaphors from stories, for example: *the writing on the wall* (a very severe warning – from the Bible, Daniel 5, where a warning to King Belshazzar appears on the wall during a banquet); *a dog in a manger* (someone who keeps something to prevent others having it but has no use for it him/herself – from Aesop's Fables).

Independent work

● Give out photocopiable page 173 'Metaphors from stories' and ask the children to read the metaphors and write their meanings, and to find out about the stories they come from. They can then choose a metaphor from the list provided and make up their own story about it.

> **Differentiation**
> ● If necessary, explain the metaphors for which the children are asked to make up stories.
> ● To increase the level of challenge, cover some or all of the meanings before copying and ask the children to look them up and explain them.

Review

● Ask the children to compare their answers with a partner and to make any corrections they think are needed. Invite volunteers to tell their metaphor stories.

Curriculum objectives
● To use knowledge of morphology and etymology in spelling and understand that the spelling of some words needs to be learned specifically, as listed in Appendix 1.

Resources
Individual whiteboards and pens; photocopiable page 174 'More /shus/ words'

5: Words ending /shus/

Introduction

● Recap adjectives, focusing on those made by adding a suffix to words to make adjectives ending with the sound /shus/.

Whole-class work

● Ask the class to write some of these /shus/ adjectives, and the words they come from, on their whiteboards: *gracious, spacious, infectious, anxious, conscious*. Ask them to underline the parts of the /shus/ suffix that differ. Ask: *Can you see why some are spelled like this?* (*Space* and *grace* already have 'c', *infectious* has 'ct'; *anxious* has 'x'.) Remind them that not all words with /shus/ endings come from words they will know, and that they have to learn their spellings, for example: *precious*.

Independent work

● Give out photocopiable page 174 'More /shus/ words' and ask them to match the /shus/ words to their meanings.

> **Differentiation**
> ● Most children should manage the activity on the photocopiable sheet. To increase the level of demand, delete the /shus/ endings from the words in the list and enter only the root words, if English, and the first part of any word with a Greek or Latin root.

Review

● Ask the class to turn over their photocopiable sheets so that they cannot see the words. Then ask different children to turn over the photocopiable sheet and read out a /shus/ word for the class to write on their whiteboards, then check it. Point out that some of the root words for these come from other languages – mainly Greek and Latin.

Week 5 lesson plans

These lessons begin with the very short myth of 'Arachne and Athena', which the children compare with other Greek myths they know and again discuss the behaviour of the Greek deities and other characters. This leads to writing about gods behaving badly and the creation of their own 'Greek myths'. It also provides an opportunity to explore word derivations, beginning with *arachnid/arachnophobia*.

1: Arachne and Athena

Introduction

● Point out Athena on the Mount Olympus display and read out her name. Share some key facts about Athena, for example: the city of Athens is named after her; she was the goddess of wisdom, warfare, arts and crafts; she was the daughter of Zeus and Metis; Athena's symbols include snakes, olive trees and owls; her Roman equivalent is Minerva.
● Tell the class that they are going to hear a very short story about how Athena treated a mortal named Arachne.
● Write up the name Arachne and remind the children of words with 'ch' pronounced /k/ and tell them that many of these come from Greek (for example, *chaos, orchid, chameleon*).

Whole-class work

● Explain that the Ancient Greeks believed that each of their gods and goddesses was in charge of part of nature and kept it working properly, and that all mortal (human) abilities and personal characteristics also came from the deities, with different gods or goddesses in charge of these. At different times the Greeks prayed to different gods to give them the strengths they needed, such as skill in a craft, and skill or luck in battle or sport. They praised and thanked their gods for these gifts.
● Tell the story of 'Arachne and Athena'. Ask: *Why did Athena turn Arachne into a spider?* (She wanted to punish her because Arachne would not agree that her gift of weaving came from Athena, the goddess of wisdom and skill in crafts; also Athena was jealous of Arachne's skill.)
● Ask: *What themes are there in this story?* (Power, jealousy, punishment.) Discuss who is powerful, and how; who is jealous, of whom, and why; who punishes whom, what for, and whether this is justified.

Independent work

● Ask the children to write character profiles for Athena and Arachne, using words such as *stubborn*, *proud*, *jealous* and *powerful* – and to justify these with evidence from the story.

> **Differentiation**
> ● Discuss the meanings of *stubborn*, *proud*, *jealous* and *powerful* in relation to everyday life, other stories or characters in television series.

Review

● Read some of the character profiles and ask the class if they agree/disagree, and why.

Expected outcomes

● All children can write a character profile and headline, give opinions about story characters' behaviour, write a story based on one read and identify root words.
● Most children can also support opinions with evidence and identify and explain a greater range of root words.
● Some children can also use knowledge of root words, prefixes and suffixes from Greek to explain new words they meet.

Curriculum objectives

● To increase their familiarity with a wide range of books, including myths.
● To identify and discuss themes and conventions across a range of writing.
● To participate in discussions about books that are read to them and those they can read for themselves, building on their own and others' ideas and challenging views courteously.

Resources

Your own adaptation of story of 'Arachne and Athena' to tell, rather than read, to the class

Curriculum objectives
● To increase their familiarity with a wide range of books, including myths.
● To make comparisons within and across books.
● To identify and discuss themes and conventions across a range of writing.
● To précis longer passages.
● To use a colon to introduce a list.

Resources
Children's versions of various Greek myths

2: Comparing myths

Introduction

● Tell the class that in this lesson they can choose which Greek myths to read: their task is to list any themes that appear in different myths and to make a note of any bad behaviour by the gods/goddesses and about ways in which the gods and goddesses try to trick or outwit one another.

Independent work

● Ask the children to write the title of any story they read and model (using the myth of 'Arachne and Athena') how to summarise the plot, listing, below the title, any themes they find in the story. Encourage them to use a colon to introduce their lists.

> **Differentiation**
> ● Read the first story with the children. Ask: *Who is the story about? What did he/she do? Why? What happened in the end?* Help them to write this down very briefly. If necessary help them to identify themes.

Review

● Invite volunteers to read out a summary of a story they read and to say what themes they noticed. Encourage the children to read more of these stories between lessons. Keep their notes for lesson 3.

Curriculum objectives
● To identify and discuss themes and conventions across a range of writing.
● In narratives, to describe settings, characters and atmosphere and integrate dialogue to convey character and advance the action.
● To choose which shape of a letter to use when given choices and deciding, as part of their personal style, whether or not to join specific letters.
● To choose the writing implement that is best suited for a task.

Resources
Children's versions of various Greek myths; the children's notes from lesson 2; newspaper headlines about bad behaviour, for example: *Thieves target elderly; Pensioners riot in post office; Playground closes due to vandalism; Drink driver injures horse*

3: Gods behaving badly

Introduction

● Tell the class that their task in this lesson is to continue reading Greek myths and to make a note of any bad behaviour by the gods and goddesses. Remind them how newspaper headlines are written and show them some headlines about people's bad behaviour. Ask: *Are headlines sentences?* (Not quite: they might have verbs but words such as *is, are* and *the* are usually omitted.) *Which tense is used?* (The present, even though the events took place in the past.) Ask: *What would you write about Athena in a headline?* Ask them to include an adjective, for example: *Jealous Athena turns nation's best weaver into spider.*

Independent work

● Ask the children to write a headline that contains an adjective for each of the Greek gods and goddesses they know. They should try these out on scrap paper and then, when they are happy with them, write them neatly (perhaps in colour) for the Mount Olympus display.

Group work

● To accompany each headline, ask the children to use their, and others' notes from the previous lesson to help them to write a summary of the god's or goddess's story.

Review

● Ask the children to read out their headlines, without the god's/goddess's name. Ask the others: *Who is the god or goddess?* Then ask the children to read out the summary that goes with the headline.

4: My own Greek myth

Introduction
- Ask a child to name a Greek god or goddess; ask another to say something about his or her character; ask another to describe something he or she did. Then give the children a minute or two to think of something that isn't in the myths but is the kind of thing the god or goddess might do. Share ideas.

Independent work
- Ask the children to choose a Greek god or goddess and to think of a story idea for their chosen deity. Maybe a mortal upsets a god, or someone has a bad olive harvest, or there is a drought. Encourage them to use pictures and books about Ancient Greece for inspiration.
- Give each child photocopiable page 175 'My Greek myth' to help them to plan their story. Keep the planning session short so that the children can get on with their story.

Paired work
- Ask the children to swap plans with a friend, to read one another's plans and to ask about anything that isn't clear to them. Ask them to discuss powerful words they could use to describe what happens and to create the atmosphere they want.

Review
- Read some of the stories, as far as they go, and indicate where more powerful vocabulary can be used. Suggest words to link paragraphs and to lead on from one sentence to another within paragraphs (cohesion).

5: Etymology

Introduction
- Remind the class of the names Arachne and Athena. If not covered before, ask: *What words does the name Arachne remind you of?* (*Arachnid* – spider; *arachnophobia* – fear of spiders.) Tell the class that the word for the group of animals that spiders belong to – *arachnids* – comes from this story, and that *phobia* comes from a Greek word for *fear*. Write up these words.

Whole-class work
- Read out a word from photocopiable page 'Words from Greek' from the CD-ROM and ask the children to write it and hold up their whiteboards. Discuss some incorrect spellings, acknowledging plausible attempts. Show the children how to look up the word in an etymological dictionary to find the Greek word(s) it comes from.
- Remind them how to speed up their dictionary work (opening the dictionary in approximately the right place, using the words at the tops of the pages). Remind them to look at the second, third and fourth letter of the word for alphabetical order.

Independent work
- Give each child the photocopiable sheets and ask them to tick what they think is the correct meaning for each word. They should then look the words up, write the Greek word they come from, check their meanings and change their answers (in a different colour) if necessary.

Review
- Ask the children if they found any words linked to stories they have read.

Curriculum objectives
- To use a wide range of devices to build cohesion within and across paragraphs.
- In narratives, to describe settings, characters and atmosphere and integrate dialogue to convey character and advance the action.
- To use and understand grammatical terminology in Appendix 2 accurately and appropriately in their writing and reading.

Resources
Pictures of Greece, including mountains, sea, coast, islands, old buildings, statues and so on; textbooks about the Ancient Greeks; photocopiable page 175 'My Greek myth'

Curriculum objectives
- To use knowledge of morphology and etymology in spelling and understand that the spelling of some words needs to be learned specifically, as listed in Appendix 1.
- To use the first three or four letters of a word to check spelling, meaning or both of these in a dictionary.

Resources
Photocopiable page 'Words from Greek' from the CD-ROM; dictionaries (as detailed as possible); etymological dictionaries; individual whiteboards and pens

Expected outcomes
● All children can identify rhymes and patterns in poems.
● Most children can identify powerful language and describe its effect on the reader, and use some language to create effects.
● Some children can consistently use powerful language to create effect on the reader.

Curriculum objectives
● To discuss and evaluate how authors use language, including figurative language, considering the impact on the reader.
● To continue to read an increasingly wide range of poetry.
● To identify and discuss themes and conventions in and across a wide range of writing.
● To identify how language, structure and presentation contribute to meaning.
● To use dictionaries to check the spelling and meaning of words.
● To use the first three or four letters of a word to check spelling, meaning or both of these in a dictionary.

Resources
Photocopiable page 'Ancient Greek odes' from the CD-ROM; dictionaries

Week 6 lesson plans

These lessons are based on the poetry of the Ancient Greeks. The poems chosen, from the victory odes of Pindar and Bacchylides, are on the theme of sport. After enjoying the poems, discussing the purpose and features of an ode and exploring the poetic language, the children read non-fiction sources to find out about the modern Olympic Games, and then write their own victory odes.

I: Ancient Greek poetry (I)

Introduction
● Tell the class that they are going to read a poem from Ancient Greece that is part of an ode. Explain that an ode is usually quite a long poem, and that the Ancient Greek odes were written to be sung or chanted to praise something or someone, or to celebrate something.
● Tell or remind the children that the Olympic Games were first held in Ancient Greece more than 2000 years ago, for men only, because the Ancient Greek leaders wanted to encourage men to be fit and healthy, so that they would be good soldiers. (Women had separate competitions.)
● Introduce the poems they will read: the first, from the 'Victory odes of Pindar', is about the winner of a race, who came to the Greek mainland because of civil war in his own country, which was famous for its springs, and became famous as a runner.
● The second, from 'Victory odes of Bacchylides' is about the race itself, giving a lively description of the race. (The race was run back and forth along a track marked with posts at each end, with spectators very close to the track.) It is a humorous poem that describes how the winner, smeared with oil (normal for Greek athletes, who ran naked), ran on into the crowd.

Group work
● Give out photocopiable page 'Ancient Greek odes' from the CD-ROM and ask the children to read the first passage together and look up any words they do not know. They should then discuss who it is about and what it tells us about him, as well as the purpose of the poem. Ask them also to mark any rhyming words and describe the rhyme pattern. (There is a half rhyme at the ends of lines 1 and 2 (*games, fame*) and lines 3 and 4 (*home, own*). Explain half-rhyme as nearly rhyming, usually with a similar but not identical consonant or vowel sound.)

> **Differentiation**
> ● Arrange mixed-ability groups and remind the children that, as for any discussion, everyone should have a chance to speak and should be listened to politely. Remind them to ask others what they think.

Review
● Ask children from different groups to answer the questions: *Who does the poem praise?* (A runner.) *What did he do?* (He won four races at the Olympic Games.) *What does the poem tell us about the runner?* (He had to leave his own country because of a war there and came to live in Greece. He wouldn't have become famous if he had stayed there.) *Which word tells us that he had to leave?* (*exiled*) *What do we know about the country he left?* (It was famous for its bubbling springs.) *What is the rhyme pattern?* Explain that the poem was translated from Greek but that translators try to match the rhyme pattern.

Curriculum objectives
● To discuss and evaluate how authors use language, including figurative language, considering the impact on the reader.
● To continue to read an increasingly wide range of poetry.
● To identify and discuss the themes and conventions in and across a wide range of writing.
● To identify how language, structure and presentation contribute to meaning.

Resources
Photocopiable page 'Ancient Greek odes' from the CD-ROM; highlighter pens

2: Ancient Greek poetry (2)

Introduction
● Tell the class that they are going to read another poem from Ancient Greece – again part of an ode. Recap the meaning of *ode*.

Whole-class work
● Read the second poem on photocopiable page 'Ancient Greek odes' with the children. Ask: *How is this different from the last poem you read about a runner?* (This describes the race in detail. The first poem praises the runner and tells his story.) Ask: *Does the poem have a fast or slow pace? What is the rhythm of this poem like?* (Running.) *How does this help to give it meaning?* (It sounds like a race.)

Group work
● Ask the children to re-read the poem and to underline any powerful words that help them to see, hear and feel what it was like watching the race. Also ask them to highlight any rhyming words and describe the rhyme pattern, and to discuss how the rhyme pattern and the lengths of the lines help to create the rhythm.

Review
● Ask children from different groups to give feedback from their discussions. Ask: *How did the poet make you feel that you were close to the runner?* (He describes the runner *spraying oil* over anyone near him. This might have meant sweat or oil or both – Ancient Greeks, like the Romans, used to rub oil into their skin – and the athletes were naked for the Games.)

Curriculum objectives
● To read books that are structured in different ways and read for a range of purposes.
● To retrieve, record and present information from non-fiction.
● To ask questions to improve their understanding of what they have read.

Resources
Information books, leaflets and online sources of information about the most recent Olympic Games and the athletes and about the Ancient Olympic Games; computers and internet access

3: The Olympic Games

Introduction
● Remind the class about the poems they read about the ancient Olympic Games. Ask: *What events did we find out about?* (Running races.) *What sports do you know in the modern Olympic Games? What did you find out about the runner who won four races?* (He came from another country to live in Greece.) *Can you name any modern Olympians who came to live in Great Britain from other countries and became champions?* Some of the best known are runner Mo Farah (Somalia), gymnast Beth Tweddle (South Africa), tennis player Laura Robson (Australia) and cyclist Bradley Wiggins (Belgium).

Paired work
● Ask the children to find out about the different sports and athletes of the ancient and modern Olympic Games and to list the similarities and differences. Remind them to write in note form. They could use a table, for example:

Ancient Olympic Games	Modern Olympic Games
At Olympia Every 4 yrs Men only Naked	Different place each time Every 4 yrs Men & women Clothed

Review
● Ask each pair to share their findings with another; repeat this with other pairs, if time allows.

Curriculum objectives
● To note and develop initial ideas, drawing on reading and research where necessary.
● To select appropriate grammar and vocabulary, understanding how such choices can change and enhance meaning.

Resources
Films (DVD or online) of modern Olympic events

4: A modern Olympic ode

Introduction

● Remind the class about the poems they read about the ancient Olympic Games. Ask: *What did you find out from the poems about the ancient Olympic Games?* Focus on the first poem's story and the second poem's depiction of the race itself and making the reader feel the atmosphere.

Whole-class work

● Show a selection of short film clips of events and medal presentations from the most recent Olympic Games and ask: *Which event did you enjoy the most? Who was it about?* (If the names are not known, ask what sport they were taking part in.) *What did you like about it? What was the atmosphere like?*

Independent work

● Ask the children to make a note of any words and phrases that come to mind when they think of their favourite events and to write their own Olympic ode. Their ode could either be in praise of an athlete, like the first poem they read, or a description of an athlete in action, like the second. As they write, help them to find expressive vocabulary to create effects or to tell the athlete's story.

> **Differentiation**
> ● Ask an adult helper to watch a film of an event again with the children and to help them to think of words to express their responses to it.

Review

● Read some of the children's odes and ask the class: *Which words help you to picture or feel what the event was like?* or *What does the poem tell you about the athlete?*

Curriculum objectives
● To use knowledge of morphology and etymology in spelling and understand that the spelling of some words needs to be learned specifically, as listed in Appendix 1.

Resources
Dictionaries; etymological dictionaries

5: Words from Greek

Introduction

● Display a list of words connected with the Olympic Games that come from Greek: *athlete, discus, gymnast, marathon, decathlon, pentathlon, triathlon, Paralympics.* Ask: *What connects all these words?* (Sports/Olympic Games; they all come from Greek.)

Paired work

● Tell the children that many English words come from Greek and ask them to look up those in the list and write their meanings. Ask them also to underline parts of the words that are also parts of other words, for example: *deca* (*decagon, Decalogue*). Ask them to write these words and their meanings and to check whether these words are really linked. For example, *decay* begins 'dec' but is not connected with *decathlon*.
● Ask them to make a note of any interesting stories they find that are connected with the words.

Review

● Ask different children to give the meaning of a word and to name any other word they found that is linked to it. Write up the words and underline the common roots, prefixes or suffixes. Invite volunteers to tell any stories they found linked to the words: for example, the first marathon, the Ten Commandments.

Curriculum objectives
● To punctuate bullet points consistently.
● To use colons to introduce a list.

Grammar and punctuation: Bullet points

Revise
● Use starter activity 9 'Bullet points'.
● Next, display a text that includes bullet points. Ask the children to name the punctuation marks they see in the text. Ask: *How do the bullet points help?* To illustrate this, change the list so that the items follow each other along the same line(s). Ask: *What difference has this made?* Point out that if we want to make an impact, for example in an advertisement or warning, bullet points highlight each item more effectively.

Assess
● Ask the children to write an advertisement for a new type of ice cream that has a soft toffee centre surrounded by a creamy layer that is covered with a thin, crisp layer of milk chocolate and crispy bits of biscuit on it.

Further practice
● Collect advertisements that make specific points about the product and ask the children what difference any bullet points make.

Curriculum objectives
● To use knowledge of morphology and etymology in spelling and understand that the spelling of some words needs to be learned specifically, as listed in Appendix 1.

Resources
Individual whiteboards and pens; dictionaries

Spelling: Words from Greek

Revise
● Use starter activity 10 'Spelling words with Greek suffixes and prefixes'.
● Next, write *television* on the board. Ask the children to read the word. Ask: *Can you split this word into two parts that can each be used in other words?* Tell them that *tele* and *vision* come from Greek. Ask for other words that contain the prefix 'tele-': *telegraph, telephone, telecommunication, telescope.* Ask: *What do you think 'tele-' means?* (Far.) Ask them to use this meaning to help them to figure out what the words mean literally. Ask them to check these using a dictionary.
● Write *telescope* on the board and ask for another word with the suffix *scope* (*microscope*). Ask: *What is a telescope used for?* (Looking at far-off objects.) *What is a microscope used for?* (Looking at small objects.) Ask if they can figure out what *scope* and *micro* mean.

Assess
● List words that contain the same prefix or suffix and ask the children to use their knowledge of one or two of the words to help them to figure out what the others mean, and then to look them up to check. For example:

graph photograph graphology	microscope microbe microchip microfilm	horoscope stethoscope kaleidoscope microscope telescope	asterisk astrology astronomy asteroid astronaut
polygon polyanthus polygamy	automatic automobile autobiography	descend ascend transcend	xylophone telephone gramophone microphone

Further practice
● Use words the children know to figure out the meanings of other Greek prefixes or suffixes: *grateful, gratitude; optician, optical.*

Curriculum objectives
● To discuss and evaluate how authors use language, including figurative language, considering the impact on the reader.

Resources
Different versions of the Christian Bible (including the King James version); the story 'The Good Samaritan' from the Good News Bible or a children's Bible

Reading: Figurative language

Revise

● Remind the class that they have read different kinds of stories and that some of these, especially myths and legends, are remembered in everyday language by metaphors that come from them. Remind the children of the example from a Greek myth – *flying too close to the sun* – and ask which myth it comes from and what it means.

● Ask them for other examples of metaphors from stories. The following should be familiar: *the Midas touch, dog in the manger, the writing on the wall.* Remind them that a metaphor describes something, someone or an action as if it is something else.

● Provide the Bible story 'The Good Samaritan' and ask the children to read it in pairs. Ask if they have heard anyone described as a *Good Samaritan*. Ask: *What do you think this metaphor means?*

● Tell them that many common metaphors come from the Christian Bible. Ask if they have heard the metaphor *he washed his hands of it*. Ask: *What do you think it means?* Give out copies of the section of the story of the Crucifixion (Matthew 27:24). Allow time for the children to read it and then invite volunteers to explain what Pilate meant when he said this. (He was having nothing more to do with the matter. Other people could take responsibility for what happened.)

Assess

● Give the children a list of metaphors and ask them to say what they think they mean (or match them to a list of meanings). Examples: *a fish out of water; bring home the bacon; out of the blue; cheek by jowl; to get cold feet; cross your fingers; a feather in your cap; on the grapevine; go haywire; left high and dry; from the horse's mouth; jump the gun; break the ice; in the limelight; mind your Ps and Qs; a skeleton in the cupboard; on tenterhooks.*

Further practice

● Read other Bible stories and look for the metaphors *bite the dust* (Psalm 72:9); *by the skin of my teeth* (Job 19:20); *Can a leopard change his spots?* (Jeremiah 13:23); *a fly in the ointment* (Ecclesiastes 10:1 [King James Version]); *put the words in his mouth* (2 Samuel 14:3): *rise and shine* (Isaiah 60:1); *scapegoat* (Leviticus 16:9 –10); *a sign of the times* (Matthew 16:3 [King James Version]); *see eye to eye* (Isaiah 52:8 [King James version]); *in the twinkling of an eye* (1 Corinthians 15:52). Explain what they mean. Look out for examples in modern usage.

Curriculum objectives

● To select appropriate grammar and vocabulary, understanding how such choices can change and enhance meaning.
● To assess the effectiveness of their own and others' writing.

Resources

An Ancient Greek myth that the children have not already read; photocopiable page 175 'My Greek myth'; dictionaries

Writing: Writing a myth

Revise

● Read an Ancient Greek myth with the class. Give them time to think about the story and to respond to it. Ask: *What caused the problem? Why? What happened because of this? How did the story end? Was the problem resolved? How?* Discuss the gods' and goddesses' wishes for power and wanting to outwit one another.

● Ask the children to imagine gods and goddesses, like those of Ancient Greece, in our time and place. What might they do here? Ask: *Can you think of a famous mortal they might think is too powerful and so want to punish (or perhaps take over this power)?* This might be a celebrity: a pop star, footballer, business leader and so on.

● Discuss useful words for the story, especially for creating effects; remind them of what they learned about using adverbs to change the effects of adjectives when they wrote holiday brochures.

Assess

● Ask the children to use their notes and photocopiable page 175 'My Greek myth' to help them to plan their story. Provide dictionaries.

Further practice

● Read other Greek myths and identify the character who wants to become more powerful or to punish another character (and why); how he or she tries to do this; what happens as a result; how the story ends. Write modern myths based on the stories.

Name: _____   Date: _____

Greek god factfile

- Create your factfile below.

Name of god or goddess
_____

God/goddess of _____
_____

Special place(s) _____
_____

Symbol
_____

A picture of _____

Magic powers _____
_____

Stories _____
_____
_____
_____
_____
_____
_____
_____
_____

I can write a factfile for a Greek god.

How did you do?

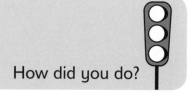

PHOTOCOPIABLE

Bullet points

■ Read each passage, and then rewrite it using bullet points to make the list stand out. Use a colon to introduce your list.

1. We wrote some safety rules for a trip to a farm: wear wellies, stay with the group, wash your hands at the end of the visit, don't touch animals without permission, don't touch your mouth or face after touching animals, don't touch machinery, at the end say thank you.	
2. When you first take your pet puppy home it will need a comfortable bed, a bowl for water, a bowl for food, a collar, a lead, some puppy toys.	
3. If you go on holiday in Greece you can enjoy sunshine, ancient buildings, good restaurants, traditional dancing, art and much more.	

I can use bullet points in a list.

How did you do?

Making verbs (2)

■ Read the sentences. Find the verbs with a suffix. Underline the suffix. Write the noun or adjective the verb comes from.

Every night we watched the sky darken.   _____

I phoned Sam to apologise for hitting him.   _____

We learned how to simplify fractions.   _____

The BBC is going to serialise the book soon.   _____

They lost their jobs so they had to economise.   _____

You can purify water using tablets.   _____

■ Add a suffix to change the noun or adjective in brackets to a verb.

The roadworker wore ear protectors so that the drill wouldn't _____ (deaf) her.

They had to _____ (wide) the road to allow buses to pass.

The teacher asked us to _____ (summary) the book.

In the 17th century the British tried to _____ (colony) parts of Africa.

I tried to _____ (active) my SIM card.

Christians sing hymns to _____ (glory) God.

■ Change these nouns to verbs. Use them in sentences on a separate sheet of paper.

television _____   memory _____   formula _____

■ Change these adjectives to verbs. Use them in sentences on a separate sheet of paper.

hard _____   false _____   solid _____

I can add a suffix to a noun or adjective to make a verb.

How did you do?

Name: _____   Date: _____

Travel guide planner

- Use this page to help you plan a travel guide to Minos and Sounion. Write notes.

Audience	What sort of tourist are you writing for? (Families, people with special interests, older people, younger people.)	Pictures	What kind of picture will attract their attention? List any you found, and where they are from.

Information to include

The land and sea	Weather/climate	Historical sites	Stories

Title/headline

What will interest your audience? Why?

Headings

Opening sentence

Useful words

Powerful verbs	Appealing adjectives	Adverbs to enhance

Summary

I can plan a travel guide that gives information and attracts tourists.

How did you do?

Add an adverb

■ Underline the adverbs.

I. Walk through lovingly tended gardens or just relax by the pool.

2. The moors provide ruggedly beautiful countryside for walking.

3. Watch local craftspeople creating intricately carved pictures.

4. Linger in the fragrantly spicy marketplace.

5. Watch the fishing boats bobbing on gently rolling waves.

6. See the eerily changing shadows in the caves at night.

■ Write the adverbs.

_____

_____

_____

■ Add an adverb to each sentence to make the adjective more meaningful.

7. Swim in the _____ clear sea.

8. Stay at one of three _____ stylish hotels.

9. Climb the hill to the _____ beautiful castle.

10. Ride a _____ swaying camel along the beach.

II. Watch _____ fast runners complete the annual uphill run.

12. Sample _____ varied loaves at the many artisan bakeries.

Useful adverbs

elegantly	amazingly	sparklingly
astonishingly	magnificently	gently

I can use adverbs to make adjectives more effective.

How did you do?

Metaphors from stories

■ Link each metaphor to its meaning.

Metaphor	Meanings
a fish out of water	look foolish
loose cannon	spend very little
let the cat out of the bag	give away a secret
get the sack	out of place
live on a shoestring	lose your job
have egg on your face	someone who might say or do something dangerous or silly

■ Look up these metaphors and write their meanings.

a) a wolf in sheep's clothing _____

b) Pandora's box _____

c) a dog in a manger _____

d) to cry wolf _____

e) the Midas touch _____

f) the straw that broke the camel's back _____

■ Choose one of them and write a summary of the story it comes from.

Metaphor (_____) is from _____

_____

I can find the meanings of metaphors.

How did you do?

More /shus/ words

- Write the endings of the /shus/ words. Read the words.
- Match the words to their meanings.

pre _____

ambi _____

deli _____

cau _____

vi _____

fero _____

atro _____

no _____

Meanings

| wanting to do |

| important or difficult tasks |

| fierce |

| poisonous |

| nasty and dangerous |

| dreadful |

| very dear |

| careful |

| tasty |

- Add a /shus/ ending to these words.
- Look them up and write their meanings.

/shus/ word   **Meaning**

nutri _____   _____

_____

mali _____   _____

_____

conscien _____   _____

_____

supersti _____   _____

_____

I can spell /shus/ endings.

How did you do?

PHOTOCOPIABLE   ■SCHOLASTIC www.scholastic.co.uk

Name: _____   Date: _____

My Greek myth

- Use this page to plan your own Greek myth.

Greek god or goddess	Other characters

Setting	The event that starts the story

What happens as a result

How the problem is resolved

Conclusion

Useful words

I can write a story in the style of a Greek myth.

How did you do?

The North Pole

These lessons begin with non-fiction texts from which the children find information about the causes of climate change, how this is affecting the Arctic ice cap and its implications for wildlife, future climate change and humans. In addition to reading about the Arctic the children watch audio-visual material and make notes on what they learn – with a focus on effective note-taking. They write summaries of the main points and use the information to help them to debate climate change, using persuasive language.

The children use their growing knowledge of the Arctic and ideas from a story about a wolf and a grizzly bear to help them to write their own adventure story featuring a polar bear. They learn about the explorer Fridtjof Nansen; their reading provides opportunities to discuss how language has changed and to write a diary of one of the explorers in the first person. The issue of overfishing is explored, with a discussion about whether we should eat fish and a focus on the characteristics of persuasive language.

Finally, the children read poetry on the environment, noting poetic devices and features of poetic language before writing their own poems on the subject.

Expected prior learning
- Can use vocabulary to explain the grammar features learned in Year 5.
- Can distinguish between fact and opinion.
- Can write brief notes.
- Can outline the basic features of an adventure story.
- Can use correct verb agreement consistently.
- Can outline the structure of a discussion text.
- Can name the poetic techniques looked at in Year 5.

Overview of progression
- The texts provide opportunities for children to develop research skills, checking facts and distinguishing between facts and opinions.
- They also explore writing styles: structural devices, grammatical features and language. They are taught how to use appropriate structural devices, cohesion, grammar and punctuation and how to proofread and redraft their writing.
- The children develop narrative skills by writing an adventure story, using a published author's work as model and drawing on their research a.
- In their reading they encounter homophones and words with silent letters.

Creative context
- This chapter has strong links with geography and environmental issues such as climate change, overfishing and the preservation of habitats.
- This can also feed into science work on animals (polar bears, sea creatures).

Preparation
For week 3, you will need *Lone Wolf* by Kathryn Lasky or another story written from the point of view of an animal struggling for its survival.

You will also need:
Pictures, information and websites about the Arctic, polar bears and climate change; world maps and globes; maps of the Arctic and Canada; a documentary about climate change (see week 2, lesson 2); pictures of Arctic exploration; labels and packaging from fish products; promotional leaflets about eating fish; internet access; individual whiteboards; dictionaries; highlighter pens.

On the CD-ROM you will find:
Media resources 'Arctic', 'Nansen and team setting off', 'Inuit people'; interactive activities 'Homophone quiz', 'Silent letters', 'Words ending in '-ant' and '-ent''; photocopiable pages 'On thin ice', 'Polar bears under threat', 'Extract from *Lone Wolf*', 'Nansen's idea', 'Madcap plan or brilliant idea?', 'Nansen's route map', 'The fish that disappeared', 'Inuit poems', 'Behold, my brothers', 'Important Notice', 'Words whose endings sound like 'shun'', 'Stop whaling campaign', 'Halloween', 'Ghosts', 'Pigeons'

■ SCHOLASTIC

Chapter at a glance

An overview of the chapter. For curriculum objective codes, please see pages 8–10.

Week	Lesson	Curriculum objectives	Summary of activities	Outcome
1	1	RC: 13, 16	Discuss what they know about the Arctic, reading a report on the effects of climate change there and identifying the main points.	• Can distinguish between facts and opinions. • Can make notes on the main points of a non-fiction text.
	2	RC: 13, 16	Read a second report on the plight of polar bears in the Arctic and compare it with the previous one read.	• Can make notes on the main points of a non-fiction text and compare two reports on the same topic.
	3	RC: 2, 13, 17, 20 WC: 6	Recap on what they know about the plight of polar bears, write questions to help with research, researching and noting answers.	• Can ask questions that will help with understanding and make notes from a range of non-fiction sources.
	4	WC: 2, 7, 8, 9, 27	Read a second report on the plight of polar bears, noting key points and comparing it with the previous report read.	• Can use organisational devices such as bullet points in presenting information from a non-fiction. • Can punctuate bullet points.
	5	WT: 3	Recap homophones. Spell a selection of homophones linked with the texts read in recent lessons.	• Can distinguish between and spell a range of homophones.
2	1	RC: 13 WT: 9	Watch, and make notes on, a documentary about climate change effects in the Arctic. Decide which points to make a note of.	• Can identify the key points in a documentary and make notes on them.
	2	RC: 13, 17, 20	Watch the documentary from lesson 2 again, checking they have not missed any key points. Plan a report on an issue connected with climate change.	• Can plan a non-chronological report.
	3	RC: 13, 17 WT: 5 WC: 2	Write a report using notes made in previous lessons.	• Can write a non-chronological report.
	4	WC: 1, 2, 4, 7, 9, 19, 21	Use what they have learned about climate change to write a persuasive text in the form of a cartoon story, using modal verbs to express choice, and for emphasis.	• Can plan and write a persuasive text in an engaging way.
	5	WT: 2	Spell words with silent letters.	• Can spell a range of words with silent letters.
3	1	RC: 9 WT: 9 WC: 2, 3	Start to read *Lone Wolf* by Kathryn Lasky. Use the opening as a model for their own story about an endangered animal. Draft the opening.	• Can use a story opening as a model for their own.
	2	RC: 9 WC: 2, 3	Continue to read *Lone Wolf*. Continue to draft their own animal story.	• Can use a story as a model for their own.
	3	WC: 2, 3	Continue to read *Lone Wolf*. Draft the ending of their own story.	• Can plan the ending of a longer story.
	4	WC: 4	Discuss how Kathryn Lasky uses language in *Lone Wolf* to create effects. Use what they have learned as they improve and redraft parts of their own stories.	• Can use language to create effects.
	5	WT: 8, 9 WC: 5, 7, 13	Examine a passage of dialogue from *Lone Wolf* and discuss how the author uses language to tell the story and to show the characters' feelings. Add dialogue to stories.	• Can integrate dialogue into a story.
4	1	RC: 1, 9, 10, 12, 17, 21	Read a non-fiction report about Fridtjof Nansen's plan for reaching the North Pole. Discuss the opinions of people at the time and write their own opinion based on the evidence supplied.	• Can express an opinion supported by evidence.
	2	RC: 1, 9, 10, 17	Look at maps and read about Nansen's planned route; ask questions about it and read to find the answers.	• Can raise questions to deepen their understanding and use non-fiction sources to find the answers.
	3	RC: 19 WC: 2, 14	Look at a photograph of the unexpected meeting between Nansen and Frederick Jackson in Franz Josef Land; discuss the explorers' feelings and re-enact the meeting.	• Can enact a scene they have read about, using dialogue.
	4	WC: 2, 8, 9, 10, 11, 13	Read a section of Nansen's journal and writing the 'journal' of one of his crew in order to tell the story.	• Can write in the first person, in the past tense, with verbs and subjects agreeing and the tense consistent.
	5	WC: 11, 12	Change a first-person recount to the third person, with appropriate agreement of verbs.	• Can write in the first or third person, with verbs and subjects agreeing.

Chapter at a glance

Week	Lesson	Curriculum objectives	Summary of activities	Outcome
5	1	RC: 1, 13, 16 WC: 26	Read labels and leaflets about fish to find the locations of fisheries. Read a (non-fiction) report about the collapse of the Grand Banks fishery off Newfoundland. Make notes. Discuss the reasons for this and give opinions.	• Can collect information from non-fiction to support and present an opinion.
	2	RC: 1, 19	State facts and opinions from the report they read in lesson 1. Enact discussions between the holders of different opinions about the fisheries' problems and what should be done about them.	• Can present an opinion in role play.
	3	RC: 15	Read a persuasive text on overfishing and note how the writer uses facts and language to persuade the reader.	• Can use persuasive language.
	4	RC: 19 WC: 4	Use what they have learned about climate change and overfishing to help them to take part in a debate on whether we should continue to eat fish.	• Can take part in a class debate.
	5	WT: 4	Spell words ending '-ant' and '-ent'. Learning clues that will help with the spelling of some of these.	• Can spell a greater range of words ending '-ant' and '-ent'.
6	1	RC: 1, 3, 5, 7	Read and discuss the poetry of the Inuit. Look at pictures of traditional and modern Inuit settlements and discuss how the poetry reflects these. Choose a poem to learn.	• Can learn a poem by heart and recite it.
	2	RC: 1, 3, 5, 15	Read a Native American speech that expresses feelings in a very poetic way. Discuss the messages and how they are expressed.	• Can answer questions about the sentiments expressed in a poem.
	3	RC: 1, 5, 15 WT: 5, 6	Read a modern poem on the environment, then look up any new words. Make and compare notes on what the poet is saying, and how.	• Can use a dictionary and discussion to help them to understand a more difficult poem.
	4	WC: 1, 2, 9, 10	Read a modern poem warning about the dangers of lack of care for the environment. Use it as a model for their own poems.	• Can use a poem as a model for their own.
	5	WT: 1, 4, 5	Discuss words from the poem they read that end '-ssion'. Spell '-ssion' words and explore their roots.	• Can spell a greater range of nouns ending '-ssion'.

Background knowledge

Command: The imperative form of a verb.

Documentary: A non-fiction film about an issue.

Exclamation: Speech that expresses a short burst of humour, surprise, shock or an urgent command.

Monologue: A speech by one person.

Non-chronological report: A report that gives information rather than narrating a sequence of events.

Third person: The form of a verb for *he*, *she*, *it* or *they*.

Week 1 lesson plans

This week's lessons are based on non-fiction texts about how climate is affecting the Arctic ice cap and its implications for wildlife, future climate change and humans. The children compare three different reports; this enables them to develop research skills, distinguish between facts and opinions and check the facts. There are also opportunities to explore writing styles: structural devices, grammatical features and language. The children use what they have learned to help them to write a report on the effects of global warming on the Arctic ice cap and how humans are contributing to the problem. Opportunities arise to practise spelling, with a focus on homophones.

1: A warning about polar bears and the Arctic ice cap

Introduction
● Show the images from media resource 'Arctic' on the CD-ROM, and ask: *Do you know where this is? How do we know that it is the Arctic and not the Antarctic?* (Polar bears live in the Arctic but not the Antarctic.) Ask the children if they know what the Arctic Circle is, and where it is. Invite a volunteer to point it out on a globe (also the Antarctic Circle and the continent of Antarctica). Explain that Antarctica has a large area of land: it is a continent, but the Arctic is not.

Whole-class work
● Ask the children what they know about the Arctic. (The North Pole is in the Arctic. Point this out on a globe.) Write their answers on the board. Ask what they know about the climate of the Arctic. Ask: *Is it always cold? Is there always ice there? What do you know about the changing climate of the Arctic?*

Paired work
● Give out photocopiable page 'On thin ice' from the CD-ROM and ask the children to read it, talk to their partner about it and to make notes of the main points and conclusion. Recap how to make notes briefly: the main words but not complete sentences.

> **Differentiation**
> ● Arrange pairs so that better readers can read aloud with a partner who needs support.

Review
● Ask: *What is the conclusion of the article?* (Summer sea ice in the Arctic is shrinking and the winter freeze is getting later. If this continues, polar bears will die out by the end of the 21st century. Human activity adds to global warming, which melts the ice; humans can reduce this by reducing the greenhouse gases they produce.)
● Ask: *What main points does it make to support this conclusion?* (Scientists have measured the sea ice. Tiny organisms live in the ice and other animals in the food web feed on them. Polar bears are at the top of the food web, so their food is disappearing. The time when they can hunt and get fat is getting shorter, so the bears are becoming thinner and weaker. They have to swim farther to hunt; this weakens them and can kill them. Females can't get to their usual safe places to make dens to give birth to cubs. Hungry males are beginning to eat the cubs and even the female bears.)
● Ask: *Which facts can we check from satellite images and maps drawn from them?* (That the area of sea ice in the Arctic is reducing and that this is getting faster.)
● Keep the children's notes for lesson 2.

Expected outcomes
● All children will be able to combine information from more than one source, with support, write an explanation, recognise and spell homophones.
● Most children will be able to use language more effectively in these, write with less support and spell a range of homophones.
● Some children will be also able to discuss how the main points contribute to a conclusion and spell a greater range of homophones.

Curriculum objectives
● To distinguish between statements of fact and opinion.
● To summarise the main ideas drawn from more than one paragraph, identifying key details that support the main ideas.

Resources
Globe; individual whiteboards and pens; photocopiable page 'On thin ice' from the CD-ROM; media resource 'Arctic' on the CD-ROM; optional: a display area about the North Pole, featuring maps, pictures of wildlife, articles about the environment set up in advance of the lesson (with room to add children's work as the week progresses)

Curriculum objectives
● To distinguish between statements of fact and opinion.
● To summarise the main ideas drawn from more than one paragraph, identifying key details that support the main ideas.

Resources
Photocopiable page 'Polar bears under threat' from the CD-ROM; the children's notes from lesson 1; globe; individual whiteboards and pens

2: A different view on global warming

Introduction
● Recap lesson 1 and ask the children about the main points of the article they read. Tell them that they are going to read and make notes about another similar article.

Paired work
● Give out photocopiable page 'Polar bears under threat' from the CD-ROM and ask the children to read the report with their partner and make notes of the main points and conclusion.

Whole-class work
● Ask: *What is the conclusion of the report?* (Areas of permanent sea ice may provide refuges for polar bears, meaning they will survive over the long term.) *What main points does it make to support this conclusion?* (It says that human activity causes the ice to melt and that the US's decision to give the bears special protection is a step in the right direction. But as many areas of sea ice are outside the US, protecting polar bears will depend on international cooperation.)

> **Differentiation**
> ● Arrange pairs so that better readers can read aloud with a partner who needs support.

Review
● Ask: *How does this report disagree with the first one you read?* (It suggests that polar bears may survive even if humans don't reduce greenhouse gases.) *What do you think people in the USA will think about reducing their own greenhouse gas production if they read the final sentence?*
● Keep the children's notes from both lessons for lesson 3.

Curriculum objectives
● To ask questions to improve their understanding of what they have read.
● To retrieve, record and present information from non-fiction.
● To summarise the main ideas drawn from more than one paragraph, identifying key details that support the main ideas.
● To précis longer passages.
● To read books that are structured in different ways and for a range of purposes.

Resources
Computers and internet access; the children's notes from lessons 1 and 2; computers with internet access; websites that give information on polar bears and climate change, bookmarked in advance of the lesson, for example: www.polarbearsinternational.org and www.wwf.org.uk

3: Finding out more

Introduction
● Compare the main points of the two reports read in lessons 1 and 2.

Group work
● Ask the children to work with their group to list the facts they know about polar bears. They should re-read their notes from the two reports they read (and re-read parts of the report, where necessary, to check). Ask them to think about polar bears' way of life, how and where they feed, how and where they breed, how they survive in extremely cold conditions and so on. They could use the format below to record the facts, their questions and what they find out.

What we know about polar bears	Our questions	The answers

● Suggest that they use the websites of Polar Bears International, WWF and other charitable organisations to find information to answer their questions. Use one of these to model how to follow links, use tools such as the site map and links to find information and return to the home page.

Review
● Ask the groups to split into two, with half the group remaining at their table to discuss their finding with others and the other half moving around the room to read what other groups found out.
● Keep the children's notes from all three lessons for lesson 4.

■SCHOLASTIC

Curriculum objectives

● To note and develop initial ideas, drawing on reading and research where necessary.
● To use a wide range of devices to build cohesion within and across paragraphs.
● To use further organisational and presentational devices to structure text and to guide the reader.
● To punctuate bullet points consistently.
● To assess the effectiveness of their own and others' writing.

Resources

The children's notes from lessons 1, 2 and 3; computers and internet access; websites that give information on polar bears and climate change, bookmarked in advance of the lesson; for example: www.polarbearsinternational. org and www.wwf.org.uk

4: Writing reports

Introduction

● Recap lesson 3 and tell the class that their task is to write an argument about how climate change is affecting polar bears and what humans can do about it. First they should consider what they know that will help them.

Whole-class work

● Ask: *How is climate change affecting the Arctic? Why is this bad for polar bears? What do scientists say are some of the causes of climate change? What do they say people can do to help to slow it down?*
● Recap how to write an argument: introduce the topic; set out each important point in a new paragraph, and support it with evidence; use words and phrases that link ideas (for example *in this way, however, because of this, in addition, at the same time*); sum up the main points and write a conclusion.
● Ask the children to check their notes so that they have all the information they need to help them as they begin to write their reports.

> **Differentiation**
> ● Read the children's notes from previous lessons with them and draw out any points they should use in their writing, explaining why.

Review

● Invite volunteers to read their arguments. Remind the class about listening to others (look at the speaker; listen; sit still; think of questions to ask at the end; ask questions politely).

Curriculum objectives

● To continue to distinguish between homophones and other words that are often confused.

Resources

Individual whiteboards and pens; interactive activity 'Homophone quiz' on the CD-ROM; photocopiable page 200 'Spot the homophones'

5: Homophones

Introduction

● Tell the class they are going to spell some homophones from the reports they have read and written. Ask: *What are homophones?* Tell the children that you are going to read out some homophones from the articles about polar bears, with clues, and that you would like them to write the words on their individual whiteboards and hold them up.

Whole-class work

● Read out some of following words and clues (or use interactive activity 'Homophone quiz' on the CD-ROM for this), allowing the children time to write them down: *bear* (polar bear)/*bare* (naked); *weather (sun or rain)*/*whether* (if), *rays* (rays of the sun)/*raise* (lift); *prey* (catch animals to eat)/*pray* (say a prayer); *current* (a flow of water)/*currant* (dried grape); *waste* (waste energy)/*waist* (middle of the body); *pole* (North Pole or a long stick)/*poll* (vote).
● After each word (and clue), ask the children to hold up their whiteboards. Compare the results. If any differ, ask: *Which are correct?* Invite the children to write another word that sounds the same but has a different spelling and suggest sentences for the homophone pairs.

Independent work

● Give out photocopiable page 200 'Spot the homophones'. Ask them to think about the meaning of each word and the other word that sounds like it.

Review

● Ask if there are any clues to help with spelling some of the homophones, for example, a plural often ends with 's' *rays, paws, rows*. Point out that most homophones just have to be learned. Where appropriate model how to use 'spell speak' to help with some of them, for example: *whales* (sound the 'h'); *waist* (sound the 'i').

Expected outcomes
● All children will be able to retrieve information from non-written sources, write a report on it, write a persuasive text and spell words with silent letters.
● Most children will also be able to use modal verbs and spell a greater range of words with silent letters.
● Some children will also be able to use modal verbs more effectively.

Curriculum objectives
● To summarise the main ideas drawn from more than one paragraph, identifying key details that support the main ideas.
● To choose the writing implement that is best suited to the task.

Resources
A documentary about climate change in the Arctic, useful documentaries: 'Eyewitness Documentary of Changes in the Arctic's Climate' www.climate.gov; 'Status and Trends of Arctic Biodiversity' from YouTube; BBC Science and Nature, Climate Change Experiment Results 'Impact on the UK' has a selection of videos on how climate change affects the UK

Week 2 lesson plans

This week's lessons are based on a documentary on climate change and its effects on the Arctic ice cap. The children take notes as they watch, raise questions and then watch again. They take more detailed notes before writing a persuasive text to convince others of the dangers of climate change to the environment, wildlife and humans, and to encourage them to take action to help to prevent further damage. Opportunities arise to practise spelling words with silent letters.

1: Documentary on climate change in the Arctic

Introduction
● Tell the class that they are going to watch a documentary about climate change in the Arctic and to make notes on the main points it makes about how climate change happens, its effects and what we can do about it. Ask: *What is a documentary?* (A non-fiction film.) Ask: *What headings can you use for your notes?* (Causes, Effects, Actions.) Tell them that it will be difficult to write down all the main points and watch at the same time, so they will have the chance to watch again to check anything they missed.

Whole-class work
● Ask: *How will you write information quickly?* Recap how to take notes: don't write in full sentences; shorten some words; use signs such as +,→ and any others that are useful. Remind them that handwriting doesn't have to be neat but that it needs be legible to them. They should also think about what they find easiest to write with – for example, a pencil might facilitate quick writing.
● Show a documentary about climate change while the children take notes. Take your own set of notes to help with the review.

Group work
● Ask the children to talk to others in their groups to find out anything they missed and to make a note of it.

> **Differentiation**
> ● Have an adult helper modelling what to make a note of, and how.

Review
● Invite volunteers to say what they noted down. Stop after main points and ask: *Did everyone else write that? Was it important?* Allow time for them to augment their notes.
● Keep the children's notes for lesson 2.

Curriculum objectives

- To summarise the main ideas drawn from more than one paragraph, identifying key details that support the main ideas.
- To ask questions to improve their understanding of what they have read (or watched or listened to).
- To retrieve, record and present information from non-fiction.

Resources

The documentary about climate change watched in lesson 1

2: Watching again

Introduction

- Recap lesson 1 and discuss any points the children were not sure of. Tell them that they are going to watch the documentary again so that they can make a note of anything they missed. Ask them also about any interesting language they noticed: for example, powerful verbs, adjectives or adverbs, and give some examples.
- Ask: *What did you find helped you to make notes quickly?* Remind them that unimportant words such as *a*, *an*, *the* and *but* can be omitted and they can use symbols such as + for *and* and arrows to link ideas.

Whole-class work

- Repeat the documentary about climate change while the children take notes.

Group work

- Ask the children to talk to others in their groups again to find out anything they missed and to make a note of it.

> **Differentiation**
> - Arrange mixed-ability groups.

Review

- Ask: *What new information did you make a note of this time? What interesting language did you notice?* If they missed any, replay sections and point it out.
- Keep the children's notes from both lessons for lesson 3.

Curriculum objectives

- To retrieve, record and present information from non-fiction.
- To summarise the main ideas drawn from more than one paragraph, identifying key details that support the main ideas.
- To note and develop initial ideas, drawing on reading and research where necessary.
- To use dictionaries to check the spelling and meaning of words.

Resources

The children's notes from lessons 1 and 2; dictionaries

3: Writing a report

Introduction

- Display some of your notes about the documentary the class watched and highlight the points that interested you. Ask: *What points did you think were important? Why?*

Independent work

- Ask the children to read through their notes about the documentary and to highlight the points they thought were important. Point out that this will be different for different people: for example, they might be interested in shrinking sea ice, polar bears, other endangered animals, endangered plants, changing weather patterns around the world or dangers to humans.
- Ask them to plan a report on an issue connected with climate change that interests them. Their plan should take only five or ten minutes, then they should begin writing their report. Remind them to include any interesting language they noted down from the documentary. Check the spelling or meaning of any unfamiliar words.

> **Differentiation**
> - Arrange for an adult helper to read through the children's notes with them – either before or during the lesson.

Review

- Invite children to read reports with different themes to the class.
- Keep their reports and their notes from the previous lessons for lesson 4.

Curriculum objectives
● To identify the audience for and the purpose of the writing, selecting the appropriate form and using other similar writing as models for their own.
● To note and develop initial ideas, drawing on reading and research where necessary.
● To select appropriate grammar and vocabulary, understanding how such choices can change and enhance meaning.
● To use a wide range of devices to build cohesion within and across paragraphs.
● To assess the effectiveness of their own and others' writing.
● To use modal verbs or adverbs to indicate degrees of possibility.
● To use and understand grammatical terminology in Appendix 2 accurately and appropriately in their writing and reading.

Resources
The children's notes from lessons 1 and 2; the children's reports form lesson 3

4: Climate change: taking action

Introduction
● Ask the children what we can all do to help to slow down or prevent climate change, for example: try not to throw away rubbish by using less disposable material such as packaging, reuse things and recycle materials; try not to waste water; wear warm clothes so that heating can be turned down slightly.

Independent work
● Ask them to plan a cartoon strip to persuade other children to help to combat climate change. Ask them to think about characters and what they can say to persuade people: for example, using evidence from the documentary and expressing it powerfully.
● Discuss useful phrases such as: *if..., what if...?, imagine..., what would you do if...? you have a choice...*
● Remind them of modal verbs such as: *must, may, might, can, could, should, will, shall, can't, won't.*
● Ask the children to sketch their ideas for the cartoon, to decide what should be shown in each scene – perhaps six scenes – and to decide how big each speech bubble should be. Ask them to draw the pictures and write the words in a way that is easy to read (print).

Differentiation
● Where appropriate, ask the children to enact their ideas for a cartoon story before drawing the pictures and writing the words.

Review
● Allow time for the children to read one another's cartoons and to comment on what worked well and what they think might convince readers, and why.

Curriculum objectives
● To spell words with 'silent' letters.

Resources
Individual whiteboards and pens; photocopiable page 201 'Silent letters'; interactive activity 'Silent letters' on the CD-ROM

5: Silent letters

Introduction
● Ask the children to listen to a sentence and then to write the word you choose from it: *If we try not to use too much **wrapping** we can reduce litter.* Ask them to hold up their whiteboards and compare the spellings. If there are differences, ask: *Which is correct?* Remind them of silent letters. Repeat this, using the following sentences and bold words: *The charity has been working on a **campaign** to reduce carbon emissions by 50 per cent in ten years; The president cast **doubt** on the link between carbon emissions and climate change; Representatives from the **Foreign** Office will be attending the global summit.*

Independent work
● Hand out photocopiable page 201 'Silent letters' (or use the interactive activity on the CD-ROM) and ask the children to read the definitions and the sentences, and to write the answers, which are words with silent letters.

Differentiation
● Edit the photocopiable sheet before copying it, giving some letters in the answers.

Review
● Ask the children which letters are often silent in English words. Ask for their ideas on how to learn to spell words with silent letters (for example, using 'spell speak' and pronouncing the letters as they learn the words: *whales* (sound the 'h'); *waist* (sound the 'i').

Week 3 lesson plans

These lessons begin with a story about a wolf and a grizzly bear – *Lone Wolf* by Kathryn Lasky – a compelling and moving story written from the point of view of the two main animal characters. Through reading the story the children also learn how an author writes the wolf's story from the inside, noticing how she uses dialogue and monologue without actually having talking animals. They use a similar technique in writing their own stories about a polar bear in the Arctic. This includes developing skills in writing and punctuating dialogue and in also editing and proofreading.

1: Animal adventure story (1)

Introduction
● Tell the class that they are going to read a story about a wolf, which has a very different life from the polar bears of the Arctic but, like them, has problems to overcome. Show them the cover and tell them that the book is the first in a series by Kathryn Lasky, an American author. Read the first few chapters and ask: *How do you think the author can write from the point of view of an animal?* (She must know a lot about wolves.) *How does she know about them?* (From research.) Ask: *Which person is the book written in? How can you tell?*

Whole-class work
● Ask the class which animal they now know quite a lot about. (The polar bear.) Ask: *How is the polar bear's life similar to that of the wolf in this story?* (For example: like the wolf, the polar bear has to find food, water and shelter; it is a carnivore and at the top of its food web, but its young are vulnerable; both animals are harmed more by humans than by any other species – through hunting and habitat destruction.) *How is the wolf different?* (It lives on land and, unlike polar bears, in packs – that is the main way in which it defends itself.)

Independent work
● Ask the children to use what they have learned about polar bears to draft the opening of a story in a similar style to *Lone Wolf*. They can write in the first or third person. The story could begin in a happy way with the polar bear having a safe life with enough food (which will provide a contrast if things change). Tell them that this is an adventure story, which means that the main character (the polar bear) will face problems. They could try to think of an interesting way to let the reader know that the main character is a polar bear rather than saying *x is a polar bear* or *I am a polar bear*. Can they include just enough details to help the reader to figure this out?
● At this stage they should just make up the opening of their story, using what they have learned. They can check details later.

Review
● Read some of the story openings and discuss how well they capture the readers' imagination and make them want to read on.
● Keep the children's initial writing for lesson 2.
● If sufficient copies are available, encourage the children to continue reading *Lone Wolf* between lessons.

Expected outcomes
● All children will be able to write a longer story based on facts and including dialogue.
● Most children will also be able to use dialogue to tell the story and show character's thoughts and feelings.
● Some children will be able to use what they know to create an authentic feel to their story.

Curriculum objectives
● To check that the book makes sense to them, discussing their understanding and exploring the meaning of words in context.
● To note and develop initial ideas, drawing on reading and research where necessary.
● In writing narratives, to consider how authors have developed characters and settings in what they have read, listened to or seen performed.
● To choose the writing implement that is best suited to a task.

Resources
Lone Wolf from the *Wolves of the Beyond* series by Kathryn Lasky – if possible, several copies for the children to read independently, or another story written from the point of view of an animal struggling for its survival and/or the survival of its young (in the first or third person); computers and internet access; useful websites about polar bears, bookmarked in advance of the lesson

Curriculum objectives

● To check that the book makes sense to them, discussing their understanding and exploring the meaning of words in context.
● To note and develop initial ideas, drawing on reading and research where necessary.
● In writing narratives, to consider how authors have developed characters and settings in what they have read, listened to or seen performed.

Resources

The children's story openings from lesson 1; information books and online sources about polar bears in the wild, including those used in previous lessons; *Lone Wolf* by Kathryn Lasky; computers and internet access; useful websites about polar bears, bookmarked in advance of the lesson

2: Animal adventure story (2)

Introduction

● Continue reading *Lone Wolf* (a short section to allow time for the children's own writing). Ask: *How is an animal story different from a report about animals?* (It is based on real animals but it is not all factual. The author makes up the story, what the animals are thinking, and so on.)

Independent work

● Ask the children to read through the story openings they wrote during the previous lesson and to check the facts about polar bears by re-reading their earlier notes as well as non-fiction texts. Ask them to check that the setting and the bear's actions are realistic. Point out that they could also include another Arctic animal, such as an Arctic fox. They could find out about Arctic foxes from information texts.
● Ask them to continue writing their story, describing a problem facing the polar bear and what happens because of it. For example, they could solve small parts of the problem but still face other, bigger issues: it might find some food but not enough, and perhaps become thinner and weaker, swimming long distances in its search for food; it might find a place to give birth to cubs but then find that it is not suitable (not sheltered enough, too near melting ice and so on).

Review

● Ask the children to swap stories with a partner and to say what they enjoyed and anything they think the reader needs to be told.
● Keep the children's stories for lesson 3. Encourage them to continue reading *Lone Wolf* between lessons.

Curriculum objectives

● To note and develop initial ideas, drawing on reading and research where necessary.
● In writing narratives, to consider how authors have developed characters and settings in what they have read, listened to or seen performed.

Resources

The children's stories from lesson 2; information books and online sources about polar bears in the wild, including those used in previous lessons; *Lone Wolf* by Kathryn Lasky; computers and internet access; useful websites about polar bears, bookmarked in advance of the lesson

3: The end of the story

Introduction

● Tell the children that they are going to think about how their story will end, and then finish it in draft form. To help them to write from the point of view of animals, they are going to look at how the author does this *in Lone Wolf* (by expressing the animal's thoughts; although she can't be sure what an animal might be thinking, her ideas are based on sound research into animal behaviour).

Whole-class work

● Read another short section of *Lone Wolf*. Ask: *What do wolves do when a pup is born very weak or with something wrong with it? How do you feel about this? Why do animals do this?* (Any weak member of the pack would slow down and weaken the rest of the pack. It would be attacked by predators and the pack would use up valuable energy defending it.) Discuss whether it would be realistic to change this behaviour in their stories.

Independent work

● Ask the children to continue their stories and, as they do, to continue checking any facts about polar bears that they think will make them more realistic.

Review

● Read some of the story drafts and ask the class: *What is the meaning of* tying up loose ends? *Do their stories do this? Are there any unresolved issues?*
● Keep the story drafts for lesson 4.

Curriculum objectives
- To select appropriate grammar and vocabulary, understanding how such choices can change and enhance meaning.

Resources
The children's story drafts from lesson 3; photocopiable page 'Extract from *Lone Wolf*' from the CD-ROM

4: A focus on language

Introduction
- Tell the children that, to help them to think of interesting language to use in their stories, they are going to look closely at some of the language in *Lone Wolf*.

Whole-class work
- Give out photocopiable page 'Extract from *Lone Wolf*' from the CD-ROM. Read the first paragraph with the children and ask: *What picture do you have in your mind of the forest? What colours would you see there? Which words create this picture? What would you hear?*
- Ask the children to think about the atmosphere. *How does Faolan feel?* (Wary and threatened.) *Which words show how he feels?* (*Warily, ears forward, tail slightly raised, hackles straight up and bristling.*) *What does it make you feel?* (It seems to be preparing for something dreadful.)

Independent work
- Ask the children to read the next two paragraphs and to draw the scene of each paragraph. They could talk to one another about them.

Review
- Invite volunteers to show and talk about the pictures they drew. Ask: *How did the author make you feel shock in the second paragraph? Which words communicate sadness in the last paragraph?*
- Allow the children to use what they have learned about the power of language to redraft parts of their stories. Keep their stories for lesson 5.

Curriculum objectives
- In narratives, to describe settings, characters and atmosphere and integrate dialogue to convey character and advance the action.
- To use a wide range of devices to build cohesion within and across paragraphs.
- To proofread for spelling and punctuation errors.
- To choose which shape of a letter to use when given choices, and deciding, as part of their personal style, whether or not to join specific letters.
- To choose the writing implement that is best suited to a task.

Resources
The children's story drafts from lesson 4; photocopiable page 'Extract from *Lone Wolf*' from the CD-ROM; photocopiable page 202 'Dialogue'

5: Dialogue

Introduction
- Recap the meaning of *dialogue*. Explain the root of the word, which comes from Greek (*dia* meaning *two* or *separate* and *logue* meaning *speech*, so *separate people speaking*). Ask: *What do you think monologue means?* (One person speaking.) *How can you spot dialogue or monologue in a text?* (The spoken words are enclosed in inverted commas.)

Independent work
- Recap inverted commas, using photocopiable page 202 'Dialogue'.

Whole-class work
- Ask the class if they think dialogue is important in *Lone Wolf*. The animals do not talk but Thunderheart's and Faolan's thoughts are written as dialogue. Ask: *Can you remember any of their words?* Read photocopiable page 'Extract from *Lone Wolf*' from the CD-ROM with the children. Ask: *How does the author tell us what the wolf is thinking?*

Independent work
- Ask the children to re-read their draft stories to see if they can add any dialogue or monologue to enhance their stories. They should also check spelling and punctuation then create a final version in their best writing.

> ### Differentiation
> - Indicate places where dialogue or monologue might help and ask: *What can the polar bear see, feel or hear happening here? How can you say this in his/her words as thoughts?*

Review
- Select some completed stories to read to the class.

Expected outcomes
- All children can write in the first person.
- Most children can ensure that subjects and verbs agree and that the tense is consistent.
- Some children can also change tense where appropriate, for example: where the diary refers to what has already happened and what is happening at the time.

Curriculum objectives
- To continue to read and discuss an increasingly wide range of non-fiction.
- To retrieve, record and present information from non-fiction.
- To ask questions to improve their understanding.
- To check that the book makes sense to them, discussing their understanding and exploring the meaning of words in context.
- To provide reasoned justification for their views.
- To predict what might happen from details stated and implied.

Resources
Pictures of Arctic exploration over the ages, added to the Arctic display; media resource 'Nansen and team setting off' on the CD-ROM; globe; atlases with a map of the Arctic, enough for one per pair or small group; photocopiable page 'Nansen's idea' from the CD-ROM; photocopiable page 'Madcap plan or brilliant idea?' from the CD-ROM; photocopiable page 203 'Nansen's voyage'; computers with internet access; the website www.frammuseum.no (in English with video clips, exhibits and photographs) and other useful sites, bookmarked in advance of the lesson

Week 4 lesson plans

These lessons are based on non-fiction reports about Arctic exploration, beginning with the Norwegian explorer Fridtjof Nansen's voyage on the *Fram*. The children read about his idea, based on the location of wreckage found from an earlier, unsuccessful, expedition to use the natural flow of the ice on currents in the region to take the ship to the North Pole. They read about his meeting in a remote icy spot, with another explorer – Frederick Jackson – whom Nansen had rejected for the *Fram* expedition. They write the diary of a crew member, based on their research on the expedition, checking tenses and verb agreement (first person).

1: Nansen's idea

Introduction
- Point out the pictures on the display. Tell the class that people from around the world have explored the Arctic for thousands of years. Even the Ancient Greeks sailed far enough north to find frozen seas. Two American explorers – Robert Peary and Frederick Cook – claimed to have been the first to reach the North Pole but many people nowadays think that neither actually reached it, although they made extremely difficult journeys and got very close.

Whole-class work
- Give the children some information about the Norwegian explorer Fridtjof Nansen (but not his dates) and show a photograph of him. Explain that he was interested in zoology and travelled to the North Pole to study wildlife there. This began his interest in exploration, and his first expedition was across the Greenland ice cap. Thousands of people applied to go with him on his North Pole expedition, including some very experienced explorers. One of those he didn't choose was the British explorer Frederick Jackson, who then planned his own expedition to Franz Josef Land. (Help the children to find these islands on a map.)
- Show media resource 'Nansen and team setting off' on the CD-ROM. Ask: *Is this modern or from some time ago? How can you tell?* (The clothing is a clue.) Tell them that it was in 1893. Give out photocopiable page 'Nansen's idea' from the CD-ROM and read it with the class. Ask: *Is there anything else you would like to know about the ship or its crew?*
- Show the children a map of the area and ask them to follow the first part of his route. Give them the following instructions, which are based on a description and map of Nansen's route: *Sail from Christiania (now Oslo), northwards up the coast to Bergen, Trondheim and then Tromso. Leave the coast of Norway from Vardo. Sail eastwards across the Baring Sea to Novaya Zemlya then to Khabarova on the northern coast of Russia. Pick up the dogs there, then sail east across the Kara Sea. Few sailors have been there before so there are no accurate sea charts.*
- Ask: *Why did they take dogs?* (To pull sledges.) Ask: *How did Nansen plan to get to the North Pole by sea?*

Independent work
- Ask the children to re-read photocopiable page 'Nansen's idea' and photocopiable page 'Madcap plan or brilliant idea' from the CD-ROM. Hand out photocopiable page 203 'Nansen's voyage' and ask them to answer the questions and to predict whether Nansen's idea would work.

Review
- Invite volunteers to read out their answers and the evidence from the passage, where relevant. Tell them that they will find out how well Nansen's idea worked in the next lesson.

■ SCHOLASTIC

Curriculum objectives
● To continue to read and discuss an increasingly wide range of non-fiction. and reference books.
● To retrieve, record and present information from non-fiction.
● To check that the book makes sense to them, discussing their understanding and exploring the meaning of words in context.
● To ask questions to improve their understanding.

Resources
Pictures of Arctic exploration over the ages; globe; atlases with a map of the Arctic; photocopiable page 'Nansen's idea' from the CD-ROM; computers with internet access; the website www.frammuseum.no (in English with video clips, exhibits and photographs) and other useful sites, bookmarked in advance of the lesson; if possible, information books about Fridtjof Nansen and the Fram

2: The voyage on the *Fram*

Introduction

● Recap lesson 1, including the children's answers about how well Nansen's idea would work. Tell them that they will now be able to find out more about the voyage.

Whole-class work

● Re-read photocopiable page 'Nansen's idea' from the CD-ROM and ask the children to look at the map. Tell them that Nansen set off from Oslo in June 1893 on the *Fram*. Ask: *What would you like to know about Nansen's voyage?* If their questions are closed (giving yes/no answers) help them to open these up for research, for example: *Did they reach the North Pole? What was their route? How long did it take? What happened on the voyage? What happened after they left the ship and continued across the ice? What problems did they face? What unexpected problems/mishaps arose?*

Paired work

● Ask them to share the task of research: finding out about the crew, plotting the sea route, marking where any mishaps took place, listing and describing key events during the voyage – also the weather and sea conditions finding out about and what the explorers saw during the expedition.

Review

● Ask: *What have you found out?* Share information and highlight the problems that polar explorers face, and the noticeable differences between exploration more than 100 years ago and today (clothing, communication, sea charts, navigation equipment).
● Keep the children's notes for lessons 3 and 4.

Curriculum objectives
● To explain and discuss their understanding of what they have read, including through formal presentations and debates, maintaining focus on the topic and using notes where necessary.
● To note and develop initial ideas, drawing on reading and research where necessary.
● To perform their own compositions, using appropriate intonations, volume and movement so that meaning is clear.

Resources
Photocopiable page 'Nansen's route map' from the CD-ROM; the children's notes from lesson 2; computers with internet access; the website www.frammuseum. no (in English with video clips, exhibits and photographs) and other useful sites, bookmarked in advance of the lesson; if possible, information books about Fridtjof Nansen and the Fram

3: An unexpected meeting

Introduction

● Recap what the children know about Nansen's expedition and show them photocopiable page 'Nansen's route map' from the CD-ROM. Remind them of the location of Franz Josef Land. Ask: *Was Nansen worried that he might not survive the expedition when he left the* Fram *and went on foot across the ice? How can you tell?* (He wrote a farewell letter to his wife.) *How were he and his companions feeling by the time they got to Franz Josef Land?* Ask: *How must they have felt when they heard voices?*

Group work

● Discuss Nansen meeting Frederick Jackson in Franz Josef Land. Ask: *Would explorers in those days expect to meet others here? Who was Frederick Jackson?* (A British explorer whom Nansen turned down for his expedition.) *How do you think each explorer felt? What did Jackson do?*
● Ask the children to re-read the information about this historic meeting, noticing the style of language in any quotations. Ask them to enact the scene. Remind them that this was more than 100 years ago and encourage them to use the more formal style of speech that people used in those days.

Review

● Invite groups to enact the meeting between Nansen and Jackson, with the others as an audience or crew members.

Curriculum objectives
● To note and develop initial ideas, drawing on reading and research where necessary.
● To use further organisational and presentational devices to structure text and to guide the reader.
● To assess the effectiveness of their own and others' writing.
● To propose changes to grammar, vocabulary and punctuation to enhance effects and clarify meaning.
● To ensure the consistent and correct use of tense throughout a piece of writing.
● To proofread for spelling and punctuation errors.

Resources
Globe; atlases inc the Arctic; photocopiable page 'Nansen's idea' from the CD-ROM; computers with internet access; the website www.frammuseum.no (in English and has video clips, exhibits and photographs) and other useful sites, bookmarked in advance of the lesson; if possible, information books about Fridtjof Nansen and the *Fram*

Curriculum objectives
● To ensure correct subject and verb agreement when using singular and plural, distinguishing between the language of speech and writing and choosing the appropriate register.
● To ensure the consistent and correct use of tense throughout a piece of writing.

Resources
The children's diaries from lesson 4; photocopiable page 204 'Nansen's diary'

4: Journal

Introduction
● Recap lesson 2 and ask the children to describe the experiences of the members of the crew of the *Fram*.

Independent work
● Ask the children to use what they know about the Arctic and what they found out about the *Fram* expedition to help them to write a section of the diary of one of Nansen's crew members. Allocate different sections of the expedition to different groups, for example: the first part of the voyage, when the ship was on course, when it began to drift in the wrong direction, when Nansen left the ship and set off across the ice, and the meeting between Nansen and Jackson.
● Recap how to set out a diary, using the actual dates of the voyage (but selecting key dates) and use of the first person.
● Ask: *Which person will you write in?* Ask for an example of a sentence in the first person. *Which tenses will you use?* (Some present tense – if writing about something happening at the time – but mainly past tense, writing up the events of the day.) Ask for examples of sentences in the present and past tense.
● Remind them to proofread the first draft for spelling and punctuation errors and provide printed diary pages for their final version for the Arctic display.

Review
● Ask the children to arrange their diary entries in chronological order for others to read. Keep these for lesson 5 before adding them to the Arctic display.

5: Verb agreement

Introduction
● Recap lesson 4. Ask: *How is writing a diary about an expedition different from writing the text for an information book about it?* (It is written from the point of view of one person and in the first person. Also, some parts are in the present tense.) Remind the children of their other writing in the first person and partly in the present tense: for example, the polar bear story.

Whole-class work
● Display a sentence or two from the diary entry of one of the children's journals for a crew member (from lesson 4). Ask: *Which words would we need to change to make this into a past-tense report in the third person?*

Independent work
● Ask the children to rewrite their crew members' journals in the third person and past tense. Compare the effects of these and their originals.

> ### Differentiation
> ● For a more challenging activity, some children could change an entry from Nansen's diary using photocopiable page 204 'Nansen's diary'.

Review
● Ask the children to swap journals and reports with a partner and to read the report, comparing it with the diary. Ask them to check that each verb is in the correct person and that the tenses are correct.

Week 5 lesson plans

This week's lessons continue the theme of the Arctic, with a focus on protecting our food supply. After reading a report about a fishery that collapsed, the children research the causes, and find out about other fisheries and about the measures being taken to protect them. They discuss these and what we can all do to help. They take part in a debate about whether we should stop eating fish.

1: The fish that disappeared

Introduction

- Recap what the children know about the Arctic. Show photographs of the area and allow time for the children to appreciate and talk about the seemingly unspoiled ice, icebergs and ocean. Ask: *Which countries are in or near the Arctic Circle?* Ask them to read the labels and leaflets about fish and fish products and to notice where the fish came from. Ask them to locate the places on maps. Ask: *Which fish do we eat that come from the North Atlantic? Does it matter if we carry on eating fish or might we use up all the fish in the sea? Should we eat the very young fish?*

Whole-class work

- Tell the children about a law of the Maori people of New Zealand hundreds of years ago: no one could take more fish than could be eaten, and that they had to give back the first fish caught as an offering to the sea god Tangaroa. Ask: *Why do you think they had this law?* Point out that nowadays fishing is an industry, so people find ways of catching larger and larger numbers of fish to make money.
- Hand out photocopiable page 'The fish that disappeared' from the CD-ROM and read it with the class. Allow time for them to comment on what they have read. Ask: *Whose fault was it that most of the fish disappeared from the Grand Banks fishery? What evidence is there for this? Could any of the following be blamed: seabirds; seals and other sea mammals; traditional fishermen who had been fishing there for a long time; modern trawlers, climate change. What evidence can you find for this? Is it fair to say that technological advances destroyed the fishery?*

Paired work

- Ask the children to re-read the report, to list the facts and opinions they find in it (encourage them to use a colon) and to make a note of any evidence to support the opinions. Ask them to answer the following questions: *Why didn't the Canadian government listen to the warnings of the fishermen? Why didn't they listen to the warnings of scientists? Were the politicians worried about the people who would lose their jobs if they closed the fishery? Why would unemployment be a problem to the government?*

> **Differentiation**
> - Where necessary, let the children record their discussions and write their answers afterwards, with help, if needed.

Review

- Invite different pairs to read out their answers. Ask if anyone disagrees, and why. Keep copies of the report, along with the children's writing, for lesson 2.

Expected outcomes

- All children will be able to write an argument, contribute to a class debate and use clues from linked words to help them spell some words ending '-ent' or '-ant'.
- Most children will also be able to write a balanced argument and prepare some answers to counter arguments.
- Some children will also be able to prepare more effective counter arguments and spell a greater range of '-ent' and '-ant' words.

Curriculum objectives

- To continue to read and discuss an increasingly wide range of non-fiction.
- To distinguish between statements of fact and opinion.
- To summarise the main ideas drawn from more than one paragraph, identifying key details that support the main ideas.
- To use a colon to introduce a list.

Resources

Labels and packaging from fish/fish products from the North Atlantic; leaflets from supermarkets/fishmongers about North Atlantic fish; photocopiable page 'The fish that disappeared' from the CD-ROM; globe; world atlases; map of Canada; arctic photographs – icebergs, wide expanses of ice and blue sea, blizzards, explorers in different weather conditions – added to the Arctic display from last week's lessons

Curriculum objectives
● To continue to read and discuss an increasingly wide range of non-fiction.
● To explain and discuss their understanding of what they have read, including through formal presentations and debates, maintaining a focus on the topic and using notes where necessary.

Resources
Photocopiable page 'The fish that disappeared' from the CD-ROM; the children's written work from lesson 1

2: Discussion

Introduction
● Recap lesson 1 and give out copies photocopiable page 'The fish that disappeared' from the CD-ROM. Ask: *What happened at Grand Banks fishery in Canada?* Ask the children to give just the facts. Ask: *How can you tell that these are facts?* (They can be checked.)
● Ask: *Which facts told people that cod in the Grand Banks were in danger of dying out? Which fact could be used to argue that they began to increase? Was this correct? Why not? Which different groups of people had an interest in the fishery?* (Fishermen, other people employed in the local fish trade, large fishing companies, the Canadian government, scientists.)

Group work
● Ask the children to discuss and make a note of the views of the different people with an interest in the fishery. They then to enact discussions between some of these, with different children taking the roles of different people: local fishermen and the Canadian government; Canadian politicians discussing the situation among themselves; owners of large fishing companies and scientists.

> **Differentiation**
> ● Remind the children that everyone should have the opportunity to take part in a discussion and the most talkative ones should not take over; they should ask others what they think.

Review
● Ask a group to present their discussion to the class, and invite others to comment. Keep the copies of the photocopiable sheet for lesson 3.

Curriculum objectives
● To discuss and evaluate how authors use language, including figurative language, considering the impact on the reader.

Resources
Computers and internet access; material from www.overfishing.org or other organisations that campaign against overfishing

3: Striking language

Introduction
● Tell the children that in this lesson their task is to look closely at the type of language that writers use in a text that is meant to warn or persuade readers.

Whole-class work
● Show a campaign resource from www.overfishing.org. Ask the children for comments about it. Ask: *What words do you remember from the presentation/ text?* Discuss why these words were memorable: perhaps they were examples of figurative language such as comparison, simile or metaphor; perhaps they included powerful vocabulary or sentence structures that were memorable such as commands, exclamations, rhyme, repeated sounds (alliteration) and so on.

Paired work
● Give out copies of texts that contain powerful language and ask the children to highlight the language they think has an impact on readers.

Review
● List examples of effective language from different pairs under headings.

Comparisons and similes	Metaphors	Adverbs to enhance adjectives	Rhyme	Alliteration	Exclamations	Commands

Curriculum objectives
● To select appropriate grammar and vocabulary, understanding how such choices can change and enhance meaning.
● To explain and discuss their understanding of what they have read, including through formal presentations and debates, maintaining a focus on the topic and using notes where necessary.

Resources
Texts used in previous lessons on overfishing/depletion of fisheries; leaflets on nutrition, including fish; texts about the health benefits of eating fish (search online for 'why eat fish?'); computers and internet access; other online materials about overfishing and depletion of fisheries, bookmarked in advance of the lesson (for example www.msc.org or at www.greenpeace.org.uk)

4: Should we eat fish?

Introduction
● Tell the class that their task in this lesson is to plan what they will say in a debate on the topic 'Should we eat fish?'.

Group work
● Split the class into groups, with half the class preparing what to say about why we should not eat fish (using information from texts read during the last three lessons and any others they can find) and the other half preparing to defend fish-eating. Tell them about possible sources of information to support their side of the argument.
● Remind them to think about the arguments the other side will present and to prepare answers for them. Also remind them to think of questions to ask the opposition and arguments against what they might say.
● Visit each group to help them to prepare for these arguments and choose a speaker to open the debate, as well as opposition speaker.
● Give a time limit and, when this is approaching, give a warning so that they can be ready for the debate.

Whole-class work
● Invite the first speaker to present their view – briefly. Invite the opposition speaker to present their view. Invite questions from the others.

Review
● Ask the class how well they think they conducted the debate. Ask: *How well did everyone listen to the speakers? How politely did they ask questions? How well did you give everyone who wanted to the chance to speak? How well did you encourage those who hadn't spoken and who might want to say something?*

Curriculum objectives
● To use knowledge of morphology and etymology in spelling and understand that the spelling of some words needs to be learned specifically, as listed in Appendix 1.

Resources
Photocopiable page 205 'Words ending in '-ant' and '-ent''; interactive activity 'Words ending in '-ant' and '-ent'' on the CD-ROM; individual whiteboards and pens

5: Spelling words ending '-ant' and '-ent'

Introduction
● Tell the class that the focus of this lesson is on spelling: practising words ending with '-ant' and '-ent'.

Whole-class work
● Ask the children to write *observant* on their whiteboards. Ask them to show their whiteboards. If there are differences, ask: *Which is correct?* Give a hint to help them to spell this word: *Think of observation.* (Stress the 'a'.) Ask them to write *expectant*. Ask: *Can you think of a hint to help?* (*Expectation.*) Repeat this for *confident* (*confidential*).

Paired work
● Tell the class that many of the words with endings that sound like '-ant' or '-ent' have to be learned but that, for some, other words from the same root can help. Give out photocopiable page 205 'Words ending in '-ant' and '-ent'' (or provide the interactive activity on the CD-ROM) and ask them to work through the examples with their partner and to discuss any words from the same root that might help.

Review
● Collect examples of hints the children have discovered using words from the same root as the '-ant'/'-ent' words.

Expected outcomes
● All children will be able to learn and recite a poem, discuss how poets use language and spell some '-ssion' words.
● Most children will also be able to describe the atmosphere of a poem and how it is created.
● Some children will also be able to spell a greater range of '-ssion' words.

Curriculum objectives
● To continue to read and discuss an increasingly wide range of poetry.
● To increase their familiarity with a wide range of books, including those from other cultures.
● To identify and discuss themes and conventions across a wide range of writing.
● To learn a wider range of poetry by heart.

Resources
Media resource 'Inuit people' on the CD-ROM; photocopiable page 'Inuit poems' from the CD-ROM; atlases; map of the Arctic

Week 6 lesson plans

These lessons are based on poetry about issues that have arisen from the texts read during the previous five weeks: care of the environment, wildlife (particularly fish), links between humanity and nature, the conflict between profit and caring for the environment, how modern industrialised nations are harming traditional ways of life, persuasion and warnings. The children discuss the message of each poem and how the poet communicates the message through poetic devices and language. They write their own poems about endangered fish using some of these poetic devices, as appropriate, and then read and evaluate their own and others' poems.

1: Inuit poems

Introduction
● Tell the children that during this week's lessons they will be reading poetry from different cultures and ages that reflect the themes they discussed during their non-fiction reading and research on the Arctic.
● Show the children pictures of traditional and modern Inuit settlements (from the media resource 'Inuit people' on the CD-ROM) and tell them about the traditional Inuit way of life and about the relatively new Inuit land, Nunavut. Help them to locate this on a map. Tell them that Inuit poetry used to be sung but not written and that they are going to read some Inuit poems translated from Inuktitut.

Whole-class work
● Give out photocopiable page 'Inuit poems' from the CD-ROM and invite different children to read a poem aloud. After each poem, ask: *What is the poem about? What does the poet say about this?*
● After reading the final poem, ask: *What is similar about the poems?* (They are all about nature and the environment the people live in.) *What, in their environment, do most of the poets mention?* (The sea or ice. Others mention the seasons and night and day.) *From reading these poems, what do you find out about how the poets felt about their environment?* (They thought it was beautiful. They seem to feel awe and respect for nature – also closeness to nature.) *Which words tell you this? What feeling do the poems have?* (A feeling of joy. Three of them end with the word *joy*. They all have a joyful feel and celebrate nature.)

Paired work
● Ask the children to re-read the poems with their partner and choose one to learn by heart. Model one way of doing this: read a line, repeat it without looking at the page, repeat this for the other lines, then try increasing the number of lines read and repeated, with their partner checking. Ask them to think about what the poet says and feels and to practise reciting the poem with expression once they know it.

> **Differentiation**
> ● Some of the poems are simpler to read and understand than the others. The children should choose one they can read, understand and learn. If necessary an adult could read it with them the first time.

Review
● Ask the children to recite their chosen poems to larger groups, who should listen, pay attention and then say what they did well and pick out one aspect they could improve (unless they think the recital perfect).
● Keep the copies of the poems for lesson 4.

Curriculum objectives
- To continue to read and discuss an increasingly wide range of poetry.
- To increase their familiarity with a wide range of books, including those from other cultures.
- To identify and discuss themes and conventions across a wide range of writing.
- To discuss and evaluate how authors use language, including figurative language, considering the impact on the reader.

Resources
Photocopiable page 'Behold, my brothers' from the CD-ROM; photocopiable page 206 'A Native American poem'

2: Native American poem

Introduction
- Tell the class that the poem they are going to read in this lesson is a speech made by a Native American leader named Tatanka Yotanka (Sitting Bull) in 1877, but it sounds like a poem.

Whole-class work
- Hand out photocopiable page 'Behold, my brothers' from the CD-ROM and read the speech with the class. Ask: *How is this speech similar to the Inuit poems?* (It expresses respect for the environment and a feeling of closeness to nature; it celebrates the coming of spring, like the Inuit poem 'Song to Spring'.) *What is the message of the speech?* The Sioux, led by Tatanka Yotanka, are prepared to die fighting to save their land – not to own it or for its value or for profit, but to care for it and look after it for generations to come.

Group work
- Hand out photocopiable page 206 'A Native American poem'. Ask the children to re-read the speech and discuss the questions, which are about the messages of the speech and on how the speaker communicates these through the images that he creates with language. Model how to answer the first question by asking the children to re-read the first three lines and highlight or underline the words that express love and care (*love, embraces*).

Review
- Ask: *Tatanka Yotanka made this speech more than 100 years ago: how could his message fit in with the modern world? Which issue that you have researched could it apply to? Which people do you think could have learned from it?*
- Keep the photocopiable sheets for lesson 4.

Curriculum objectives
- To continue to read and discuss an increasingly wide range of poetry.
- To identify and discuss themes and conventions across a wide range of writing.
- To discuss evaluate how authors use language, including figurative language, considering the impact on the reader.
- To use dictionaries to check the spelling and meanings of words.
- To use the first three or four letters of a word to check spelling, meaning or both of these in a dictionary.

Resources
Photocopiable page 'Important Notice' from the CD-ROM; dictionaries; computers and internet access

3: A modern poem on the environment

Introduction
- Using photocopiable page 'Important Notice' from the CD-ROM, read the poem by Philip Waddell as if reading a corporate press announcement. Ask: *What does this poem sound like?* (A managing director of a business giving a report.) *What is the business? Is it a good report? What makes it good/not so good?*

Paired work
- Give out copies of the poem and let the children re-read it. Ask them to look up and write the meanings of any words they don't know – and to find out a bit more about any animals they haven't heard of. Ask them to discuss the message of the poem and how it relates to issues they have read about and researched, and to make notes about these.

> **Differentiation**
> - Where necessary, help the children to read and look up the meanings of any difficult words.

Review
- Ask each pair to join another pair and compare their notes about the poem. Allow a few minutes for this, then ask: *What do the quagga, dodo and passenger pigeon have in common?* (They are all extinct. Invite volunteers to say, briefly, what they found out about them.)
- Keep the copies of the poem for lesson 4.

Curriculum objectives
● To identify the audience for and purpose of, the writing, selecting the appropriate form and using other similar writing as models for their own.
● To note and develop initial ideas, drawing on reading and research where necessary.
● To assess the effectiveness of their own and others' writing.
● To propose changes to vocabulary, grammar and punctuation to enhance effects and clarify meaning.

Resources
Photocopiable page 206 'A Native American poem'; photocopiable page 'Inuit poems' and 'Important Notice' from the CD-ROM

4: A warning poem

Introduction
● Recap what the children learned about the Arctic, the Inuit and Native Americans.

Independent work
● Ask the children to re-read the poems and to choose a style for their own poem – either like 'Behold, my brothers' or 'Important Notice', to write from the point of view of the Inuit. Ask them to use what they learned about language for impact on the audience to write their own poem.
● Encourage them to begin by just writing what they want to say. Give them time to write their ideas, then suggest parts in which they could change the language, use a metaphor or simile and alter the structure of the poem to change its effect. Tell them to think about the sounds of the words and the images they conjure up, but that the poem need not rhyme. However, if they come up with any effective rhymes that help to create the effect they want, then they should use them.

Paired work
● Ask the children to swap poems with a partner and suggest any changes they think would improve their partner's poem.

Review
● Read out some of the poems and ask: *Does this express what the Inuit people might feel? Does it give a warning? Does the language give the warning impact? Which words do this well?*

Curriculum objectives
● To use knowledge of morphology and etymology in spelling and understanding that the spellings of some words need to be learned specifically, as listed in Appendix 1.
● To use dictionaries to check the spelling and meaning of words.
● To use further prefixes and suffixes and know the guidelines for adding them.

Resources
Photocopiable page 207 'Nouns ending with '-ssion''; individual whiteboards and pens; dictionaries

5: Spelling '-ssion' words

Introduction
● Remind the children of the following lines of 'Behold, my brothers':
  ● *And the love and of possession is a disease with them.*
  ● *First kill me before you take possession of my Fatherland.*
● Discuss the repetition of *possession*. (It emphasises that the Native Americans don't want anyone to *possess* their land – but to share it and care for it.)

Whole-class work
● Ask the children to write *possession* on their whiteboards and hold them up. Show the different spellings and point out the difficult parts of the word (the double 's', twice). Ask them to write the root word (*possess*). Ask: *Does this help you to get the two double 's's right?* Give them some other '-ssion' words to spell (and their root words): *discussion* (*discuss*), *admission* (*admit*), *recession* (*recede*). Point out that the root words for '-ssion' words do not always end with '-ss' (*admit*, *recede*) and that some are roots words (*mission*).

Independent work
● Give out photocopiable page 207 'Nouns ending with '-ssion''. Ask the children to complete the table, writing the '-ssion' word or the root word (or both), as required.

Review
● Invite volunteers to use '-ssion' words in sentences. Ask: *What kind of word ends in '-ssion'?* (A noun. It names something in a sentence.) *What type of word is this suffix usually added to?* (A verb. It says what something does in a sentence.)

Curriculum objectives
● To ensure correct subject and verb agreement when using singular and plural, distinguishing between the language of speech and writing and choosing the appropriate register.

Grammar and punctuation: Verb agreement

Revise

● Begin with starter activity 11 'Verb agreement'.
● Next, display the sentences below on the whiteboard.
  ● *In the desert there was sand everywhere.*
  ● *There was no trees – just sand.*
● Ask: *Are the sentences written correctly? Which word would you change? Why?*
● Repeat this for the following sentences.
  ● *I went into the shop but no one seemed to be there.*
  ● *I went into the shop but there were no one there.*
  ● *I went into the shop but only one person were there.*

Assess

● Provide a set of up to ten pairs of sentences (see examples below), for the children to add the correct form of the verb *to be*.

1. I _____ at home now.

2. Last week Mr and Mrs Khan _____ on holiday in France, but this week they _____ back at work in their offices.

3. The thief stole the radio when no one _____ looking, but it was strange that no one saw him because the shop _____ full of people.

4. We _____ having a street party and everyone _____ welcome, but please let us know if you _____ coming.

5. Today _____ the day of the party and there _____ 84 people seated at 12 big tables.

6. Many of them _____ wearing fancy dress: one _____ dressed as an astronaut, there _____ several witches and a lot of police officers.

7. Now it _____ evening and many of the people from the party _____ helping us to tidy up.

8. We'll make sure the street _____ just as it _____ before the party.

9. It _____ be so tidy that no one will be able to tell that there _____ 84 people here.

10. There _____ a large number of plastic bags full of plastic bottles but we _____ take them to the recycling centre later.

Further practice

● Investigate common expressions from familiar dialects in which the verbs and subjects do not agree.

Curriculum objectives
● To use further prefixes and suffixes and understand the guidelines for adding them.

Resources
A set of cards with the first parts of words that end with '-cian' or '-ssion' written on them (for example: 'mi-', 'Ru-', 'profe-'); cards with '-cian' and '-ssion' written on them (one per pair of children); photocopiable page 'Words whose endings sound like 'shun' from the CD-ROM

Spelling: Words ending in '-ssion' and '-cian'

Revise

● Begin with starter activity 12 'Spelling nouns with '-ssion' suffixes'.
● Next, hold up a word-beginning card (such as 'mi-', 'Ru-', 'profe-', and ask the children to hold up the correct ending. Choose a pair that were correct and ask them to say the word. Ask: *Can you tell me any other words from the same root?*

Assess

● Give out photocopiable page 'Words whose endings sound like 'shun'' from the CD-ROM. The children read the sentences then underline and rewrite any misspelled words.

Further practice

● From reading, collect examples of words with /shon/ suffixes. Compile a word bank of these words, split into two columns ('-cian' and '-ssion').

Curriculum objectives
● To distinguish between statements of fact and opinion.

Resources
Photocopiable pages 'Stop whaling campaign' and 'Halloween' from the CD-ROM; highlighter pens in two different colours

Reading: Non-fiction

Revise

● Hand out photocopiable page 'Stop whaling campaign' from the CD-ROM and give each child a highlighter pen. Allow time for them to read the story. If an adult helper is not available you could pair children who need more support with able readers who could read with them. Ask: *What kind of text is this?* They should be able to identify it as non-fiction – a news report. Ask how they can tell. They should recognise that it gives facts (that could be checked).
● Ask the children to highlight (in a given colour) any facts that can be checked. They should note any statements about what people have done, also figures. Invite feedback and discuss how the facts can be checked.
● Ask: *Does the report include any opinions? What do you think is the opinion of the writer?* (That whale meat should not be eaten.) Ask: *Which words in the first two paragraphs suggest opinions?* Point out adjectives (*staggering, cruel*) and powerful verbs (*slaughtered*). Ask what each suggests about the opinion of the writer. (That Icelandic whalers kill huge numbers of whales; they act cruelly.)
● Ask them to work in pairs to highlight words in a different colour the rest of the text that suggest opinions. Visit each group to discuss the words they highlight, which should include adjectives (*amazing country, inhumane, magnificent and intelligent, long and slow, exotic*), also contrast: *tourists walking off whale-watching vessels and straight into restaurants that serve whale meat.*
● Ask: *Who is the audience for this report?* (Tourists to Iceland.) *How does it try to influence them?* (It tells them things they might not have thought of, for example: going on whale-watching trips is harmful because it helps to support the whaling industry; they might want to try local foods, but they could be eating the whales they like to watch; whales do not reduce local fish stocks. It mentions restaurants they should avoid.)

Assess

● Hand out photocopiable page 'Halloween' from the CD-ROM and ask the children to highlight facts in one colour and opinions in another. They should then and then to rewrite the article, using the same facts but changing the language to suggest a different opinion.

Further practice

● Collect reports from newspapers that express opinions as well as giving facts. Ask the children to identify facts and opinions and to rewrite the reports to suggest a different opinion. Useful reports include anything on local planning issues, wind turbines, building developments or plans to convert buildings for different uses.

Curriculum objectives

● To select appropriate grammar and vocabulary, understanding how such choices can change and enhance meaning.
● To use a wide range of devices to build cohesion within and across paragraphs.

Resources

Photocopiable pages 'Ghosts' and 'Pigeons' from the CD-ROM

Writing: A balanced argument

Revise

● Ask: *Do you believe in ghosts? What makes you think that?* Ask the children to give some evidence to support their opinions.
● Tell them that they are going to read some statements people have made about ghosts. They will present a balanced argument in writing. Their writing may have a conclusion about whether or not they think ghosts exist, but does not try to persuade the reader.
● Hand out photocopiable page 'Ghosts' from the CD-ROM and ask the children to read and discuss the statements about ghosts with a partner. Ask them to arrange them in pairs: argument and counter-argument. To explain this use an example: *people say they have seen ghosts/light could play tricks; they say they have heard ghosts/the wind and creaking wood and metal can make ghostly sounds.*
● Begin a shared writing activity by writing or keying in and displaying an opening for an argument about whether ghosts exist. It could be a question, for example: *Do ghosts really exist? Many people believe this because, they say, they have seen or heard them or felt their presence.*
● Ask for a suggestion about what to write next (perhaps something about people who say ghosts do not exist, for example: *On the other hand, there are many who say that there are explanations for what they have seen, heard or felt.*
● Highlight the words that link the sentences (*this, them, their, on the other hand*) and point out the importance of linking ideas rather than just giving a list of statements.
● Continue the balanced argument by asking the children to suggest an idea from the photocopiable sheet including how to link it to what has already been written, and then to suggest a counter-argument, using the pairs of statements they listed. Invite volunteers to read the argument aloud and ask the class what they could do to help a reader to see at a glance what arguments are used, for example, by using bullet points or subheadings.

Assess

● Hand out photocopiable page 'Pigeons' from the CD-ROM and ask the children to use the statements to help them to write a balanced argument about what should be done about pigeons in the town. Remind them to balance arguments and counter-arguments, and to find ways to link the paragraphs and the sentences in them. Also remind them to think about ways of guiding the reader, for example, by using bullet points or subheadings.

Further practice

● Discuss issues of local interest, collect facts and write short but balanced arguments about them. Examples could include: what should happen to bus routes, extensions or closures of local leisure facilities; whether a fish and chip shop, fast food outlet or supermarket should be allowed; one-way traffic systems, parking regulations. You could also use ideas purely for fun: *Should ghosts be allowed to haunt the old castle/derelict house? Should flying broomsticks be banned from the high street?*

Spot the homophones

- Read the passage and underline any words that are spelled wrongly.
- Number them and write the correct spellings in the homophone note book.

As we past the abbey the floodlights came on and eliminated the hole of the front of the building. It seemed like a waist of electricity. Dad guest it must cost thousands of pounds each year. I herd him muttering about it as we went in. He was still muttering as we began the assent of the old stone stares up the tower.

"But it has a lovely affect, and it brings in the tourists," said Mum, and preceded up the steps.

"It's against environmental principals," said Dad. Father on we came to a balcony that overlooked the knave of the abbey. The high alter was illuminated, too (more waste).

"Where's that draft coming from?" asked Mum, and we looked up. There was a big hole in the roof. That was knew. We made a quick dissent to the bottom of the steps.

We found a churchwarden, who's job is to check the building, and told her about it.

"Not again," she said. "Thieves keep steeling the led. We can't keep up with them, even with modern security systems."

- Write the homophones that these past-tense verbs are often confused with.

missed _____   sent _____

seen _____   packed _____

tracked _____   wrapped _____

Homophone note book

1. _____
2. _____
3. _____
4. _____
5. _____
6. _____
7. _____
8. _____
9. _____
10. _____
11. _____
12. _____
13. _____
14. _____
15. _____
16. _____
17. _____
18. _____
19. _____
20. _____

I can spell common homophones.

How did you do?

Silent letters

- Write the words with silent letters next to their definitions.

1. A little fly that bites. _____

2. Brushes have these. _____

3. Broken remains of a damaged ship, plane, car or building. _____

4. Bump into people in a crowd. _____

5. Serious and grave. _____

6. Think something might not be right. _____

7. A circle of flowers and leaves used as a decoration or at a funeral. _____

8. The rule of a king or queen. _____

Silent letter word list

reign

wreckage

wreath

gnat

jostle

doubt

solemn

bristles

- Write the words with silent letters that match the definitions and highlight the silent letters.

1. Not right. _____

2. Young sheep. _____

3. Prickly plant from Scotland. _____

4. A sport in which opponents try to throw one another to the ground. _____

5. A football referee blows this. _____

6. The season after summer. _____

7. A worm does this when it moves. _____

8. You have four fingers and one of these one each hand. _____

I can spell words with silent letters.

How did you do?

Dialogue

- You can change sentences from recount to dialogue, for example:

| Jack told his dog, Skye, to lie down. | → | "Lie down, Skye," said Jack. |

- Change these sentences to dialogue.

Shazia and Danayal's father told them he would take them to Alton Towers.	→	
He asked the children playing football if he might play with them.	→	
She whispered to Ellie that she would see her later.	→	
Fiona asked the waiter for a cup of coffee.	→	
Mrs Patel's neighbour waved and wished her good morning.	→	
Jade said she had seen someone breaking a window next door the night before.	→	

- Proofread your dialogue sentences to check the punctuation.

I can write and punctuate dialogue.

How did you do?

Nansen's voyage

■ Research the answers to these questions about Fridtjof Nansen's voyage on the *Fram.*

What was Nansen's destination? _____

How did he plan to get there? _____

In which year did he tell the Norwegian Geographical Society about his plan? _____

How did Nansen know about the sea current that would help him?

_____

Where did the sea current flow from?

_____

Which ship's route would Nansen and his crew follow?

_____

What had happened to that ship?

_____

How would Nansen avoid this happening to his ship?

_____

_____

What did other explorers think about Nansen's plan?

_____

_____

Who offered to pay for the trip?

_____

Nansen turned this offer down. See if you can find out why.

_____

_____

I can find information from different non-fiction texts.
I can give opinions on this and justify them with evidence.

How did you do?

Nansen's diary

■ Read this extract from Fridtjof Nansen's diary. Rewrite it as a report in the third person and in the past tense. Continue on a separate sheet of paper.

Friday, October 13th: The ice is pressing and packing round us with a noise like thunder. It is piling itself up into long walls, and heaps high enough to reach a good way up the Fram's rigging; in fact, it is trying its very utmost to grind the Fram into powder. But here we sit quite tranquil, not even going up to look at all the hurly-burly, but just chatting and laughing as usual. Last night the ice had towered up higher than the highest point of the floe, and hustled down upon it. It had quite spoilt a well, where we till now had found good drinking water, filling it with brine. Furthermore, it had cast itself over our stern ice anchor and part of the steel cable which held it, burying them so effectually that we had afterwards to cut the cable. Then it covered our planks and sledges, which stood on the ice. Before long the dogs were in danger, and the watch had to turn out all hands to save them. At last the floe was split in two. This morning the ice was one scene of melancholy confusion, gleaming in the most glorious sunshine. Piled up all round us were high, steep ice walls. Strangely enough, we had lain on the very verge of the worst confusion, and had escaped with the loss of an ice anchor, a piece of steel cable, a few planks and half a sledge, all of which might have been saved if we had looked after them in time.

_____

_____

_____

_____

_____

I can write in the past tense and third person.

How did you do?

PHOTOCOPIABLE

Words ending in '-ant' and '-ent'

■ Complete the adjectives using the suffixes '-ant' or '-ent'.

1. He was sil_____ because he couldn't think of anything to say.

2. They looked towards the horizon and could see the dist_____ hills.

3. We were hesit_____ because we wondered what we should do.

4. He was a frequ_____ visitor to our house.

5. As soon as she opened her mouth it was evid_____ that she couldn't sing.

6. Border collies are said to be the most intellig_____ dogs.

7. We did an experiment to find the most absorb_____ paper towel.

8. The newspaper had a report about a rec_____ earthquake.

9. The passengers became very impati_____ when the train was delayed.

10. The girl was arrested for viol_____ behaviour.

■ List other words from the same root.

Adjective	Words from the same root
tolerant	
confident	
assistant	
obedient	
independent	
recent	
magnificent	
important	

I can spell adjectives ending with the suffixes '-ant' or '-ent'.

How did you do?

A Native American poem

■ Answer the questions about Tatanka Yotanka's 'Behold, my brothers' speech.

1. Which words in the first verse show that the Sioux people loved their land?

_____

2. What feeling does verse 2 show about the land?

_____

3. In verse 2, what does Tatanka Yotanka say about the neighbours of the Sioux, including animals, who also wanted to use the land?

_____

4. Which people do you think are 'another race' in verse 3?

_____

5. What does verse 3 say about how this other race thought of the land?

_____

Write the metaphor the writer uses for this.

_____

6. What metaphor in verse 4 says how the other race treats the land?

_____

_____

_____

7. What is the writer's feeling at the end of the poem? _____

_____

8. What are the most powerful words he uses to show this?

_____

_____

_____

I can identify the language that expresses feelings in a poem.

How did you do?

PHOTOCOPIABLE ■SCHOLASTIC www.scholastic.co.uk

Nouns ending with '-ssion'

- Fill in the gaps in the table.
- Don't write in the shaded boxes.

Verb	Noun ending '-ssion'	Adjective
admit	admission	
		aggressive
compress		
		compassionate
concuss		
confess		
discuss		
express		
		possessive
omit		
remit		
proceed		
recede		
transmit		
submit		submissive
depress		
		oppressive
		professional

I can spell adjectives that end with the suffix '-ssion'.

How did you do?